ALT-RIGHT GANGS

ALT-RIGHT GANGS

A Hazy Shade of White

———

**Shannon E. Reid and
Matthew Valasik**

UNIVERSITY OF CALIFORNIA PRESS

University of California Press
Oakland, California

Library of Congress Cataloging-in-Publication Data

Names: Reid, Shannon E., 1981– author. | Valasik, Matthew, author.
Title: Alt-right gangs : a hazy shade of white / Shannon E. Reid and
    Matthew Valasik.
Description: Oakland, California : University of California Press, [2020] |
    Includes bibliographical references and index.
Identifiers: LCCN 2020017106 (print) | LCCN 2020017107 (ebook) |
    ISBN 9780520300446 (cloth) | ISBN 9780520300453 (paperback) |
    ISBN 9780520971844 (epub)
Subjects: LCSH: Right-wing extremists—United States.
Classification: LCC HN90.R3 R398 2020 (print) | LCC HN90.R3 (ebook) |
    DDC 322.4/20973—dc23
LC record available at https://lccn.loc.gov/2020017106
LC ebook record available at https://lccn.loc.gov/2020017107

Manufactured in the United States of America

28   27   26   25   24   23   22   21   20
10   9   8   7   6   5   4   3   2   1

CONTENTS

ILLUSTRATIONS

FIGURES

MAPS

BOX ILLUSTRATIONS

ACKNOWLEDGMENTS

To E and D, for their tolerance, humor, and willingness to sit next to me while I try and explain what I study. D, keep asking questions and always be true to you. Thank you both for putting up with me. To my coauthor, Matt, thank you for taking this ride with me; I doubt I could have done all this with anyone else. Thanks for being a great friend, and thanks to M for tolerating all our phone calls.
—Shannon

I am extremely grateful for my family, especially M, for your enduring encouragement, patience, and support throughout the writing process. I would not be the scholar I am today without you! To O, Q, and E, thank you for reminding me daily that life moves fast, and without stopping and enjoying it I will miss out on the journey. Lastly, I would like to thank Shannon for prompting this endeavor, for being a devoted coauthor, but most of all for continuing to be a trusted friend.
—Matt

This book would not have been possible without the insights and support of our colleagues. We appreciate all the feedback and discussions during conference presentations, workshops, and bar chats. This is especially true for the members of the Eurogang research program, who have been invaluable throughout this process, especially in the early stages of crafting our research agenda into better understanding white power groups, particularly alt-right gangs. We must also thank James R. who deserves a research assistant award for putting up with us and our last-minute requests. We would also like to thank David Neiwert for contributing the photographs used in this book. They greatly enrich the narrative and provide a visual sense of just how successful alt-right gangs have been at mainstreaming their public persona. We would also like to thank the University of California Press, especially our editor and editorial staff who believed in the project and helped us so much along the way. Lastly, we would like to thank all the other researchers across the academic spectrum who are involved in this important work of better understanding the white power movement, as many of them have helped lay the ground work for our research agenda and continue to expand our understanding of the alt-/radical-/far-/extreme-/racist-right.

INTRODUCTION

Blood and soil. . . . Jews will not replace us. . . . White lives matter.
CHARLOTTESVILLE MARCHERS (VICE, 2017)

We talk to these young people, we give them literature . . . they go and they
start their own white youth gangs to counter the terrorism of the black youth
gangs.
SKINHEADS USA (KEANE, 1993)

At 8:45 p.m. on Friday, August 11, 2017, in Charlottesville, Virginia, America's
white power movement (WPM) reemerged from the secluded spaces it had been
festering in for the last 25 years (Heim 2017; Lyons 2018; McAuliffe 2019). Over
the next few days, the level of vitriol, along with barefaced far-right messaging
expressed by the alt-right (short for alternative right) shocked people around
the world. The images of bellowing white males brandishing flaming tiki torches
harkened back to a history of Ku Klux Klan (KKK) rallies (see Chalmers 1987;
L. Gordon 2018; Wade 1998), while violent clashes with counterprotesters and bystanders seemed aggressively new (First Vigil 2019; McAuliffe 2019; PBS 2018a;
VICE 2017). It was at this moment that the WPM blipped back onto the radar
of mainstream America, creating a turning point in US history. For many, the
anti-Semitism, xenophobia, and racist rhetoric combined with youthful adoption
of neo-Nazi, neo-Confederate, and far-right imagery was horrifying, given the
belief that this sort of blatant white supremacy had dissipated in our "post-racial"
society (see Anderson 2016; Bhopal 2018; Bonilla-Silva 2015; Walton 2018; Ward
2018; Wise 2010). The fact that youth were now adopting these alt-right designations was all the more disturbing. Law enforcement, policy makers, and the
general public continue to be stumped trying to understand why youth are joining
these groups and how to deal with them (see Reitman 2018). Yet, for those who
investigate the far right, the Charlottesville protest was simply the visible face of
a movement that has never disappeared (Belew 2018; Daniels 2018; Futrell & Simi
2017; Lyons 2018; Neiwert 2017). Additionally, for those who study street gangs,
such alt-right youth groups and the violence they participate in are not surprising
(Reid & Valasik 2018; Simi 2006, 2009; Simi, Smith & Reeser 2008; Valasik &

Reid 2018a, 2019). In fact, gang researchers, in particular, are uniquely situated to help demystify these groups. As such, the purpose of *Alt-Right Gangs* is twofold. First, we wish to provide a timely and necessary discussion of present-day youth-oriented groups in the WPM, which we refer to in this text as alt-right gangs, and how they need to be integrated into the current paradigm of street gang research. The goal is to provide researchers, students (graduate and undergraduate), law enforcement officials, and policy makers with knowledge aimed at understanding and, hopefully, combating membership in these groups. Second, this book provides a pathway to guide future research in studying these alt-right groups and their members. *Alt-Right Gangs* is the first book to conceptualize alt-right youth groups and situate their appearance across a broad array of academic literature. The interdisciplinary nature of this book synthesizes research from criminology, sociology, communication studies, social movements, political science, history, cultural studies, religious studies, media and information, and computer science to underscore the need to take alt-right gangs seriously and not dismiss them as just a youthful phase or subculture (e.g., Hamm 1993).

While the book is aimed at discussing the intersection of conventional street gangs and alt-right gangs, there remains a great deal of research to be done to fully understand the overlap between these groups, especially in terms of how gang prevention, intervention, and suppression programs and policies apply to these youth. The current understanding of alt-right gangs has been greatly hindered by historical decisions about who is and is not considered to be a gang member. For over three decades, gang scholars have explicitly disregarded white youth who are active in overt white power groups (e.g., neo-Nazis, racist skinheads, and white separatists) or influenced by implicit white power ideologies (e.g., Christian Identity, Creativity, manosphere, and the patriot movement). This resistance to acknowledging or discussing alt-right gangs in such foundational and accessible texts has only aggravated our lack of knowledge (e.g., Curry, Decker & Pyrooz 2014; Hamm 1993; Klein 1995).

As a new wave of culture wars and identity politics continues to inundate the United States and Europe, scholars and policy makers have grown concerned over the radicalization of youth, both domestically and internationally (Dandurand 2015; Decker & Pyrooz 2011, 2015a; Pyrooz, La Free, Decker & James 2018; Valasik & Phillips 2017, 2018). The "alt-right," a term coined, arguably, in 2008 by Richard Spencer, a white supremacist, consists of young, white identitists who present themselves as a leaderless, loosely organized "fun movement, one using Internet jargon familiar to tech-savvy millennials" and who are striving to redefine the American political landscape (Hawley 2017: 20). "Free speech" demonstrations by white supremacists in cities that are seen as liberal bastions, such as Charlottesville, Virginia; Berkeley, California; and Portland, Oregon (see figure I.1), have resulted in hate/bias-related crimes, violence, and even murder (First Vigil 2019;

FIGURE I.1. Proud Boys among others in the far right protesting at a "free speech" rally (photo by David Neiwert).

McAuliffe 2019; Stern 2019; VICE 2017) (see chapter 7). Despite the desire to treat alt-right groups as nothing more than atypical or radical youth, a substantial subset of alt-righters, such as racist skinheads, are also involved in delinquent, street-oriented youth groups (Woods 2017). It is these youth and their groups—alt-right gangs—that this book endeavors to understand.

WHAT IS A STREET GANG?

After nearly one hundred years of research examining street gangs, a universal definition for what constitutes a gang, who is considered to be a gang member, and what constitutes a gang-related incident still eludes researchers, law enforcement agencies, and policy makers (see Curry 2015). Howell and Griffiths (2018: 51) highlight just how challenging it has been to attempt to reach a consensus between scholars and criminal justice practitioners, with "no other deviant group [being] shrouded in more mythic and misleading attributes than gangs." This lack of agreement in defining gangs, gang members, and gang-related crimes has often meant the explicit exclusion of white power groups in both street gang research and law enforcement's gang databases, or at best a mere implicit acknowledgment of them (Brosseau 2016; Flores 2017; Howell 2015; Howle 2016; Reid & Valasik

2018; Simi 2006; Simi et al. 2008). As such, it is important to recognize the variations that exist in defining street gangs, paying particular attention to the similarities and differences of these descriptions.

The earliest studies examining gangs were based on school surveys of youth. Sheldon (1898: 428) describes fighting gangs as "predatory organizations" and "the typical association of small boys." The common age for youth in these predatory gangs was between 10 and 13. Puffer (1912) suggested that beyond the family and the neighborhood, the gang (i.e., the play group) is one of youth's three primary social groups. Puffer (1912) argues that youth's instinctive tendency to group themselves, combined with a lack of parental supervision, explains the existence of gangs.

Puffer's (1912) typical gang had a distinct name and included youth between the ages of 10 and 16, who gathered together daily in a claimed area, participated in initiation rituals, engaged in delinquent/criminal activities, and were likely to have a designated leader. According to Puffer a gang was a "social organism . . . with a life of its own which is beyond the lives of its members" (1912: 38), not only instilling antisocial behaviors in its members, but possibly also encouraging and reinforcing prosocial behaviors.

Thrasher's (1927) seminal work on street gangs was so thorough and detailed that it took half a century before gang researchers again raised definitional issues. Thrasher, known as the father of gang research, defined a gang as "an interstitial group originally formed spontaneously and then integrated through conflict. It is characterized by the following types of behavior: meeting face to face, milling, movement through space as a unit, conflict and planning. The result of this collective behavior is the development of tradition, unreflective internal structure, esprit de corps, solidarity, morale, group awareness, and attachment to a local territory" (1927: 57). Other renowned gang scholars have subsequently built upon Thrasher's definition, competing to better describe the social phenomenon and failing to reach accord (see Howell & Griffiths 2018 for an in-depth discussion).

Regardless of the definition embraced by gang researchers, a level of variability exists in the characteristics required for a group to be considered a street gang. This intense focus on attempting to decipher specific features that transform a group into a street gang has greatly contributed to gang researchers' inability to achieve a universal definition of a gang. Yet, as Papachristos (2005: 644) points out, "Such distinctions mean little to the cop on the street, the victim of gang violence, or even gang members." Papachristos (2005) adapts Everett C. Hughes's ([1948] 1984) definition of an ethnic group, contending that a gang is not a gang because of some measurable or observable features distinguishing it from other groups. Instead, a gang exists because the members in a gang, and those individuals outside of it, know that it is a gang, because both the ins and outs socialize, believe, feel, and act as if it is a distinct group. Thus, "gangs take their meaning instead from their function and from the consequences of their actions"

(Papachristos 2005: 644), and the group boundaries of a gang are amorphous, with members fluidly joining and leaving the group (see Fleisher 2005; Klein & Crawford 1967), unconcerned about scholarly semantics and the legal definitions of a street gang. In fact, gangs are dynamic, adapting and evolving, not conforming to a static definition (see Ayling 2011; Densley 2013; Valasik & Phillips 2017).

Based on these characteristics, it is clear that white power youth groups would easily qualify as a gang under these scholarly definitions (see chapter 1 for an explicit definition of an alt-right gang). Researchers are not the only ones interested in classifying what constitutes a street gang. Every state law in the United States includes a definition for a criminal street gang. For instance, looking at the state law for the gang capital of America—Los Angeles—a criminal street gang is defined as "any ongoing organization, association, or group of three or more persons, whether formal or informal, having as one of its primary activities the commission of one or more of the criminal acts . . . , having a common name or common identifying sign or symbol, and whose members individually or collectively engage in, or have engaged in, a pattern of criminal gang activity" (section 186.22(f) of the California Penal Code).

According to the National Gang Center (2016), every state's definition for a gang includes illegal/criminal behavior or activity. Forty-four states and Washington, D.C., have legislation explicitly defining a gang. Forty states consider gangs to be an "organization, association, or group." Thirty-six states require a gang to consist of three or more individuals. Thirty states indicate that a gang must have a common name, sign, or symbol that clearly identifies the group. Clearly, variation exists in how each state defines a criminal street gang.

The takeaway point, however, is that many white power youth groups, along with other youth social groups (e.g., fraternities), are able to fit within these legal criteria. Yet white power groups are routinely not considered to be criminal street gangs by law enforcement and remain generally overlooked from gang databases (Brosseau 2016; Flores 2017; Howell 2015; Howle 2016).

As a response to the lack of consensus among researchers, policy makers, and law enforcement in defining a street gang, a group of international gang scholars began to network and convene, forming the Eurogang Program of Research (Esbensen & Maxson 2018; Klein, Kerner, Maxson & Weitekamp 2001; Weerman et al. 2009). The initial objective driving the Eurogang Program of Research was to ascertain if the troublesome youth groups observed in Europe were comparable to American street gangs (Esbensen & Maxson 2018). To accomplish this cross-national comparison, the Eurogang Program of Research created survey instruments within an integrated research design and developed a common definition for a street gang or troublesome youth group (since the term *gang* does not always translate precisely). A systematic approach with a multi-method, multisite, comparative research design allowed for the ability to measure street gangs around the world (Esbensen & Maxson 2018). The Eurogang definition identifies a street gang as "any durable, street-oriented youth group whose own identity includes involvement in illegal activity" (Weerman et al. 2009: 20). This definition, developed meticulously over the course of several years and multiple conferences, contains four crucial components required for a group to be considered a street gang: *durability, street orientation, youthfulness,* and a *group identity revolving around illegal behavior* (Esbensen & Maxson 2018; Weerman et al. 2009). Despite the failure of the overall field of gang researchers to reach a consensus, the Eurogang definition "has become widely adopted and appears regularly in publications," with the Eurogang Program of Research publishing six edited volumes of scholarship (see Decker & Weerman 2005; Esbensen & Maxson 2011; Klein et al. 2001; Maxson & Esbensen 2016; Melde & Weerman 2020; van Gemert, Peterson & Lien 2008) and is the most widely employed modern definition for ascertaining whether a group should be considered a street gang (Maxson & Esbensen 2016: 7).

Despite white power youth groups, particularly long-standing racist skinheads, being treated as the "Schrödinger's cat" of street gangs (i.e., simultaneously being regarded as a street gang and not being regarded as a street gang), they easily qualify as a street gang based on the Eurogang definition (Klein 1996, 2001, 2009; Klein & Maxson 2006; Pyrooz et al. 2018; Reid & Valasik 2018; Reid, Valasik & Bagavathi 2020; Simi 2006; Valasik & Reid 2018b, 2019). This definitional tension between whether or not white power youth groups are considered a street gang is discussed in much more depth in chapter 1, where the features required for a group to be defined as an alt-right gang are described. Now that it is established that white power youth groups satisfy the requirements to be considered a street gang, either by researchers or law enforcement, an overview of the most recent iteration of the WPM mobilizing today's youth, the alt-right, is in order (see Daniels 2018; Futrell & Simi 2017).

WHAT IS THE ALT-RIGHT?

The WPM in American society has been extremely resilient, continuing to evolve and adapt since the Reconstruction Era (1863–1877) (see Lewis & Serbu 1999; McVeigh & Estep 2019; Parsons 2015). With the advent and ubiquity of digital communications (the internet, social media, etc.) the WPM has undergone a noticeable transformation over the last three decades (Daniels 2018; Futrell & Simi 2017; Levin 2002). Based on the blueprint of "leaderless resistance" laid out by Louis Beam ([1983] 1992), a prominent white supremacist strategist, digital communications (e.g., online message boards) could be used asymmetrically and with minimal resources to spread the WPM's messages, maintain communication between individuals not spatially proximate, and recruit new members (see Belew

2018; Gardell 2018; Joosse 2016; Kaplan 1997; Levin 2002; Michael 2012; T. Morris 2017; Simpson & Druxes 2015). Under this guiding principle white power groups have been able to covertly expand and extend their footprint, growing a base of support for issues of white identity (Daniels 2018; Futrell & Simi 2018; Hawley 2018). Throughout this transformation, the WPM continues to reinvent their groups' image and branding in order to offset the general stigma associated with white supremacy's racial and anti-Semitic hate (Futrell & Simi 2018; Mudde 2018, 2019). The alt-right is just the WPM's most recent veneer.

The term *alt-right* was conceived of in the important context of an unpopular and frustrating war in Iraq and the burgeoning financial crisis of the Great Recession, both of which were being filtered through new forms of news media (e.g., cable news, the internet, and social media) to discontented Americans (see Crothers 2019; Hawley 2017, 2019; Hermansson, Lawrence, Mulhall & Murdoch 2020; Lewis 2018; Main 2018; Neiwert 2017; Waring 2019; Wendling 2018). The constellation of far-right groups and individuals falling under the alt-right umbrella has shifted since Richard Spencer's christening over a decade ago. Today the alt-right projects itself as being a loosely organized, leaderless far-right social/political movement of young, tech-savvy millennials employing facetious internet jargon to revamp and mainstream white supremacist beliefs behind a facade of white identity politics or Western chauvinist convictions (Hawley 2018, 2019; Hermansson et al 2020; Johnson 2019; McVeigh & Estep 2019; Mudde 2018, 2019; Stern 2019; Valasik & Reid 2018b). Yet there has been some questioning about just how youth-centric the alt-right as a social movement actually is, and whether figureheads in the alt-right (e.g., Richard Spencer) and alt-lite media personalities (e.g., Milo Yiannopoulos) may be overstating the youth-orientedness of the alt-right (see Hawley 2018; Main 2018). The alt-right is also not just a bunch of trolls on the internet, nor are they simply "lone shooter" extremists like those who attacked two mosques in Christchurch, New Zealand, and the Tree of Life Synagogue in Pittsburgh, Pennsylvania (Jipson & Becker 2019; Phillips et al. 2018). While it may be impossible to truly assess the age makeup of the alt-right, what has been documented is that throngs of young, white males routinely participate in "free speech" demonstrations across the United States in "liberal" cities (see chapters 5 and 7) (Crothers 2019; Marcotte 2018; McAuliffe 2019; Wilson 2019).

The alt-right is not a monolith, unified by a strict ideology. Instead, the alt-right is a confederated movement composed of a variety of factions that are generally against feminism, globalism, immigration, multiculturalism, establishment politics, and political correctness, but are supportive of President Trump (Berger 2018; Hawley 2019; Hermansson et al 2020; Perry & Scrivens 2019; Vitolo-Haddad 2019; Waring 2019; Wendling 2018; Winter 2019). In fact, the alt-right is very "disjointed and more clearly focused on external enemies than its own internal cohesion" (Berger 2018: 53). Thus, the term *alt-right* has been used to encompass a range of groups and ideologies. Among them are online trolls who only seek *lulz*, or "amusement at other people's distress" (Phillips 2015: 27) (see chapter 6). Next, there is the manosphere, composed of misogynistic "meninists," focused on issues of men's rights, or "incels" (short for "involuntarily celibates") (see Baele, Brace & Coan, 2019; Beauchamp 2018; Enloe, Graff, Kapur & Walters 2019; Hawley 2019; Hermansson et al 2020). Then there are survivalists, or members supportive of the patriot (or militia) movement, such as the Oath Keepers or Three Percenters (see Aho 1990; Belew 2018; Crothers 2019; Klein 2019; Lyons 2018; Michael 2015; Neiwert 2017; Simi, Windisch & Sporer 2016). There are also the intellectuals—a group of academics including paleoconservatives (the antithesis of the neoconservative movement, opposing free trade, foreign wars, multiculturalism, and immigration) and racialists (those adhering to questionable race-based theories, such as human biodiversity, who attest to differences in intelligence between racial groups)—who are attempting to establish an intellectual far right outside of mainstream conservatism (Hawley 2019; Hermansson et al 2020; Main 2018; Saini 2019; Stern 2019; Wendling 2018). Another faction within the alt-right is conspiracy theorists (e.g., QAnon, Pizzagate, New World Order [NWO]), white genocide) (see Berger 2018; Berlet & Vysotsky 2006; Coaston 2018a; Hodge & Hallgrimsdottir 2019; Marcotte 2018; Neiwert 2018b; Pollard 2016; Saslow 2018; Stern 2019; Wendling 2018). Lastly, the most prominent factions are the individuals at the core of the alt-right who fully endorse the WPM (see Atkinson 2018; Daniels 2018; Hawley 2017, 2019; Hermansson et al 2020; Klein 2019; Lyons 2018; Main 2018; Neiwert 2017; Stern 2019; Waring 2019). While white supremacist notions may be present among intellectuals, conspiracy theorists, and the other factions, they are not necessarily the beliefs that inspire members in these groups.

The alt-right contends that they are not a racist movement, but only use caustic and ironic humor as an instrument to facilitate their far-right arguments criticizing social justice warriors (liberals), and condemning the political, social, and cultural status quo. When we apply Ken White's (2017) slightly paraphrased rule of goats, however, we see that this argument does not hold up. The rule asserts that if you kiss a goat, whether you do it to prove a larger point or ironically, you're still a goat-kisser. As such, the alt-right are goat-kissers and not some band of ironic, transgressive humorists. As Hawley (2017) states, there is no more appropriate word to describe the alt-right than *racist*.

While racists are at the core of the alt-right and remain relatively limited in number, they are able, however, to exert substantial influence. For instance, compared to the 197 million Caucasian Americans living in the United States, only about 11 million individuals, or about 6%, are supportive of the rhetoric espoused by the alt-right (Hawley 2018). Nevertheless, there is a larger swath of Caucasian Americans who feel that the status, privileges, and authority of being white in America are deteriorating, what Du Bois (1935: 700) called the "psychological wage of whiteness" (see also Roediger 1999). Kimmel (2013: 18) calls this "aggrieved entitlement," or the belief that white Americans feel they are being swindled out of the benefits to which they are entitled under the conditions of the current political environment and economic market (see also Hochschild 2016; Kimmel 2018; Norris 2018). Berry (2017: 14) takes this concept further with the notion of "racial protectionism" in which a mythologized racial community (whites) feels obligated to fight for their preservation against imagined racial enemies. This concept is illustrated best with Derek Black's white supremacist propaganda suggesting that a "white genocide," also referred to as the "Great Replacement," a mass extinction of white, European culture through immigration, assimilation, and higher reproduction rates by individuals of non-European descent, is taking place in America (Moses 2019; Saslow 2018). While the "silent majority" of individuals who support the views of the alt-right will most likely remain within the digital realm, the number of individuals that publicly support the alt-right is not insubstantial and exceeds the 4% of the population that supported the KKK in the 1920s (Chalmers 1987; MacLean 1994; McVeigh 2009; McVeigh & Estep 2019). There is still much to be learned about the transitioning of the alt-right from a mostly online phenomenon to a real-world social movement (see chapter 6).

ALT-RIGHT GANGS: FROM TWEETS TO THE STREETS

While there may be some questions about the decision to use the term *alt-right gang*, this decision was purposeful for several reasons. First, this term is contemporary in a way that speaks to the current iteration of youth involved in these groups. The definition is explicit in that this book is focused on a very particular subset of individuals who are involved in public delinquent behavior, not the broader social movement that is associated with the term *alt-right*. Second, other terms like *racist skinhead* or *far right* or *extreme right* have a history and a set of preconceived notions attached to them. For example, the term *racist skinhead* often invokes an image of a bald thug fighting in the street, and *far right* or *extreme right* overemphasizes ideology-based activities (private meetings, propaganda distribution, etc.). In order to avoid the historical connotations of these terms, and to acknowledge that, while these youth-oriented groups in the WPM are not "new," they are also not the same as they were in the 1980s and 1990s, we employ the term *alt-right gang*.

The manifestation and initial evolution of the alt-right began across the digital landscape, primarily on Twitter and Facebook; however, over the last few years they have manifested in the public sphere (see DeCook 2018; Fielitz & Thurston 2019; Stern 2019). This sudden escalation of activity in the public limelight has been documented by the ever-increasing number of "free speech" rallies (in cities such as Berkeley, Charlottesville, New York, and Portland), which regularly conclude with violence (see KPIX 2017; McAuliffe 2019; Neiwert 2019; Stern 2019; Vice 2017; Wilson 2019) (see chapter 7). The public exhibitions of criminality and violence documented at these alt-right gatherings unambiguously demonstrate a "cafeteria-style" pattern of criminal offending, commonly observed by conventional street gangs (see Klein 1995; Klein & Maxson 2006). Such criminal offenses include harassment, larceny, assault, possessing illegal weapons, hate-related crimes, murder, and serial killings (Duggan 2018; First Vigil 2019; Heim 2018; Martinez 2018; PBS 2018b; Shallwani & Weill 2018; Thompson, Winston & Hanrahan 2018;). The breadth of these criminal offenses shows that dismissing alt-right youth as merely a bunch of online trolls is misaligned with the realities of the alt-right. Given the confederated nature of the alt-right, there are various subgroups whose members also associate with street-oriented delinquent groups (e.g., 211 Bootboys, B49, Proud Boys, and the Rise Above Movement, or R.A.M.). In the wake of the Unite the Right rally in 2017, it was surmised that the alt-right would recede from public view, limiting their activities to Aryan free spaces online (see chapters 6 and 8). Instead, the incendiary rhetoric of President Trump at rallies and on Twitter, using dog whistles and coded language (e.g., *globalist, invader, nationalist*), has produced an atmosphere receptive to the increased boldness of alt-right gangs in the United States (e.g., racist skinheads, Proud Boys, Atomwaffen Division, The Base, R.A.M.) to engage in street violence (Strickland 2018; Burke 2018; Dickson 2019; Lamoureux & Makuch 2018a, 2018b, 2019; G. Lopez 2017; Reitman 2018; Roose & Winston 2018; Valasik & Reid 2018a; Ware 2008). In fact, the "branching out from internet activism" has actually allowed these alt-right gangs to strengthen their connections with other far-right groups (e.g., the patriot movement, manosphere, and traditional white supremacists) and forge more extensive ties within the larger alt-right movement (Crothers 2019; Hawley 2019; Klein 2019; Lyons 2018; Main 2018; Nagle 2017; Stern 2019; Wendling 2018). It is this combination of having both a digital and physical footprint that differentiates alt-right gangs from traditional white power groups (e.g., KKK, neo-Nazis) and conventional street gangs.

Additionally, that membership overlaps between factions in the alt-right is also an important consideration when categorizing these groups. Researchers and law enforcement have noted that youth can and do switch between racist and non-racist skinhead groups, marking a fluidity present in alt-right gang membership (Borgenson & Valeri 2018; Christensen 1994). Similar patterns have been documented among conventional street gangs, commonly referred to as "hybrid gangs," where members switch affiliations or join multiple groups (see Bolden 2012, 2014; Howell, Starbuck & Lindquist 2001; Starbuck, Howell & Lindquist 2004). For example, following an event at the Metropolitan Republican Club in New York City, several Proud Boys members who attacked counterprotesters were also affiliated with street-based racist skinhead gangs such as 211 Bootboys and Battalion 49 (B49) (First Vigil 2019; Holt 2018). Of 10 Proud Boys arrested, seven pleaded guilty; two members were found guilty of gang assault, attempted assault, and rioting; and at the time of this writing, one is still awaiting trial (Moynihan 2019). While the Proud Boys label may give these individuals a more hip, mainstream persona, a Proud Boys member still fits the definition of being an alt-right gang member (see chapter 1).

As with conventional street gangs, alt-right gangs exist on a spectrum from loosely organized, neighborhood-based gangs all the way to highly structured organizations focused on just a particular subset of crimes (e.g., drugs, fraud, and extortion). Similar patterns also exist for alt-right gangs' criminal activity and their political motivations.

PURPOSE AND ORGANIZATION

In *Alt-Right Gangs*, we utilize our interdisciplinary training to inform our perspectives as gang scholars. This allows for a look beyond the specific academic discipline of criminology to engage with the broader WPM literature. The result of this perspective is a book that engages with a diverse set of literature across a range of academic backgrounds to provide a concise synthesis of alt-right gangs. By harnessing and integrating this assorted literature, a more inclusive characterization of alt-right gangs is developed. This highlights just how substantial the similarities are between alt-right gangs and conventional street gangs. Even though our expertise as gang researchers frames our perspective about alt-right gangs, it is through the marriage of these different literatures that a more comprehensive picture and nuanced understanding of what is known about alt-right gangs is developed. This perspective also allows the identification of what research is still lacking or limited.

The goal of this book is to give students, academics, law enforcement, policy makers, and legislators an incisive look into alt-right gangs and establish a usable definition that can be operationalized to systematically examine alt-right gangs in future research and/or policy initiatives. Additionally, this book draws on our own unique research analyzing conventional street gangs, gang-related violence, incarcerated youth, and alt-right gangs (e.g., racist skinheads). There are three primary audiences for this book. The central audience is scholars of criminology or academics studying the broader WPM. As an essential primer on alt-right gangs, this book fills a void in the gang literature, supplementing any graduate or undergraduate course on juvenile delinquency, hate or bias-related crimes, violent extremism, or juvenile subcultures. It may also serve as a primary text in special-topics courses focused on modern gangs or the WPM. The second group benefiting from this book is law enforcement agencies and policy makers bewildered by the dramatic manifestation of the alt-right movement (see Reitman

2018). Finally, the book will provide the public at large with an accessible general background about the WPM and alt-right gangs and offer some possible strategies to effectively intervene.

The format of *Alt-Right Gangs* is designed to apply nearly 100 years of gang scholarship to an understanding of these specific gangs. Chapter 1 discusses the definitional issues surrounding the historical exclusion of white power groups from street gang studies. The chapter focuses on the unique role that ideology plays in excluding these white power groups from gang studies and proposes an interdisciplinary definition for alt-right gangs that can be used to systematically study them. Chapter 2 not only lays out the myths and realities about alt-right gangs, but also unveils the myths that alt-right gangs promote to their membership. Chapters 3 through 7 provide a detailed analysis of specific aspects of alt-right gangs, paying particular attention to the overlap that exists with our knowledge of street gangs and highlighting just how well situated gang researchers are to examine these alt-right groups. Chapter 3 synthesizes the street gang and racist skinhead literatures to consider the risk factors that are associated with joining an alt-right gang. Chapter 4 discusses the integral role that white power music and culture play as a facilitator and recruiter for alt-right gangs. Chapter 5 moves on to the importance and use of space, both physical and digital, for alt-right gangs. Chapter 6 continues to build on alt-right gangs' utilization of the virtual world by focusing on how the internet and social media connect members and have evolved and adapted over time. Chapter 7 examines the "cafeteria-style" criminality and use of violence by alt-right gangs. Chapter 8 concludes with a discussion of the policy implications and next steps needed to better understand and address the public resurgence of the WPM in the form of alt-right gangs.

Most criminological texts discussing street gangs attempt to provide a comprehensive overview of the topic but routinely dismiss alt-right gangs (see Curry, Decker & Pyrooz 2014; Hamm 1993; Klein 1995), fail to acknowledge their inclusion (see Decker & Pyrooz 2015b; Esbensen, Tibbetts & Gaines 2004; Maxson, Egely, Miller & Klein 2014; Howell & Griffiths 2018; Huff 2002; Fraser 2017; Kontos, Brotherton & Barrios 2003), or provide only a cursory discussion or history (see Barker 2019; Delaney 2014; Sanders 2017; Shelden, Tracy & Brown 2012). The failure of these texts to adequately address just how much compatibility exists between conventional street gangs and alt-right gangs is an oversight this book strives to remedy. Guided by an interdisciplinary approach, *Alt-Right Gangs* synthesizes an expansive set of literatures, including emerging and groundbreaking texts analyzing the rise of the alt-right (see Crothers 2019; Fielitz & Thurston 2019; Finn 2019; Hawley 2017, 2019; Hermansson et al 2020; Lyons 2017, 2018; Main 2018; Nagle 2017; Neiwert 2017; Stern 2019; Waring 2018, 2019; Wendling 2018). The integration of scholarly research across a variety of disciplines provides the most coherent and complete understanding of alt-right gangs today.

Incorporating these diverse literatures into a singular definition not only provides a broad categorization of alt-right gangs but allows for a more insightful understanding of those involved in these gangs. This work provides scholars and policy makers with prevention, intervention, and suppression strategies that are not pigeonholed to only to a subsample of individuals involved in the WPM.

1

THE DILEMMA OF DEFINITIONS
AND CATEGORIZATIONS

I started this gang called the Proud Boys!
GAVIN MCINNES (*JOE ROGAN EXPERIENCE* [FEBRUARY 23, 2017])

We [PENI] were a group of fucken white boys that formed together to pro-
tect each other, gang style. It wasn't nothing fucken political at all. Some of
the members might have been more political . . . but generally we were only
interested in being gangsters.
SIMI, SMITH & REESER (2008: 766)

INTRODUCTION

This chapter aims to orient the reader to the definitional and categorization issues that impact the study of youth-oriented white power groups. That is, groups where the majority of members fall between the ages of 12 and 25 (Weerman et al. 2009). In order to address the current state of literature about white power youth, we need to examine how definitions and categorizations have shifted the dialogue in possibly unexpected and unanticipated ways. This discussion is even more critical since the research has seen both the exclusion (whether explicit or implicit) of these youth by gang researchers, and the inclusion of these youth by researchers focused on the more expansive WPM. This definitional gap has had long-term consequences for how white power youth are studied. Properly categorizing youth-dominated, street-oriented groups, such as racist skinhead groups, allows for the development of more appropriate research questions and data collection protocols so that findings from these studies can be generalizable and used effectively.

To better understand these issues, it is necessary to first consider how the inclusion of white power gang youth in studies that attempt to encapsulate the entire WPM and its iterations potentially misclassifies these youth. Second, we must examine how the definitional decisions of early skinhead and street gang researchers have influenced the divide between these two groups (e.g., Curry & Decker 1998; Hamm 1993; Klein 1995). This examination allows the reader to understand how and why these group distinctions were made so that we can then center the study of white power gang youth within the broader lens of gang research. It is important to note that our reference to, and usage of, the term *white power youth* is meant to limit our focus on youth who are members of street-based youth groups that have adopted white power ideology and/or signs and symbols. Youth involved in these groups have previously been referred to colloquially as racist skinheads (Baron 1997; Blazak 2001; Borgeson & Valeri 2018; Brake 1974; Cooter 2006; Fangen 1998; Hicks 2004; Moore 1993; Moore 1994; Pilkington, Omel'chenko & Garifzianova 2010; Pollard 2016; Reid & Valasik 2018; Sarabia & Shriver 2004; Simi 2006, 2009; Simi & Futrell 2015; Simi, Smith & Reeser 2008; Tarasov 2001, 2008; Valasik & Reid 2019). We use the term *alt-right gangs* to avoid limiting our discussion to only those youth who have adopted the "skinhead" label for their group or identity (since skinheads can be both racist and non-racist) (see Borgeson & Valeri 2018).

CATEGORIZING WHITE POWER GANG YOUTH

While many books and articles aggregate these youth (aged 12–25) into the larger WPM, we contend that including these youth in studies also containing and discussing long-established white power groups organized around older individuals, such as the Ku Klux Klan (KKK), neo-Confederates (e.g., League of the South), Christian Identity sects (e.g., The Covenant, The Sword, and the Arm of the Lord), Creativity (formerly known as The Church of the Creator) sects (e.g., Creativity Movement, Creativity Alliance), racialized Odinists (e.g., The Silent Brotherhood), and neo-Nazis (e.g., National Socialist Movement, White Aryan Resistance) is a misclassification of these youth. While it makes sense, from a social-movements perspective, to aggregate all individuals who use white power symbols and language together, this is an oversimplification. These white power groups are not interchangeable and are very likely to have distinct risk factors and behavioral characteristics. The inclusion of youth in these larger studies has a number of negative implications, including an overemphasis on the roll and impact of ideology, an underestimation of the prevalence of cafeteria-style offending patterns, and an inability to develop generalizable findings. While the need for larger sample sizes may have driven many of the definitional and aggregation decisions made by researchers (see Blee 1996; Hamm 1993), the consequences of these decisions have greatly limited our ability to create effective prevention, intervention, and suppression policies and programs that can be utilized by policy makers, law enforcement, or local stakeholders to address white power groups (see Reitman 2018).

By examining the different samples from some key studies, one can see how this aggregation can affect policy makers' and practitioners' use of research findings. The purpose of these examples is not to call out any particular researcher but rather to highlight the over-inclusion of youth in larger white power studies.

1.   Freilich and colleagues (2009) use Berlet and Vysotky's (2006) typology organizing far-right groups into three categories: religious, political, and youth cultural. For their study, Freilich et al. (2009) focused on (in order) Aryan Nations, National Alliance, and Public Enemy #1 (PEN1).
2.   Blee (2003) uses a broad definition, sampling women with an association to a group that is considered an active racist group (i.e., racist skinheads, Christian Identity, Ku Klux Klan, and neo-Nazi groups).
3.   Simi and colleagues collected data from members of any white supremacist group, with participants ranging in age from 19 to 61 (Simi, Sporer & Bubolz, 2016; Simi, Blee, DeMichele & Windisch 2017).

All of these definitions make several assumptions that are yet to be supported in the literature. First is the notion that each type of white power group has the same motivations and risk factors for membership as the others. Among other problems with this idea is the substantial age range within many of these groups. Can we expect that a 16-year-old who joins a racist skinhead gang has the same motivations and risk factors for membership as a 40-year-old who joins the KKK? Second is the view that ideology is the principal motivator for membership. For this to be accepted, one must assume that an individual joins a gang such as PEN1 solely because of white supremacist motivations instead of other reasons (e.g., protection, economic interest, self-identity, etc.) (see Borgeson & Valeri 2018). When we consider the race-based organization of prisons (see Goodman 2008), it seems difficult to believe that individuals choose to join PEN1 or Aryan Brotherhood because they are seeking out like-minded racists rather than because there are a limited number of groups providing protection for white prisoners. On the street, similar constraints about group availability in the criminal market may play a role in group selection. For instance, Christensen (1994) found that skinhead gang members will switch between racist and non-racist skinhead gangs based on a desire to be a member of a group, underscoring the role of social relationships over ideology in membership choices. Third is the idea that adhering to a white power ideology is a definer for all of these groups, rather than just being a descriptor. Currently, the aggregation of different types of far-right groups together for research purposes assumes that they all share a common ideology (see Belew 2018). However, as we have seen with racist skinhead gangs in Europe, the ideological signs and symbols of these groups are used for intimidation purposes rather than to assert a belief (van Gemert, Peterson & Lien 2008). Instead, if ideology is treated as a descriptor, then more appropriate distinctions can be utilized to delineate similarities and differences not only between the various types of white power groups but also between those groups and other types of subcultural groups (e.g., street gangs, extremist groups, criminal syndicates).

It is not only social movement studies, that have unnecessarily limited or expanded their samples to the detriment of the understanding of youth in white power groups. For example, Klein (1995: 22) states in *The American Street Gang* that his book is a discussion "of street gangs, not skinheads" partly because of what he perceived as a lack of street orientation on the part of racist skinhead groups. Racist skinheads are "inside; they're working on their written materials; or if outside, they're looking for a target, not lounging around." However, since street gang survey research does not ask questions that could identify membership in a white power gang, these youth may be captured in these studies without researchers being aware they are in the sample (e.g., the G.R.E.A.T. survey, see Esbensen, Osgood, Peterson, Taylor & Carson 2013; Esbensen, Peterson, Taylor & Osgood 2012). In these surveys, researchers are unable to distinguish racist skinheads from other white youth that claim gang membership. For example, youth captured in the Division of Juvenile Justice study include white power youth (i.e., members of different skinhead gangs) that all analyses count as gang members. However, were it not for the data, qualitative and official, collected directly by the researchers, their membership in these groups would have been unknown and they would have been assumed to be members in conventional gangs (see Magnus & Scott 2020; Maxson et al. 2012; Reid & Maxson 2016; Scott 2018a, 2018b, 2019; Scott & Maxson 2016; Valasik & Reid 2019). As we will see next, if these youth were not identified by very particular indicators, they would be categorized as conventional gang members across a range of gang definitions.

DEFINING WHITE POWER GANG YOUTH
(A.K.A. ALT-RIGHT GANGS)

The next major issue surrounding the study of white power youth is the question of definitions. We consider how definitions have been used to disqualify youth, and their groups, that fall under the white power/alt-right heading from street gang studies. At the core of the distinction between street gangs and racist skinheads lies a definitional quandary. The definitional distinction between racist skinheads and street gangs is in the role of ideology (Reid & Valasik 2018). A review of the racist skinhead literature finds that the "otherness" of skinhead youth, as compared to street gang youth, is often focused on the mythology around skinheads as "the foot soldiers" of the far right (Christensen 1994; Keane 1993; Moore 1993) and bastions of the working-class ideal (Pollard 2016). This chapter lays out our argument that ideology should not be the limiting factor in excluding racist skinheads from research on street gangs. Ideology itself is neither adhered to in such a strict way nor so unique to youth in white power groups that it places them outside of the street gang spectrum (Simi 2006, 2009; Simi et al. 2008; Valasik & Reid 2019). Thus, to focus on the ideology or race-based orientation of skinheads is to ignore or minimize the role that ideology and racial/ethnic pride play in the formation, maintenance, and membership of non-white street gangs (see Brotherton & Barrios 2004; Cureton 2011; Francisco & Martinez 2003; Helmreich 1973; Moore 1978, 1991; Short 1974; Short & Moland 1976; Vigil 1996). The use of ideology as a reason to limit the inclusion of racist skinheads in gang studies has directly impacted how researchers study white power youth, how their findings influence the training of law enforcement officers, and how policies are supported and implemented to deal with white power youth groups (Reitman 2018; Valasik & Reid 2018a).

Next, consider some common definitions used to identify gangs and gang members. These definitions are used to analyze how white power youth groups fit into these street gang definitions.

1. The California Street Terrorism Enforcement and Prevention Act, California Penal Code section 186.22(f), states that a criminal street gang is defined as "any ongoing organization, association or group of three or more persons, whether formal or informal, having as one of its primary activities the commission of one or more of the criminal acts [. . .], having a common name or common identifying sign or symbol, and whose members individually or collectively engage in or have engaged in a pattern of criminal gang activity."[1]

2. In social science research the definition of a gang has varied widely, but Esbensen and colleagues point out that most definitions include, at minimum: (1) a focus on youth status (i.e., the majority of their members are between 10 and early 20s); and (2) group members engage in delinquent or law-violating behavior (Esbensen, Winfree, He & Taylor 2001). Other research definitions expand upon this to include, but are not limited to, control of and/or demarcation of territory, a sense of permanence, utilization of signs and symbols (i.e., tattoos, hand signs, graffiti) to designate in-group/out-group status, and participation in violence (see Fleisher 1998; Klein 1971; Puffer 1912; Short 1996; Thrasher 1927).

3. The Eurogang definition identifies a street gang as "any durable, street-oriented youth group whose involvement in illegal activity is part of their group identity" (Weerman et al. 2009: 20).

4. Self-nomination of gang membership (Decker, Pyrooz, Sweeten & Moule 2014; Esbensen, Winfree, et al. 2001; Esbensen, Osgood, et al. 2001; Esbensen & Osgood 1999; Webb, Katz & Decker 2006).

---

1. It should be noted that the criteria used to define a criminal street gang in California are quite common; most state and federal criminal codes look analogous.

The review of these definitions underscores how youth who join alt-right gangs would clearly fall under these definitions. Other white power groups, such as the National Socialist Movement or the League of the South, would not fall under this definitional umbrella due to the majority of these groups' membership being beyond the 12–25 age range, lacking a street-orientation, and criminal activity not being part of their group's collective identity. In California, members of groups such as PEN1, Aryan Brotherhood, Nazi Low Riders, La Mirada Punks, West Coast Costa Mesa Skins, and the Orange County Skins have been charged with crimes that were "for the benefit of, at the direction of, or in association with any criminal street gang" (California Penal Code section 186.22(f)), with several members having gang enhancements added to their sentences. In 2010, the California Department of Justice's Division of Law Enforcement put out a report on Organized Crime in California with a section on "White Street Gangs" highlighting both racist and non-racist white street gangs. The report states, "Today's white gangs in California and across the nation consist of white males from the ages of 12 to 27 years old. Law enforcement officials report rising levels of criminal activity by the white gangs, including credit card theft, fraudulent checks, vehicle theft, home invasion robberies, aggravated assault, and murder" (Harris 2010). For law enforcement purposes, these white power youth groups would be considered a gang (e.g., PEN1), while other white power groups, with their older members, are not (e.g., National Socialist Movement). Law enforcement also focuses on these youths' participation in a range of offenses, rather than focusing on hate/bias crime (see also Simi et al. 2008).

As mentioned above, it is not a true definitional distinction between street gangs and white power gangs that has researchers "removing" white power youth from larger gang studies, but rather a reliance on an outdated understanding of these groups and their members. Even though the field of gang research still fails to agree on a common description for street gangs, the Eurogang definition "has become widely adopted and appears regularly in publications" and could be considered the most appropriate definition for determining what is a street gang (Maxson & Esbensen 2016: 7). Under this definition, racist skinhead groups would clearly be considered a street gang, as indicated by Pyrooz and colleagues' (2018) recent study. Furthermore, over the last two decades many edited volumes of street gang scholarship include research that discusses or focuses on such white power gang groups (see Dekleva 2001; De Waele & Pauwels 2016; Kersten 2001; Lien 2001; Reid et al. 2020; Salagaev, Shashkin, Sherbakova & Touriyanskiy 2005; Sela-Shayovitz 2012; Shashkin 2008; Simi 2006). For example, Klein (2001: 17) stated in *The Eurogang Paradox*, "Skinheads—more prominent in Europe than in the U.S.—stretch the meaning of street gangs; they are less street-oriented, and more focused on a particular crime pattern, for example. Yet I find I am comfortable placing them in the Specialty gang category of the paradigm."

Could it be bc they're white?

It seems that Klein's (1996; 2009; Klein & Maxson 2006) reversal to include skinheads as "specialty" street gangs has been greatly ignored by gang scholars (e.g., Curry et al. 2014). Defining white power groups (e.g., racist skinheads/alt-right gangs) as outside of the street gang spectrum remains a post-hoc decision, and their inclusion or exclusion from studies is more fluid than would be expected given the emphasis placed upon ideological differences (see Pyrooz et al. 2018). Regardless of scholars' receptiveness to the Eurogang definition, street gangs do not need to have some observable or measurable difference from another group to be considered a street gang. Instead, street gangs exist because members belonging to the group and individuals external to the group believe, feel, socialize, and act as if a gang is a distinct social entity (Papachristos 2005).

Additionally, a discussion about who is or who is not a gang member cannot be had without considering an individual's self-nomination in a gang. For gang studies, self-nomination has been a validated and robust measure of gang membership (Esbensen & Carson 2012; Pyrooz & Decker 2019). With this in mind, it is important to note that in several more recent studies, white power youth identify themselves as gang members (Simi et al. 2008; Valasik & Reid 2019) and their group as a gang (Simi et al. 2008; Wooden & Blazak 2001). This self-identification is considered a reasonable standard for inclusion in gang studies and should not be dismissed due to a desire to exclude them for unsupported reasons.

For the rest of the book, the reader should be oriented by a few points: Traditionally, white power gangs have been referred to as (racist) skinheads; however, this term is narrow and traditionally elicits stereotypes and bias (see Curry et al. 2014; Etter 1999; Klein 1995; Hamm 1993; Schneider 1999). Instead, we use the term *alt-right gang* (or *alternative-right gang*) defined as: *"A durable, public-oriented group (both digitally and physically) whose adoption of signs and symbols of the white power movement and involvement in illegal activity are part of its group identity"* Our definition incorporates aspects of the Eurogang definition and is focused on explicitly identifying alt-right gangs and their members. The appendix provides a questionnaire for operationalizing our definition of an alt-right gang that can be utilized in researchers' future studies. In addition, alt-right gangs that fall under this definition would also be included as gangs in the broader Eurogang definition.

The following is a breakdown of each of the elements in the definition. For the element of *durability*, it is important to acknowledge that gang-like groups coalesce and dissipate within a short period of time, something not uncommon among white power groups (Belew 2018; Tenold 2018). Therefore, to be classified an alt-right gang, the group should exist for at least several months and remain in existence even when membership turns over.

With regard to the element of *public-orientation*, alt-right gangs direct their attention, activities, and behaviors, both digitally and physically, toward public *lt* '

spaces. Physically, this translates into being out in public places. This could mean a street location, but it also includes bars, clubs, parks, and such. Digitally, a public virtual space would include most social networking sites (e.g., Twitter, Facebook, Instagram, Gab) or public forums/imageboards (e.g., 4chan, 8kun, Reddit) where alt-right gang members are able to interact with, including harass and pressure, others publicly (May & Feldman 2019; Nagle 2017; Tuters 2019). The idea is that alt-right gangs can only be intimidating to others if they are not cloistered away from the general populace but instead are present in public venues, either in the digital or material realm. In both these spheres, however, Alt-right gangs manifest where effective supervision by social control agents is lacking.

The *adoption of signs and symbols of the white power movement* as a component of the group's identity includes ideological imagery (e.g., swastikas, SS bolts, 88, 14) that might be visibly displayed on clothing or banners or as tattoos (ADL 1995; Fangen 1998; Forbes & Stampton 2015; Miller-Idriss 2018, 2019; Moore 1993; Pollard 2016; Sarabia & Shriver 2003; Simi & Futrell 2015; Tuters 2019).[2] Thus, the collective culture and identity of the group validates the imagery of the WPM as being acceptable and normal to display openly. Additionally, there has been a mainstreaming of the WPM, and the blatant use of traditional symbols has begun to diminish as more members have begun to normalize and conform to conventional society (Cooter 2006; Hermansson, Mulhall & Murdoch 2020; Miller-Idriss 2018, 2019; Simi and Futrell 2015). The mainstreaming of the WPM has also brought a commercialization of clothing brands (e.g., Thor Steinar, Erik and Sons, Ansgar Aryan) that intentionally use coded symbols historically associated with white power rhetoric and market their apparel to individuals on the far right, producing clothing that is essentially identical to popular brands like Abercrombie and Fitch or Aeropostale (Miller-Idriss 2018, 2019). White power groups also have a history of adopting clothing brands, in spite of a brand not condoning the adoption (e.g., Fred Perry or Ben Sherman polo shirts, Dr (Doc) Marten boots, Alpha Industries Bomber Jacket, etc.) (Cooter 2006; Hermansson et al. 2020; Miller-Idriss 2018, 2019; Simi and Futrell 2015). Similarly, alt-right gangs have also adopted brands as mainstream symbols to represent the white power movement (e.g., Cadillac, Fred Perry, New Balance, Wendy's, Papa John's) (Jan 2017; Hermansson et al. 2020; Mettler 2016; Miller-Idriss 2019).

The other component comprising a group's identity, *involvement in illegal activity*, refers to antisocial behaviors and activities engaged in by the group. These go beyond just annoying conduct and fall under activities that would be considered delinquent or criminal (see chapter 7).

---

2. The SPLC (2012) has a much more complete list of white power symbology (see also Miller-Idriss, 2018).

One element that is purposefully not included in our definition is adherence to any particular form of ideology. As highlighted earlier in this chapter, we argue that ideology is better used as a descriptor for alt-right gangs than as a definer. While the general ideological beliefs of white identity and racial superiority permeate throughout various white power groups, there are also varied and sometimes contradictory beliefs that can be more complex (e.g., mythologies and religious beliefs such as Odinism, the World Church of the Creator, or National Socialism) (see Berry 2017; Burlein 2002; Gardell 2003; Goodrick-Clarke 2002; Pollard 2016; Simi and Futrell 2015). Furthermore, when considering the role ideology plays in alt-right gang membership, there is a spectrum of how integral white power is to either the group's or an individual's identity. The American flavor of white supremacy being focused on white racial purity has influenced who is eligible to join a white power group, shifting the focus away from ethnicity and toward skin color (see Dyck 2017; Miller-Idriss 2018; Mudde 2005; Saini 2019; Simi & Futrell 2015; Wooden & Blazak 2001). For instance, Pollard (2016) highlights that the traditional adherence to the rigid racial hierarchies of Nazism have largely been dispensed with as more and more individuals with Slavic backgrounds join white power groups throughout the United States and Europe. Such a shift allows non-Aryan members to be able to participate in these groups or for members to have meaningful relationships with nonwhite individuals.

The Venn diagram in figure 1.1 provides an illustration of our definition for an alt-right gang. Three sets compose the diagram: conventional street gangs, white power groups, and online trolls. While the first two sets perhaps seem to be intuitive choices, online trolls may come as a surprise. Even though white supremacists have utilized the internet for decades (see Back 2002; Borgeson & Valeri 2005, 2018; Daniels 2009a, 2009b, 2018; Donovan et al. 2019; T. Morris 2017), the larger alt-right movement readily employs digital communications (e.g., social media, imageboards, forums) to downplay the extreme rhetoric of white supremacist ideology through irony and humor, typically by using memes (see DeCook 2018; Frielitz & Thurston 2019; Froio & Ganesh 2019; Hawley 2018, 2019; Nagle 2017; Neiwert 2017; Reid et al. 2020; Tuters 2019; Wendling 2018). The intersection of conventional street gangs and white power groups corresponds to traditional white supremacist gangs (e.g., Aryan Brotherhood, Nazi Lowriders, Peckerwoods). As discussed above, these groups have had a contentious history of being included in street gang studies (see Klein 1996, 2001; Pyrooz et al. 2018; Simi 2006, 2009; Simi et al. 2008; Reid & Valasik 2018; Valasik & Reid 2019). The intersection of conventional street gangs and online trolls is embodied by "Trap Rap" gangs (see Irwin-Rogers, Densley & Pinkney 2018; Lauger & Densley 2018; Storrod & Densley 2017 for a full discussion). The intersection of white power groups and online trolls embodies the alt-lite, which includes personalities like Mike Cernovich, Lauren Southern, Steve Bannon, Milo Yiannopoulos, Alex Jones

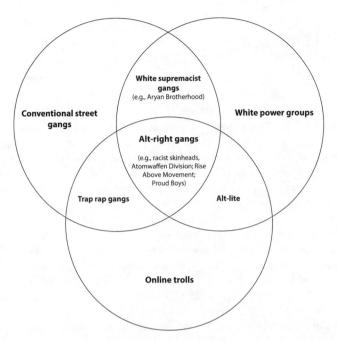

FIGURE 1.1. Venn diagram depicting alt-right gangs.

(host of *Infowars*), and Ann Coulter (Hawley 2018, 2019; Main 2018; Wendling 2018). The alt-lite is considered to be in a peripheral orbit to the extreme racist core of the alt-right movement. Specifically, alt-lite members "want white people and white culture to be openly dominant in the United States once again" in contrast to members of the alt-right, which "want to split off from the United States or destroy it altogether" (Lyons 2018: 220).

It is the intersection of all three sets (i.e., conventional street gangs, white power groups, and online trolls) that personifies an alt-right gang. This includes novel groups that have more recently made the news in the United States (e.g., Proud Boys, R.A.M., Atomwaffen Division, The Base) and throughout Europe (e.g., Erkenbrand, English Defence League, Feuerkrieg Division, Azov Battalion, Russian National Unity) (Hawley 2019; Klapsis 2019; Lamoureux & Makuch 2018a, 2018b; Lopez 2017; Makuch & Lamoureux 2019a; McVeigh & Estep 2019; Pilkington 2016; PBS 2018a, 2018b; Reitman 2018; Roose & Winston 2018; Reid et al. 2020; Valasik & Reid, 2018a; van der Valk 2019; Ware 2008). Alt-right gangs have generally adopted a more mainstream aesthetic (e.g., collared shirts and khaki pants) and intensified their digital footprint on the internet (e.g., social media, imageboards, forums, etc.). Despite contention among scholars about using the term *alt-right* to describe these far-right groups (see Fielitz &

FOCUS BOX

Proud Boys: A Prototypical Alt-Right Gang

In 2016, Gavin McInnes founded Proud Boys, a self-described "western chauvinist" men's club (DeCook 2018; Hawley 2019; McVeigh & Estep 2019; NPR 2018; PBS 2018a, 2018b; Proud Boys 2019; Valasik & Reid 2018a). DeCook (2018: 7) points out that Proud Boys "very much function like a fraternity or more accurately, a gang; their gatherings often involve heavy amounts of drinking and violence, there are rituals involved in gaining status in the group, and there is a uniform and agreed upon logo (including colors) to signify their group identity." While non-gang scholars contend that Proud Boys are clearly a gang, let's see how the group compares to what is known about conventional street gangs and the definition of an alt-right gang (see also Reid et al. 2020).

First and foremost, during an interview on the *Joe Rogan Experience* (February 23, 2017), Gavin McInnes publicly designated the group as being a gang. This process of self-nomination is one of the most robust predictors of gang embeddedness and involvement (Decker et al. 2014; Esbensen, Osgood, et al. 2001; Esbensen, Winfree, et al. 2001 Esbensen & Osgood 1999; Webb et al. 2006). While self-nomination is not an element in the alt-right gang definition, Proud Boys have many other descriptors, behavioral and organizational, analogous with conventional street gangs. For instance, like conventional street gangs, members of Proud Boys share a collective identity. That identity is one of a hipster persona that uses irony and humor to facilitate far-right arguments that attack the political, social, and cultural status quo, generally opposing feminism, immigration, political correctness, and establishment politics (DeCook 2018; Hall 2018; Hawley 2019; McVeigh & Estep 2019; Nagle 2017; NPR 2018; Reid et al. 2020; SPLC 2019a). Similar to the routine behaviors that members of street gangs participate in (Klein 1995), Proud Boys members focus the majority of their attention around hanging out together and drinking beer (Hawley 2019; NPR 2018; Rogan 2017).

The similarities between Proud Boys and conventional street gangs do not end there. Proud Boys members wear clothing of a specific set of colors, yellow and black, which usually includes the group's mascot, a cockerel. These colors and logo regularly adorn the Proud Boys' unique uniform, a black Fred Perry polo shirt accentuated with yellow piping (see figure B.1) (Beery 2017; Cauterucci 2017; Hermansson et al 2020; SPLC 2019a; Swenson 2017). Coincidently or not, Fred Perry polo shirts have a long history of being part of the uniform worn by racist skinheads (Beery 2017; Brown 2004; Cooter 2006; Hicks 2004; Miller-Idriss 2018; Pilkington 2010; Sarabia & Shriver 2004; Smolik 2015).

In addition to having a cultural style and aesthetic, Proud Boys, along with many other white supremacists, use hand signals (i.e., the "OK" sign) as another means of group identification in the larger WPM (Allyn 2019; Neiwert 2018b). Whether the "OK" sign is explicitly a white power symbol or is being deployed

FIGURE B.1. Proud Boys members wearing their signature black and yellow Fred Perry polo shirts and MAGA hats (photo by David Neiwert).

in an ironic manner as a way to troll and "trigger liberals" remains in contention (see figure B.2) (Hermansson et al 2020; Neiwert 2018b). Regardless of the motives driving the use of the "OK" sign, the fact that these groups publicly employ it produces the same result of signaling to others that these individuals are part of a larger group (see Allyn 2019; Densley 2013; Gambetta 2009; Van Hellmont & Densley 2019).

Similar to how conventional street gangs "jump in" new members (see Bolden 2012; Duran 2009; Moore, Vigil, & Garcia 1983; Padilla 1996; Petersen & Valdez 2005; Pyrooz & Decker 2011; Vigil 1996), Proud Boys also have a bizarre and violent initiation process in which a member must endure being assaulted and beaten until he is able to name five breakfast cereals (Hall 2017; Hawley 2019; Nagle 2017; Rogan 2017; SPLC 2019a). Another Proud Boys identifier is that they routinely brand themselves by getting a group tattoo, which is a common trend among both street gangs and white power groups (Hall 2017; Hawley 2019; Rogan 2017; SPLC 2019a). Members are also encouraged to utilize violence when confronting adversaries, and they have a sordid history of engaging in criminal acts of violence (see figure B.3) (Coaston 2018b; First Vigil 2019; SPLC 2019a). Additionally, there is a militant, paramilitary division called the Fraternal Order of Alt-Knights (FOAK) intent on protecting right-wing activists at political demonstrations (DeCook 2018; Finn 2019; SPLC 2019b; Vitolo-Haddad 2019). The combination of criminality and affinity toward white power symbology

FIGURE B.2. Proud Boys members making the "OK" hand sign (photo by David Neiwert).

being entwined in Proud Boys' collective identity satisfies two necessary elements required to be considered an alt-right gang.

Another analogous feature with conventional street gangs is that Proud Boys have a loose organizational structure (Decker & Curry 2002; Klein & Maxson 2006; Moore 1991; Short & Strodtbeck 1965). Following Gavin McInnes's renouncement of his leadership of Proud Boys and desistance from them, a group of "elders" (reminiscent of "shotcallers," "veteranos," or "OGs" in a street gang) stepped in to fill the void and manage the group (Campbell 2018; Crosbie 2018). Originally, it only took five like-minded individuals to create a Proud Boys chapter, with each being nominally independent; however, following attention from the FBI, arrests of members by the NYPD after a fight in Manhattan, and Gavin McInnes's departure, increased vetting of chapters and more oversight by the Elders Chapter began in hopes of minimizing law enforcement attention (IGD 2018; Shallwani & Weill 2018; Templeton & Wilson 2018). The internal structure of a Proud Boys chapter consists of different degrees that a member is able to occupy. The higher the degree status of a member, the more committed that individual is to the group. A first-degree Proud Boy is simply one who self-nominates, declaring himself to be a Proud Boy. To become a second-degree Proud Boy a member must refrain from masturbating and go through the "cereal beating" initiation ritual. Third-degree Proud Boys are required to get a group tattoo. Fourth-degree Proud Boys have to have been arrested or observed participating in a serious act

FIGURE B.3. A Proud Boys member wearing protective gear in preparation for a violent confrontation (photo by David Neiwert).

of violence in front of the police (Rogan 2017). In addition to the "men only" group, there are female auxiliary groups called "Proud Boys' Girls" specifically for women enthusiasts of Proud Boys (DeCook 2018; Proud Boys 2019; SPLC 2019a). The presence of female-specific auxiliary groups as supportive entities is commonly observed in street gangs and white power groups (Belew 2018; Blee 1991, 2002, 2005; Blee & Linden 2012; Borgeson 2003; Fangen 1997; Ferber 1998; Hughes, Botchkovar, & Short 2019; Miller 1973; Miller 2001; Moore 1991; Peterson, Miller, & Esebensen 2001). This delineates another element of the alt-right gang definition—durability. Proud Boys cliques have been established since 2016 (see Reid et al. 2020).

Unlike conventional street gangs, Proud Boys regularly use the internet and strategically employ various forms of digital media to reinforce the group's identity and maintain collective solidarity but also to spread their propaganda and recruit new members across a range of platforms (e.g., Facebook, Instagram, YouTube, Gab, etc.) (DeCook 2018; Hatmaker 2018; Reid et al. 2020). While the ubiquitous use of digital technology is unremarkable among the larger alt-right movement, or even among jihadi terrorist groups (e.g., the Islamic State of Iraq and Syria), it has traditionally been used with much less frequency by conventional street gangs (Densley 2013; Sela-Shayovitz 2012; Storrod & Densley

2016; Valasik & Phillips 2017, 2018). Proud Boys minimize the extreme rhetoric of white supremacist ideology through absurdity, irony, and humor, typically through the use of memes (see DeCook 2018; Frielitz & Thurston 2018; Froio & Ganesh 2019; Hawley 2018, 2019; Nagle 2017; Neiwert 2018b; Phillips 2015; Reid et al. 2020; Tuter 2019; Wendling 2018). As with conventional street gangs, Proud Boys appeal to marginalized men who feel they have no place in modern society. They are seeking a group that desires a return to a nostalgic past where the hegemony of being a white man bestowed privileges that were not questioned. Additionally, Gavin McInnes regularly compares Proud Boys to the Elk's Lodge (see Rogan 2017), another fraternal, exclusionary organization created in response to the increased "crisis of masculinity" as progressiveness and the feminization of society was increasing (see Kimmel 1996, 2013). Today, as youth socialization becomes more and more enmeshed with social media, it is this proficiency with the internet, social media platforms specifically and digital technologies more broadly, that sets Proud Boys apart from both conventional street gangs and traditional white power groups, making them more dangerous and disconcerting in their ability to spread their propaganda and worldview (see Coutts 2017; DeCook 2018; Hermansson et al 2020). Thus, Proud Boys do not just manifest in the material world but also have a robust digital footprint, another element of the alt-right definition.

Proud Boys also demonstrate what Felson (2006) refers to as "Big Gang Theory," an exaggerated view that a group is highly organized, controls a lot of territory, has hierarchical leadership, and drives local crime patterns. For instance, Gavin McInnes has claimed that there are Proud Boys chapters sprouting up all over the globe. However, there remain approximately 30 chapters in the United States, a half dozen in Canada, even fewer across Europe, and merely a promise that chapters are "coming soon" to the rest of the globe (Proud Boys 2019; Rogan 2017). It is possible that the organization has just failed to maintain an accurate count on the number of chapters in existence. More likely is that given Proud Boys' notoriety, local groups are just imitating them, thereby giving the impression that this alt-right gang is bigger and more imposing than it is in reality. Additionally, Proud Boys' digital footprint (i.e., website, social media, online magazine) contributes to the perception that the group is a highly organized entity, large and intimidating. The reality of Proud Boys, fortunately, fails to live up to the promise of Proud Boys.

Yet, Proud Boys are just one of these emerging alt-right gangs. In the United States others include Rise Above Movement (R.A.M.), Atomwaffen Division, and The Base (Bharath 2018; Hawley 2019; Lamoureux & Makuch 2018a, 2019; Makuch & Lamoureux 2019a; PBS 2018a, 2018b; Reitman 2018; Thompson 2018). Alt-right gangs in Europe include Erkenbrand, English Defence League, Feuerkrieg Division, Azov Battalion, and Russian National Unity (Klapsis 2019; Makuch & Lamoureux 2019b; Miller 2018; Pilkington 2016; van der Valk 2019;

Winston 2019). Like Proud Boys, these groups regularly participate in violence against counterprotesters at public demonstrations, but also more deliberately against perceived enemies. They have also been stockpiling weapons, and they celebrate anti-Semitic violence (Bharath 2018; Bromwich 2018; Lavoie & Kunzelman 2018; PBS 2018a, 2018b; Thompson 2018). Furthermore, each of these alt-right gangs exists at a different stage on an evolutionary spectrum, with Proud Boys being the least extreme; groups like Atomwaffen Division, The Base, Feuerkrieg Division, and Azov Battalion the most extreme; and others, such as R.A.M., Erkenbrand, and English Defence League, falling somewhere in between (see chapter 2 for more on alt-right gang evolution).

[handwritten margin note: Now that I remember I've heard of PB, but didn't know it was a gang]

Thurston 2019; Mudde 2018), however, alt-right gangs are both a continuation of traditional white power gangs and something new as well (Daniels 2018; Futrell & Simi 2017). As such, we use the term *alt-right gangs* to encompass all youth gangs with white power leanings that have both a real-world and digital presence. Since the vast majority of the existing research on white power youth groups has focused on racist skinheads, this term will be used when we are engaging with that specific literature, but as we reflect more broadly on the larger literature and the future directions of this research, we will use the term *alt-right gang*.

RESEARCHING ALT-RIGHT GANGS

Blee (2013) discusses how studying white power groups elicits concerns around researcher safety due to the illegal (and therefore often hidden) nature of these groups' activities. Fears about personal safety and population access have limited some alt-right gang researchers to alternative data sources, such as social media posts, online magazines, newspapers, group-based publications, and music lyrics (see also Froio & Ganesh 2019; Klein 2019; Main 2018; Reid et al. 2020). The focus on small groups for qualitative research helps to limit the risk to researchers and has been used effectively to get in-depth knowledge about a subset of individuals, but it has greatly limited the generalizability of research findings. While concerns about safety and access to group members are important considerations when designing and implementing research studies, one must consider how fear of these populations may directly affect the understanding of these groups. One way to address these concerns is to separate alt-right gangs from studies of the larger WPM. By focusing on only alt-right gangs, these studies may be more methodologically feasible and, therefore, easier to control in terms of potential risk. Another benefit is it helps focus our studies more narrowly, allowing for the opportunity to better inform policy and practice when dealing with these youth. Studies on alt-right gangs are also able to utilize best practices from gang researchers to develop robust methodological studies (see Esbensen & Maxson 2011; Vigil 2016).

Just as white power research has limitations, gang research is not without its methodological difficulties. Gang members are a population that are often young, criminally active, and distrustful of people outside of their communities. Decades of gang research have demonstrated the wide range of ways to reach this population (see Decker & Van Winkle 1995; Esbensen et al. 2012; Miller 2001). Gang researchers have leveraged relationships with law enforcement, social workers, youth outreach workers, and school administrators to access these populations. Since gang youth (even those with white power leanings) are younger and more active in public than other traditional white power members, they have greater potential to be known to a wider range of agencies and also more likely to be present in school. This allows for greater access to these youth. It is also important to note that while local law enforcement has come under scrutiny for bias in gang databases (Brosseau 2016; Dumke 2018b; Flores 2017; Howell 2015; Howle 2016), that does not mean alt-right gang youth are unknown to law enforcement. Rather, it means that instead of only utilizing gang databases for gang information, deeper discussions need to occur about youth whom researchers want to study. It is also important to note that while local law enforcement is inconsistent with how they track alt-right gang members in the community, once those youth make it into a correctional setting (i.e., detention, jail, prison, etc.), these agencies do routinely identify and track them (Fleisher & Decker 2001; Fong 1990; Pyrooz & Decker 2019).

As one moves through the chapters of this book, it is important to keep in mind how the prior research has sampled and accessed the youth in their studies. How one defines a gang, whether alt-right or conventional, has a range of important implications for which youth we study and how studies are conducted. Without being definitionally clear and consistent, researchers will continue to struggle to target the appropriate populations for prevention, intervention, and suppression programs and policies. Throughout this book, we refer to these youth as alt-right gang members to reflect the definition we outlined above, but this includes youth previously referred to as racist skinheads in the extant literature.

2

MYTHS AND REALITIES
SURROUNDING ALT-RIGHT GANGS

I think it's a small group of people that have very, very serious problems.

PRESIDENT DONALD TRUMP (MARCH 15, 2019)

*Because of their overt racism, political violence, and international links to
a broader hate movement, the skinheads are properly defined as a* terrorist
youth subculture.

MARK S. HAMM (1993: 71)

INTRODUCTION

Just like conventional street gangs, alt-right gangs are often portrayed by academics (Curry et al. 2014), policy makers (Cohan 2017; Coppins 2018; Wilson
2018a), the media (Posner & Neiwert 2016; Thompson, Young & Burns 2000;
Wendling 2018), and even themselves (Tenold 2018; Wendling 2018) as being an
international, and highly structured organization. This mythological status that is
placed upon and praised by alt-right gangs actually acts like a cloak, hiding these
groups in plain sight, instead of making them a more noticeable target for law enforcement interventions (Reid & Valasik 2018). For instance, if police are looking
for members of a large international criminal conglomerate within their jurisdiction, but are unable to locate such an organization or any individuals belonging
to this crime syndicate, then that community must not have alt-right gangs. The
lack of local police attention toward alt-right gangs is clearly (un)documented
throughout the United States with the underreporting of white gang members in
gang databases. Racial/ethnic disproportionality favoring white gang members
has been revealed in New York City (1%), Chicago (4.3%), Charlotte (4%), Denver (1.76%), California (8.2%), and Minnesota (18.5%) (Aba-Onu, Levy-Pounds,
Salmen & Tyner 2010; Durán 2013; Flores 2017; Howell 2011; 2015; Howle 2016).
Additionally, the broad criteria, particularly dress and association, used by many

[handwritten margin note: not talked about b/c they arn't given much attention]

law enforcement agencies to label an individual a gang member are strongly biased toward urban youth culture (Aba-Onu et al. 2010; Howell 2011).

The reliability of such police gang databases becomes a question in itself (see Densley & Pyrooz 2019b; Howell 2011; 2015). In fact, officers of the Chicago Police Department (CPD) regularly rely on gang information from the Regional Gang Intelligence Database maintained by the Cook County Sheriff's office (Dumke 2018b). Yet, even this more reliable database, which captures gang intelligence from both local jails and state prisons, only identifies 13.1% of the population of 25,063 as being white, and only about 2.6% have ties to an alt-right gang, which is vastly greater than CPD's gang database having fewer than 50 of 128,836 individuals tied to an alt-right gang (Dumke 2018a; PBS 2018b). Howell (2011: 653) contends that "the disparity between law enforcement estimates based on broad criteria . . . leads to substantial over-inclusion of young men of color."

Another example of this continued apathy by local police toward alt-right gangs is observed in Portland. The Portland Police Bureau's Gang Database listed 359 gang members; however, only 32 of those individuals were listed as being a member of a white power group, or less than 9% of all known gang members (Brosseau 2016). Yet, Portland is not lacking in violent white power groups (Berlet & Vysotsky 2006; Blazak 2018; Brown 2017; Campuzano 2018; Capatides 2017; Feagin, Vera & Butler 2001; Kaplan, Weinberg & Oleson 2003; Horowitz 1999; Levin & Grisham 2016; Wilson 2017; Zeskind 2009). In fact, Portland's legacy of segregationist policies, being a "sundown town" (see O'Connell 2019; Wilson 2017), and overt racism (Geiling 2015; Neiwert 2019; Semuels 2016; Shapiro 2017) has only facilitated the growth and persistence of white supremacy groups seeking to make Portland a "White Utopia" (Novak 2015). Ward (2018: 5) refers to this legacy of under-policing white power groups by legal authorities and using racist political actions as "white supremacy in policing" (see also Durán 2013).

The public resurgence of the WPM with alt-right groups' recurrent participation in demonstrations, rallies, and protests throughout the United States, particularly in more liberal and progressive urban centers, has alarmed many in society; however, there remains a lack of knowledge in how to deal with these individuals on the street (Reid & Valasik 2018; Reitman 2018). Presently, the only time members of white power groups are systematically categorized in a database is upon entering a correctional facility (Goodman 2008, 2014), resulting in policies of segregating inmates by race. Developed originally as a policy solution to curb inmate violence (Gaston & Huebner 2015), the separation of inmates by race has instead fueled the rise and dominance of prison gangs (i.e., security threat groups) in carceral settings (Blazak 2009; Pyrooz & Decker 2019; Skarbek 2014; Trammell 2011).

This chapter puts forward several common myths about alt-right gangs and myths instigated by members of alt-right gangs themselves. After presenting each myth and a brief explanation, the research revealing the realities of these myths is discussed. It is important to note that myths are collectively held narratives that are created to confirm a group's values and norms and establish patterns of behavior that are to be imitated (Honko 1972). In fact, these foundational tales may or may not be based at all on factual information. Most depictions of alt-right gangs by the media highlight at least one myth presented below. By moving away from the myths about these gangs, researchers, practitioners, and policy makers can more effectively identify these youth and consider appropriate intervention strategies (see Kimmel 2018; Koehler 2017; Windisch, Ligon & Simi 2017; Windisch, Simi, Ligon & McNeel 2016).

CONSIDERATION OF KEY MYTHS
ABOUT ALT-RIGHT GANGS

Alt-right gangs are routinely misrepresented in the media, or confused with groups that oppose these far-right groups, such as Antifa (Campbell 2019; Pyrooz & Densley 2018; Touchberry 2018). Similarly, academics have traditionally treated alt-right gangs as a type of group that is qualitatively different from conventional street gangs (Blazak 1998; Curry et al. 2014; Hamm 1993; Klein 1995; Pyrooz & Densley 2018). Such othering has both inhibited the creation of legislation specifically targeting these white power groups and limiting the application of existing laws with harsh penalties for individuals involved in gang-related activity (see Reitman 2018). Street gangs are often depicted as a uniquely urban phenomenon, being composed of members from racial/ethnic groups that are demographically nonwhite, yet federal and state criminal codes eschew any racial language in their gang statutes, leaving the application of these laws far reaching (see Barrows & Huff 2009; Bjerregaard 2015). Thus, the interpretation and implementation of these laws targeting street gangs falls primarily on local law enforcement agencies and prosecutors, which, we have pointed out, does not systematically include all possible individuals that are members of a street gang, most notably people who are white (see Ward 2018). Six of the most common myths surrounding alt-right gangs and the realities being misconceived are now discussed.

Myth 1: Alt-Right Gangs Are Not "Real" Gangs

Scholars have resisted including members of alt-right groups in the same category as conventional street gangs due to the perception that these youth are part of the larger far-right movement (e.g., Christian Identity, Ku Klux Klan [KKK], neo-Nazis, etc.) and lack a street orientation. Either members are "inside; they're working on their written materials; or if outside, they're looking for a target, not lounging around" (Klein 1995: 22). And when these racist members are outside, their "overt racism, political violence, and links to a homologous international subculture" is focused on acts of terrorism designed to overthrow the government and should be solely considered a "terrorist youth subculture" (Hamm 1993: 65).

Reality

The focus by scholars (Blazak 1998; Curry et al. 2014; Hamm 1993; Kinsella 1994; Terrell 1989) on the ideological underpinnings and radicalization of alt-right gangs to prioritize political violence over all other crime types is misguided. Hamm (1993: 65) argues that such alt-right gangs violate the "classic criminological definition of a street gang"; however, the gang literature to date—let alone policy makers or practitioners—does not agree on a uniform definition of a street gang (Howell & Griffiths 2018; Klein & Maxson 2006; Papachristos 2005). Though conformity across the broad field of gang research on a common description for street gangs is nonexistent, the Eurogang definition "has become widely adopted and appears regularly in publications," becoming one of the most appropriated definitions used by gang scholars (Maxson & Esbensen 2016: 7). According to the Eurogang definition, a street gang is "any durable, street-oriented youth group whose involvement in illegal activity is part of their group identity" (Weerman et al. 2009). Based upon the Eurogang definition, alt-right gangs would clearly be classified as a street gang. In fact, over the last two decades many edited volumes of gang scholarship include research that discusses or focuses on these alt-right gangs (see Dekleva 2001; De Waele & Pauwels 2016; Kersten 2001; Lien 2001; Salagaev, Shashkin, Sherbakova & Touriyanskiy 2005; Sela-Shayovitz 2012; Shashkin 2008; Simi 2006). Historically, white supremacist street gangs, such as the Spook Hunters in Los Angeles, would terrorize black youth with violent intent to restrict residency and mobility, counter school integration, and maintain racial purity (see Alonso 2004; Howell & Griffiths 2018). It seems that whether or not an alt-right gang is considered to be too extreme (i.e., falling outside of the street gang definitional spectrum) is a post-hoc decision, with these white power groups' inclusion or exclusion from studies being more fluid than would be expected given the emphasis placed upon alt-right gangs' ideological differences. The selective emphasis on the ideology attached to these groups has led to their inconsistent categorization. For instance, the unfocused classification of alt-right gang members as conventional street gang members is seen in Pyrooz and colleagues' (2018: 9) comparative study between domestic extremists and gangs, which distinctly categorizes members of alt-right gangs as being part of a street gang. They find that while these organizations have "some ideological motivation . . . [they] nonetheless possess the organization attributes of street-oriented youth gangs." This contrasts with Pyrooz and colleagues' own earlier contestation of the idea that "while these groups share some features in common with gangs, they fall outside the definition of what a gang is" (Curry et al. 2014: 58).

Myth 2: Alt-Right Gangs Focus on Hate Crimes

Curry and colleagues (2014: 59) contend that white power groups, such as alt-right gangs, "have a strong ideological set of beliefs." These ideological principles include anti-Semitism, Islamophobia, homophobia, opposition to immigration, and general fear that "white genocide" is occurring (Saslow 2018). Simi (2010: 256) defines a hate crime as an incident that is "initiated by members of the dominant racial group targeting individuals who represent minority out groups perceived, for varying reasons, to be threats." Etter (1999: 19) states, "Skinhead crimes are usually violent and chosen for their political or racial impact rather than for the profit motive." As such, being driven by ideological principles propels alt-right gang members to focus most of their criminal involvement on hate/bias-related activities.

Reality

In fact, alt-right gang members have demonstrated a generalist pattern of cafeteria-style offending, as opposed to a specialized pattern of offending (e.g., hate- and bias-related crimes). It is true that alt-right gang members participate in hate crimes and bias-related offences, but this is only one aspect of their criminal offending. Alt-right gang members have been arrested, indicted, and convicted for engaging in assault, harassment, larceny, auto theft, drug possession, drug trafficking, criminal possession of firearms and/or explosives, kidnapping, murder, and serial killings (First Vigil 2019; Simi et al. 2008; Thompson, Winston & Hanrahan 2018). In 2010, the Attorney General's Division of Law Enforcement for the state of California circulated a report on organized crime in California with a section on "white street gangs" asserting that "law enforcement officials report rising levels of criminal activity by the white gangs, including credit card theft, fraudulent checks, vehicle theft, home invasion robberies, aggravated assault, and murder" (Harris 2010). The seriousness and variety of these crimes highlights just how divergent the realities of alt-right gang members are from the public's perceptions and stereotypes. It should also be noted that hate/bias-related violence against people of color does not solely rest on alt-right gangs but also involves black gang members attacking Latinx and vice versa (see Kun & Pulido 2013).

Myth 3: Alt-Right Gangs Are Part of
a Large International Conglomerate

Alt-right gangs are generally perceived by academics, law enforcement, the media, and the public as criminal syndicates that "tend to be organized internationally" (Curry et al. 2014: 58). Their ultimate goal is to establish a Pan-Aryan world that transcends national borders (Blee 2002; Dobratz & Shanks-Meile 2000; Hermansson et al. 2020). The internet (Daniels 2009a, 2009b; Hermansson et al. 2020;

T. Morris 2017) and white power music (Dyck 2017; Futrell, Simi & Gottschalk 2006; Windisch & Simi 2017) are the two principal instruments that have facilitated a transnational white power community, where individuals across the globe are able to connect and communicate with each other or rendezvous in person (Back 2002; Cooter 2011; Corb 2011; Corte & Edwards 2008; Dobratz & Waldner 2006; Hamm 1993). Dyck (2017: 3) more cautiously conceives of this network as a web of interconnected "groups and individuals who may agree with one another on a few key points and work together when necessary, but who sometimes also maintain separate spheres of influence and differ in important regards" (see also Belew 2018).

Reality

Blee (2002: 4) warns that a great deal of the existing scholarship on white power groups has emphasized "the organized facade of racism—the structure, leadership, and propaganda issued by racist groups—creates a strong impression of uniformity, which may be undermined by an examination of *individual* racists" (emphasis in the original). Such focus has led to a false impression of homogeneity and unity within the larger WPM, which is not supported in reality (Tenold 2018). This includes the recent alt-right manifestation that resembles more of a loose coalition of varying groups competing for dominance in the movement than a uniform collective (Atkinson 2018; Hawley 2017, 2019; Hermansson et al. 2020; Lyons 2017; Nagle 2017; Neiwert 2017; Stern, 2019; Waring 2019; Waring & Paxton 2018; Wendling 2018). If we narrow our focus on particular white power groups (e.g., National Alliance, Aryan Nations, KKK, Traditionalist Worker Party, Proud Boys, World Church of the Creator), we find similar patterns of infighting and competition for dominance among members, limiting the capacity for these groups to work together in a concerted manner (Balch 2006; Belew 2018; Berry 2017; Cunningham 2013; Freilich, Chermak & Caspi 2009; Kaplan, Weinberg & Oleson 2003; Picciolini 2018; Tenold 2018). The most recent example of the inability of far-right groups to amicably get along to benefit the larger WPM has been the subsequent implosion of the alt-right following the murder of Heather Heyer and the injuring of nineteen others at the 2017 Unite the Right Rally in Charlottesville, Virginia (McAuliffe 2019). This has left the alt-right in greater disarray and decreased the confidence in leading members (Hermansson et al. 2020; Wendling 2018). For instance, alt-right gangs like Proud Boys disavowed members that attended and organized the event in an effort to distance themselves from the public backlash after the deadly rally (Woodhouse 2017).

Simi and colleagues (2008: 755–756) further contend that gang scholars' exclusion of racist skinheads and, for that matter, today's alt-right gangs from conventional gang research "is based upon inadequate assessments of the empirical evidence," with a disproportionate focus being placed upon white power groups' "ideological perceptions, overt racism, political violence and international connections" (see Curry et al. 2014; Etter 1999; Hamm 1993; Klein 1995). These "international connections" or the interconnected web of transnational groups is typically discussed in reference to the white power music scene. Both scholars and de-radicalized individuals have documented the ability of white power music to connect members of various racist groups to the larger WPM, virtually over the internet or face-to-face at concerts or festivals (Dyck 2017; Futrell et al. 2006; Love 2016; Picciolini 2018; Pieslak 2015; Simi & Futrell 2015; Teitelbaum 2017; Windisch & Simi 2017). Unarguably, white power music is a medium that can be used to readily transmit the virulent hate and viewpoints of the WPM; however, the strength of those connections remains unknown. The amount of infighting that exists within many white power groups, particularly after charismatic leadership concludes (see Eatwell 2018; Fangen 1998; Freilich et al. 2009), and between various white power groups (see Hawley 2019; Tenold 2018, VICE 2017) makes it unlikely that an organized, international syndicate exists. Furthermore, the doctrine of "leaderless resistance," a paramilitary strategy intentionally limiting the size of any one group goes against the very notion of organizing the WPM into a large, structured organization (Beam 1992; Burris, Smith & Strahm 2000; Michael 2012) (see chapter 6 for more on this).

A prime example of alt-right gangs being incorrectly perceived as being some type of international organization can be illustrated by Proud Boys. Gavin McInnes, the charismatic founder, who recently disavowed leadership of Proud Boys, claims that the gang has chapters sprouting up all over the globe, with over 10,000 members (ABC 2018). However, their website only has about 30 recognized chapters listed in the United States, with most of these being statewide groups. Only about a half dozen chapters are present in Canada. Even fewer exist across Europe, with a mere promise that chapters are "coming soon" to the rest of the globe (Proud Boys 2019). While it only takes five like-minded individuals to create a Proud Boys chapter, it is possible that the group has been unable to maintain an accurate count and to update their webpage. Given the state of other administrator postings on their website this seems unlikely (Proud Boys 2019). Instead, it seems more likely that, given all the media attention that Proud Boys receive, imitators are mimicking the group and creating the impression that these local gangs are bigger and more imposing than they are in reality (Howell & Griffiths 2018). As such, Proud Boys suffer from what is known as "Big Gang Theory," the exaggerated view that street gangs are highly organized, control a lot of territory, have hierarchical leadership, and drive local crime patterns (Felson 2006). This model is reminiscent of the Hammerskins, the largest racist skinhead gang in the United States, which only had about 500 members, despite there being around 5,000 racist skinheads nationwide (Picciolini 2018).

Myth 4: Alt-Right Gangs Focus Their Activities on Political Action

It is often put forward that alt-right gangs "seek to radicalize their members to take political action" (Curry et al. 2014: 58). Furthermore, alt-right gangs' criminal activities "are usually violent and chosen for their political and racial impact rather than for the profit motive," targeting victims "by race, religion, ethnic origin, and sexuality" (Etter 1999: 19). When profit-motive criminal activities transpire, they are done with the intention of providing revenue to further the interests of a variety of white power groups in the upcoming "Racial Holy War" (see Belew 2018; Flynn & Gerhart 1989; Hamm 2001; Lyons 2018; Sottile 2019). Thus, the dominant feature of alt-right gangs is the emphasis on political activism (see Hamm 1993).

Reality

Simi and colleagues (2008: 756) point out that exclusion from conventional gang studies is based upon the incorrect portrayal of alt-right gangs as "Nazis" whose primary focus is "bias-motivated political violence" (see also Simi 2006, 2009). Generalized statements that "the majority of skinheads across the country are racist, neo-Nazi whites who feel threatened by Jews, non-whites, and homosexuals" further characterize alt-right gangs as indistinguishable from other white power groups (e.g., the KKK, Aryan Republican Army, Silent Brotherhood), which is not the case (Landre, Miller & Porter 1997: 83). Klein's (2009: 134) travels across Europe highlight that the public perceives skinheads as being portrayed "more in political terms rather than as a street gang," viewing them as a "mob, hooligans, extremists, and in one area a bunch of psychopaths, without seeing the group aspect that holds these youth together." Yet, Klein's (2009) empirical data clearly puts skinheads into the "specialty" category of street gangs. Furthermore, when talking about neo-Nazis and skinheads in Europe, van Gemert and colleagues (2012: 8) highlight that "these groups may or may not be linked to political organizations. In some countries, juvenile gangs exist that merely use extremist symbols to add to their identity."

In the United States, the image that alt-right gangs are the foot soldiers of the far right is often contradicted with evidence presenting these groups (e.g., racist skinheads) as lacking the shared beliefs and the definitive goals necessary to make them an organized far-right insurgent group (Blazak 2001; Hamm 1993; Suall and Lowe 1988; Wooden and Blazak 2001). Even Hamm (1993: 42) who staunchly argues that racist skinheads are driven by their political motivations, and thereby different from street gangs, dismisses these individuals as "idiots with ideology" (quoting Coplon 1988: 87). Simi and colleagues' (2008: 766) interviews with members of PEN1 highlights the lack of political orientation of this alt-right gang: "We [PENI] were a group of fucken white boys that formed together to protect each other, gang style. It wasn't nothing fucken political at all. Some of the members might have been more political . . . but generally we were only interested in being gangsters." Even the broader alt-right movement is less interested in direct political action, instead focusing their energy on "red-pilling" as much of the populace as possible (Dignam & Rohlinger 2019; Hawley 2017, 2019; Hermansson et al. 2020; Stern 2019; Tuters 2019; Wendling 2018; Winter 2019).[3] That is, the alt-right wants to reveal society's supposed hidden overlords (e.g., Zionist Occupied Government [ZOG], New World Order [NWO], or Jewish people more generally). Not surprisingly, the alt-right focuses on influencing meta-politics, or how people think about politics (Hawley 2017, 2019; Hermansson et al. 2020; Lyons 2017; Main 2018; Stern 2019). The idea behind meta-politics is that the only way to successfully change political culture is to shift the "Overton window" by popularizing, mainstreaming, and normalizing their viewpoints and beliefs in the national conversation. Only through shifting society's cultural attitudes, beliefs, and values can extensive political change transpire (Hawley 2017, 2019; Hermansson et al. 2020; Lyons 2017; Main 2018; Paxton 2018; Stern 2019).

Myth 5: Alt-Right Gangs Are an Online Phenomenon

The alt-right is a unique online movement of tech-savvy millennials familiar with internet jargon who spend the majority of their time trolling others on social media or in online message/image boards (Berger 2018; Bokhari & Yiannopoulos 2016; Ellis 2018; Lewis 2018; Pollard 2018; SPLC 2018). That is, alt-right groups focus their activities and attention in the digital realm on virtual Aryan free spaces (Futrell & Simi 2004; Simi & Futrell 2006, 2015) to recruit and connect with fellow members.

Reality

Internet use by white power groups is nothing new (Belew 2018; Berlet & Mason 2015; Daniels 2009a, 2009b, 2013, 2018; Hawley 2019; Kimmel 2013, 2018; Michael 2012; T. Morris 2017; Schafer 2002; Simi & Futrell 2015). In fact, white supremacists were some of the earliest adopters to use the internet for digital communication (see chapter 6). In the early 1980s, Louis Beam, a prominent neo-Nazi strategist, figured out that digital communications, through online message boards, could be used asymmetrically to (1) maintain correspondence between

---

3. The "red pill" reference is from the science fiction film *The Matrix* by the Wachowskis in 1999. Neo, the protagonist in the story gets presented with a choice between learning the truth about reality (swallowing the "red pill") or returning to his simulated life and remaining uninformed about the real world and the robotic overlords that control society (swallowing the "blue pill"). Neo chooses the red pill and wakes up to a harsh and dangerous world but one with greater meaning, while taking the blue pill would have resulted in him remaining in his life of comfort and contentment but remaining ignorant to the truth (Wachowski & Wachowski 1999).

individual white supremacists and white power groups that are not spatially proximate to each other, (2) efficiently spread the message of white supremacy using
minimal resources, and (3) recruit new members (Beam [1983] 1992; Berlet 2008;
Berlet & Mason 2015; Michael 2012; T. Morris 2017). Beam ([1983] 1992) advocates
for a "leaderless resistance" in which large, centralized white power organizations
(e.g., KKK, Aryan Nations) are abandoned in favor of smaller groups or cells that
are better at avoiding disruption and detection by the law enforcement agencies
(see also Belew 2018; Michael 2012; T. Morris 2017). The adoption of "leaderless
resistance" has greatly contributed to the proliferation of white power websites
across the globe (Burris et al. 2000; Daniels 2009a, 2009b, 2018; T. Morris 2017;
Simi & Futrell 2015). In addition to such websites providing a means of communication between white power members and groups, these virtual spaces also are
resources that members can use to post social media, plan activities, educate children, listen to music, and play games (Burris et al. 2000; Daniels 2009a, 2009b,
2018; Hermansson et al. 2020; T. Morris 2017; Sela-Shayovitz 2012; Simi & Futrell
2006, 2015).

Even if alt-right gangs emerged from an online collective, members of these
groups still participate in activities in the physical world that adversely impact
residents of local communities (Castle & Parsons 2017). While several critical lawsuits and criminal cases (see the *Berhanu v. Metzger* lawsuit against WAR in 1990)
helped push some aspects of racist skinhead gangs online, these groups have never
been a completely online phenomenon, operating in the streets of the United
States since the 1980s and abroad since the 1960s (Belew 2018; Berlet & Vysotsky
2006; Dobratz & Shanks-Meile 2006; Gerstenfeld & Grant 2004; Kaplan, Weinberg & Oleson 2003; Langer 2003; Lyons 2018; Tenold 2018). Even "new" alt-right
gangs are no longer confined to just the digital realm, as witnessed by the numerous rallies and demonstrations that have taken place throughout the United States
and have usually ended in violence (e.g., Berkeley, Charlottesville, New York City,
Portland) (Atkinson 2018; Hawley 2017, 2019; Nagle 2017; Phillips 2015; Reid et
al. 2020; Stern 2019; Wendling 2018). In fact, alt-right gangs' public exhibitions
demonstrate a cafeteria-style offending pattern, including engaging in assault,
harassment, larceny, criminal possession of a weapon, hate-related crimes, murder, and serial killings (Duggan 2018; First Vigil 2019; Heim 2018; Martinez 2018;
Shallwani & Weill 2018; Thompson, Winston & Hanrahan 2018). The seriousness
of these offenses highlights how the realities of the alt-right gangs and the stereo-
type of the alt-right being merely an online phenomenon are misaligned. In fact,
the alt-right is not a monolith but consists of a variety of subsets, some of which
include individuals who are members of street-oriented delinquent groups in the
United States (e.g., Proud Boys, Rise Above Movement, Atomwaffen Division,
The Base) but also across Europe (e.g., Erkenbrand, English Defence League,
Feuerkrieg Division, Azov Battalion, Russian National Unity) (G. Lopez 2017;

Klapsis 2019; Lamoureux & Makuch 2018a, 2018b; Makuch & Lamoureux 2019a; PBS 2018a, 2018b; Pilkington 2016; Reitman 2018; Roose & Winston 2018; van der Valk 2019; Ware 2008).

Myth 6: Alt-Right Gangs Are Domestic Terrorists

Alt-right gangs are routinely portrayed in the media and particularly by opposition groups (e.g., Antifa) as being "domestic terrorists" (Klein 2019; Templeton & Wilson 2018). Hamm (1993: 65), focusing on racist skinheads in particular, establishes an argument that alt-right gangs "do not conform to the classical criminological definition of a street gang" but "represent something else; something with a wider agenda that is potentially more dangerous to society" due to "their overt racism, political violence and links to a homologous international subculture of neo-Nazism" and "can best be described as a *terrorist youth subculture.*"

Reality

Due to the methodological complexity of investigating white power groups (e.g., personal safety, population access) (see Blee 2018; Massanari 2018), prior research has included alt-right gang members (e.g., racist skinheads) in studies with the KKK, Aryan Nations, White Aryan Resistance, and the Council of Conservative Citizens. Yet the grouping of alt-right gangs with other groups in the WPM misrepresents them as being structured and organized, an illusion not supported by the literature (Baron 1997; Simi 2006, 2009; Tarasov 2001, 2008; Wooden & Blazak 2001). When the group structure of alt-right gangs is mentioned within these broader studies of the WPM, it is clearly articulated that these groups lack the discipline, management, and organizational structure needed to achieve political change (e.g., Atkinson 2018; Campbell 2018; Crosbie 2018; Simi 2006; Tarasov 2008; Tenold 2018). The limited research on the group structure of alt-right gangs, primarily racist skinheads, generally finds groups lacking strong leadership or a centralized hierarchy and having an unorganized character (Baron 1997; Simi 2006, 2009; Wooden & Blazak 2001). Scholars have also suggested that alt-right gangs exist on a spectrum (Reid & Valasik 2018; Simi 2006; Valasik & Reid 2019). Simi (2006) contends that on one end you have loosely organized groups that act independently while on the other end you have more traditionally structured groups that look comparable to a street gang. This has been seen outside of the United States as well. In the city of Kazan, Russia, as Stephenson (2012) documents, residents consider the local skinheads to be just another gang, having similarities with local street gangs and other crime groups but with greater levels of brutality when engaging in violent acts.

A similar evolutionary perspective has been presented for the organizational transformation of street gangs, emerging from a local neighborhood group and progressing over time in a criminal enterprise that is more professional and structured (Ayling 2011; Densley 2013; Stephenson 2015; Valasik & Phillips 2017). Densley (2013: 43) contends that street gangs in fact exist on a spectrum naturally evolving from their origins as a "neighborhood group to delinquent collectives to full-scale criminal enterprises to providers of extra-legal governance." Based upon this explanation, it is no surprise that gang research has diversely documented street gangs as confederations of loosely organized individuals or small cliques of friends that "coalesce irregularly over issues that emerge and vanish from the street" (Decker & Curry 2002: 351) as well as groups having a hierarchical structure whose vertical orientation of manpower allows for the "corporatization" of street gangs to focus their criminal activities around specific economic pursuits (e.g., drug sales, extortion) (Densley 2013; Levitt & Venkatesh 2000; Stephenson 2015). Thus, any observed differences by gang scholars in the structure of a street gang is based upon that gang's position on the evolutionary spectrum.

Although the progression from a conventional street gang to an organized crime group is well documented in the gang literature (Densley 2013; Papachristos 2005; Stephenson 2015; Sullivan 1989), the progression between a street gang and a terrorist organization is less understood. Building upon the popular conceptualization of the crime-terror continuum by adding a street gang axis, Valasik and Phillips (2017) introduced a gang-terror continuum that connects street gangs and terrorist groups (see also Phillips & Valasik 2017).[4] As terrorist organizations today exhibit more loosely affiliated cells that operate independently without requiring centralized direction and vertical hierarchies with rigid chains of command, they become more resemblant of street gangs than paramilitaries (Phillips & Valasik 2017; Valasik & Phillips 2017, 2018).

The conceptual framework proposed by Valasik and Phillips (2017) easily extends to alt-right gangs, as white power groups exist on this gang-terror continuum. For instance, Proud Boys chapters fall closer to the street gang end of the spectrum, with many of the group's characteristics, behaviors, and cafeteria-style criminal offending resembling a conventional street gang (see the Focus Box in chapter 1). In fact, much of Proud Boys' hateful rhetoric and violence is aimed at Antifa (DeCook 2018; Klein 2019; Reitman 2018), a pattern no different than the violent rivalries between racist skinheads groups and traditional street gangs (King 1988; Simi 2006; Simi et al. 2008). On the other side of the spectrum are groups such as Atomwaffen Division, The Base, Feuerkrieg Division, Azov Battalion and Russian National Unity that operate more like terrorist organizations, with extremely violent

---

4. Originally conceptualized by Makarenko (2004), the crime-terror continuum proposes that there is a continuum that bridges terrorism and organized crime. At one end of the spectrum are terrorist organizations (e.g., ISIS, al-Qaeda, Irish Republican Army [IRA], Silent Brotherhood, etc.) that work toward political or religious goals through threats or acts of violence. At the other end of the spectrum are organized crime groups (e.g., Cosa Nostra, Yakuza, Organizivannaia Prestupnaia Gruppa, Sinaloa Cartel, etc.) that pursue economic goals, striving for profit maximization by avoiding scrutiny.

FIGURE 2.1. Atomawaffen Division propaganda flyer.

behavior being documented, including the stockpiling of firearms and explosives, plotting of terror attacks, and premeditated murders (Bromwich 2018; First Vigil 2019; Hawley 2019; Klapsis 2019; Lamoureux & Makuch 2018a; 2018b; PBS 2018b; Thompson et al. 2018; van der Valk 2019; Ware 2008; Waring & Paxton 2018b). As figure 2.1 illustrates, Atomwaffen Division and other groups on this end of the gang-terror continuum do not attempt to mask their adherence to white supremacy. They use extreme images in their propaganda materials, and require members to maintain paramilitary/military training to be prepared for the upcoming race war (Hanrahan 2018; Hawley 2019; Kestenbaum 2018; Makuch & Lamoureux 2019a; Thompson et al. 2018).[5] Falling somewhere in the middle of the gang-terror

5. It should be noted that figure 2.1 is a modest advertisement of the propaganda released by Atomwaffen Division, most of which is extremely offensive and volatile.

continuum are groups like Erkenbrand, English Defence League, and R.A.M. (PBS 2018a; Pilkington 2016; Reitman 2018; van der Valk 2019). Newly established R.A.M. resembles a far-right "fight club" that trains members in mixed martial arts (MMA) fighting techniques that are designed to be used at "free speech" rallies and demonstrations to assault counterprotesters (Coaston 2018; First Vigil 2019; PBS 2018a; SPLC 2019; Thompson 2017). Erkenbrand, in The Netherlands, also molds itself in this manner (see van der Valk 2019).

"The structure and behavior of a gang is molded in part through its accommodation to its life conditions," with no two street gangs being identical (Thrasher 1927: 144). The same observation is true for alt-right gangs. Hamm's (1993) misconception of racist skinheads as being a *terrorist youth subculture*, placing alt-right gangs apart from conventional street gangs, provided justification for scholars to write off these white power groups from gang studies (see Curry et al. 2014; Klein 1995; Schneider 1999). Despite Klein's (1996, 2001, 2009; Klein & Maxson 2006) reversal that racist skinheads fit the criteria of a street gang and Simi and colleagues' (2008; Simi 2006, 2009) repeated contestation and evidence, gang scholars have excluded racist skinheads from street gang research until recently (see Pyrooz et al. 2018; Reid & Valasik 2018; Valasik & Reid 2018a, 2019). In fact, Pyrooz and colleagues' (2018: 9) study comparing members of domestic extremist groups to street gang members stated that racist skinhead groups have "some ideological motivation but nonetheless possess the organization attributes of street-oriented youth gangs." We can hope this is an indicator that established gang scholars are finally acknowledging the methodological limitations of Hamm's (1993) study and reexamining white power groups that can be categorized as alt-right gangs.

CONSIDERATION OF KEY MYTHS
IMPOSED BY ALT-RIGHT GANGS

Just like with conventional street gangs, the promise of being a member in an alt-right gang sharply diverges from the reality. The charismatic figureheads of alt-right gangs generally misrepresent their beliefs and values, producing a distorted image of the group that they can peddle in order to enlist members and justify their antisocial behavior (Hall 2017; Hawley 2019; Hermansson et al. 2020; NPR 2018; Rogan 2017; SPLC 2019a). It should be noted that this process of aggrandizing a troublesome group is also routinely practiced by leaders of jihadi terrorist groups as a means of recruiting members by normalizing and popularizing the group, thereby expanding the potential pool of applicants (Atran 2017; Makuch & Lamoureux 2019b; T. Morris 2017; Valasik & Phillips 2017, 2018). This phenomenon, referred to as "Big Gang Theory" in the street gang literature, can be recognized as a gang trying to make itself look larger and more impactful than it actually is (Felson, 2006; Howell 2007). Two of the most common myths propagated by alt-right gangs and the realities of each fallacy are now discussed.

Myth 1: Members of Alt-Right Gangs
Adhere to a Strict Racial Ideology

A popular belief is that alt-right gang members adhere to a homogeneous white power ideology with discrete racial hierarchies (typically associated with Nazism) (see Whitman 2018). Members of alt-right gangs are required to be entirely ethnically "white." Racist movements have historically been concerned about the preservation of ethnic purity and maintenance of racial hierarchies (Goodrick-Clarke 1985, 2002; Whitman 2017). Nazism under Hitler's Germany determined that Aryans (i.e., people of Nordic descent including Germany, England, Denmark, The Netherlands, Sweden, and Norway) were Ubermenschen, or the superior race, followed by hierarchical gradations and the inferior or subhuman races on the bottom (i.e., individuals of Jewish, Roma, Polish, Serbian, Russian, or Slavic descent) (Ehrenreich 2007; Hitler [1925] 2018; Longerich 2012; Whitman 2017). During the 1920s in the United States, the eugenics movement, in addition to being concerned about the inferiority of non-Europeans, also considered many European groups (primarily Southern and Eastern) of a lower status and endorsed restrictions and quotas to reduce their immigrating into the country (Lombardo 2011; Saini 2019; Whitman 2017). Similarly, the KKK emphasized not just race but also religion, striving for the United States to remain a white, Anglo-Saxon, and Protestant ("WASP") nation. Thus, they were openly hostile to not only Blacks but also Jewish and Catholic populations, immigrants, and communists (Blee 1991, 2002, 2005; Chalmers 1987; Cunningham 2013; L. Gordon 2018; Horowitz 1999; MacLean 1994; McVeigh 2009; McVeigh & Estep 2019).

Reality

Pollard (2016) attests that the tradition of strict racial hierarchies, commonly associated with Nazism, have been abandoned, with an influx of people of Slavic heritage joining alt-right gangs in America and Eastern Europe (see also Dyck 2017; Pilkington et al. 2010; Tenold 2018). American white supremacy has also shifted attention away from an individual's genotype (i.e., ethnicity) to their phenotype (i.e., skin color) to measure racial purity. This change allows non-Aryans to join and become members and permits Aryans to have relationships with non-Aryans (see Borgeson & Valeri 2018; Mudde 2005; Simi & Futrell 2015; Picciolini 2018; Wooden & Blazak 2001). Contributing to even more ambiguity in defining an individual's "whiteness" is the interest in genetic ancestry testing services (e.g., Ancestry.com or 23andMe) and the production of genealogy results that contradict the presumptions of white supremacists (Mitto, Zannettou & Blackburn 2019; Panofsky & Donovan 2019; Saini 2019).

Proud Boys, for instance, regularly claim that their groups are full of nonwhite members (Proud Boys 2019). One of Proud Boys' ideological underpinnings—abstaining from masturbation—is even derived from a black, male comedian, Dante Nero, a former Proud Boys member and figurehead (NPR 2017). For Dante Nero, in addition to the tragic death of Heather Heyer in Charlottesville, it was the free use of racial slurs and white supremacist rhetoric among members that forced him to reevaluate being a member of Proud Boys (NPR 2017). As Dante points out, it is not a big ideological jump from believing that "the West is the best" to "white people are the best" (NPR 2017). While nonwhites are encouraged to join Proud Boys, they must readily subscribe to the fact that (1) being white is not a problem in modern society and (2) Western civilization is the highest form human development (DeCook 2018; Proud Boys 2019).

Proud Boys, being only the newest iteration of alt-right gangs in the WPM that admit nonwhite members, are not unique. The Nazi Low Riders (NLR) is another example of an alt-right gang from Southern California that has overlooked racial restrictions for membership for years. The NLR has strong ties to California's Division of Juvenile Justice, highlighting the youthful age range of their membership. Due perhaps to the overall demographics of Southern California, the NLR allowed members with Latinx and Asian heritage to join, with the standard of "at least half white blood, but no black blood" (Valdez 1999: 46). Members of the NLR have been linked to murders, robberies, assaults, and drug sales, especially methamphetamine (Finnegan 1997; Valdez 1999). For the NLR, the white supremacy aspect has a more anti-black, anti-Semitic, and anti-Norteño (a Northern California Latnix gang member) focus, rather than the idealization of a "pure" white race. Inflexibility in this regard could get in the way of profitability and safety, which are higher priorities for these gangs. In Southern California, it is difficult to imagine that a gang would successfully manage a drug market without opening the group up to any other races or ethnicities, such as Latinx or Asian. By being "selective" in their choices, the gang can still symbolically "manage" their ideology without hindering their ability to sell drugs (see chapter 4 for more on the role of ideology).

Myth 2: Only Racists Join Alt-Right Gangs

The general belief is that only white supremacists or those with far-right attitudes join racist groups (e.g., John Birch Society, KKK, skinheads) (see Blazak 1998, 2001; Duckitt & Sibley 2010; Etter 1999; Forscher & Kteily 2019; Hamm 1993; Saini 2019; Sibley, Robertson & Wilson 2006). Therefore, if a group's membership is not racist, then it would follow by extension that the group cannot be racist. Proud Boys in particular attest that they are neither part of the alt-right nor racist because members may be of any race or sexuality and just have to subscribe to the belief that "the West is best" (Hermansson et al. 2020; Klein 2019). Yet, despite the rhetoric uttered by Gavin McInnes and other Proud Boys elders, members' sentiments and opinions daily posted on social media show "derogatory statements about the transgender community, Muslims, Jews and 'non-Europeans' as well as evocative allegiances to 'blood and soil'" (Klein 2019: 300).

Reality

This myth is based on the adage "birds of a feather flock together." The idea in this case is that only individuals who have some predisposition toward white supremacy would join an alt-right gang (see chapter 3 for more on risk factors). Yet, the larger question that needs to be asked is whether the feathering comes before the flocking or the flocking comes before the feathering (Boman 2016; Gottfredson & Hirschi 1990; Gravel, Allison, West-Fagan, McBride & Tita 2018). That is, do individuals with white supremacist points of view associate with others having similar perspectives and then form a group, or do individuals without any white supremacist convictions join the group and develop racist attitudes through socializing with established group members? It has been documented that individuals who are exposed to and familiarized with white supremacy by family or friends are at greater risk of joining an alt-right gang or participate more broadly in the WPM (Saslow 2018). Yet most members in alt-right gangs lack exposure to white supremacist rhetoric until after joining the group (Blee 1996, 2002; Blee & Yates 2015; Bjørgo, Carlsson & Haaland 2004; Picciolini 2018; Simi & Futrell 2015; Wendling 2018). In fact, the traditional recruiting method for white power groups, including alt-right gangs, follows the boiling frog metaphor. If a frog is placed in boiling water, it immediately jumps out; however, if the frog is paced in tepid water and the temperature of the water is slowly increased to a boil, the frog will not become cognizant of any danger and will be cooked alive. This progression of slowly exposing recruits to white supremacist rhetoric and violence allows alt-right gangs to have a considerably larger pool of potential individuals to pull from (Daniels 2009; DeCook 2018; Hawley 2019; Love 2016; Saslow 2018; Simi & Futrell 2015; Tenold 2018; Valasik, Reling & Reid forthcoming; Wendling 2018). Figure 2.2 shows how the alt-right has perverted this classic metaphor to its own ends with the meme, "Don't be a boiling frog. Jump, Pepe." The meme is expressing to potential recruits that they are unknowingly being boiled to death, and by jumping onto the side of the alt-right, they can save themselves.

Blazak's (2001) research on the recruitment of racist skinheads finds that members will look for high school students who may be experiencing anomie and economic strain (e.g., from a parent being laid off) and target these youth (see also Picciolini 2018). A skinhead may tell a youth whose parent has been laid off about how "the money hungry Jews sent his job to China" (Blazak 2001: 992). One of the individuals Blazak (2001: 993) interviews discusses the process stating:

FIGURE 2.2. "Don't be a boiling frog, jump" (alt-right meme).

> It's really easy. You find out what's happening in a school and then find out where the
> kids hang out. You get some stupid conversation going and then you ask them about
> school. They bitch and moan and you say, "Yeah, it was a lot better in my day when
> we didn't have gangs and people who can't even speak English and all this multicul-
> tural shit." I'd say, "Don't you think it's fucked up that you can have a Black student
> union but not a White student union? Why are the Blacks allowed to be racist?" And
> you can see them agreeing. . . . Then I tell them they should hang out with us or start
> an "unofficial" White student club.

McVeigh and Estep (2019) document a similar phenomenon with the national
rise of the KKK in 1920s. They successfully recruited members across communities throughout the United States through identifying local issues and attesting
that the Klan would be able to solve them (see also Blee & McDowell 2013; Chalmers 1987; MacLean 1994; McVeigh 2009).

Furthermore, DeCook (2018: 13) provides a great example of how the meme
"Take Back Our Future" was endorsed by Proud Boys members and spread across

FIGURE 2.3. "Because its the future son" (alt-right meme).

the digital landscape as a call for the return to an idealized (and nonexistent) past, a 1950s-esque American society before the civil rights and feminist movements (see also Bogerts & Fielitz 2019; Daniels 2009b; Hawley 2019; Jefferies 2018; Klein 2019; May & Feldman 2018; Nagle 2017; Philips 2015; Pollard 2018; Zannettou et al. 2018b). This meme was regularly combined with science fiction shows, such as *Star Trek*, and presented in a 1950s aesthetic in response to a specific question (DeCook 2018). Figure 2.3 illustrates one version of the meme where a young boy asks his father, "Dad Why are there no Jews, Christians, and Muslims on Star Trek?" followed by the father responding that it's because it takes place in the future. The implication, of course, is that in the reimagined, nostalgic future, these groups will have been eliminated from society, representing "part of the far-right's goals in participating in ethnic and religious genocide" (DeCook 2018: 497).

As Hawley (2018) points out, approximately 6% of non-Hispanic, white Americans, or about 11 million individuals, are sympathetic to the identity politics of the alt-right (see also Beauchamp 2018). This is not an insubstantial number. Interestingly, these numbers are approximately double the membership of the KKK in 1925, the group's peak year, which was 2–6 million and represented about 4%

of the population in the United States (Chalmers 1987; MacLean 1994; McVeigh 2009; McVeigh & Estep 2019). As Waring (2018: 75) points out, "While some [alt-right supporters] will actively support far-right groups such as the KKK in the United States and attend their rallies and protest marches, far more show their support in online blog comments to newspapers or on social media."

Lastly, the alt-lite, which orbits the outskirts of the larger alt-right movement, employs similar talking points, such as white identity politics and anti-immigration, but does not use the explicitly bigoted language of the extreme racist core of the alt-right (Hawley 2017, 2019; Hermansson et al. 2020; Lyons 2018; Main 2018; McVeigh & Estep 2019; Neiwert 2017; Wendling 2018). Alt-lite personalities like Milo Yiannopoulos, Ann Coulter, Mike Cernovich, Lauren Southern, Steve Bannon, and Alex Jones are able to slowly move the "Overton window," mainstreaming and normalizing the racist beliefs of the alt-right and making it easier for recruits to not realize they are being boiled alive until it's too late (see Picciolini 2018; Saslow 2018; Stern 2019). It is this "penchant for generating fake facts to counter actual facts . . . to discredit experts whose information is inconvenient" that makes the alt-right and alt-lite so successful at appealing to the average person through racism, anti-elitism, anti-intellectualism, and resentment, stoking the flames of nativism among a broad range of supporters (see chapter 6 for more detail) (Paxton 2018; Waring 2018: 66).

3

ALT-RIGHT GANGS' BROKEN TOYS

Risk Factors for Membership and Gang Formation

We want the broken toys. Send us your broken toys and we will fix them for ya.

BILL RICCIO, NATIONAL DIRECTOR, ARYAN NATIONAL FRONT
(SKINHEADS USA, KEANE 1993)

The idea that there is a firm barrier between any one person and an alternate, extremist version of them is a misconception.

DARYL JOHNSON (2019: 15)

INTRODUCTION

Since not all youth join gangs and not all communities have gangs, researchers continue to try to understand why some youth are more likely to join than others, and why some communities or neighborhoods are more susceptible to gang formation and persistence. Risk-factor research tries to understand the range of individual-, family-, social- (i.e., peers), and community-level risk domains (e.g., neighborhood disadvantage, ethnic heterogeneity) that impact gang joining and gang formation. Understanding risk factors allows researchers, policy makers, and practitioners to develop appropriate policies and programs to reduce the number of youth who join gangs, help them leave the gang faster and more effectively, and suppress the most dangerous gang-related activities. It is important to note that having a risk factor, such as school failure, does not automatically mean an individual will join a gang. Rather, the risk for joining has simply increased.

Gang researchers have highlighted that the vulnerability of gang membership increases with the number of risk factors a youth has across multiple domains. (For a larger discussion see Freng, Davis, McCord & Roussell 2012; Hill et al. 1999; Howell & Egley 2005; Howell & Griffiths 2018; Peterson, Taylor & Esbensen 2004; Taylor et al. 2008; Thornberry et al. 2003.) For example, if a youth has had negative life events (individual domain), poor parental supervision (family domain), and gangs in their neighborhood (community domain), the convergence of these three domains increases a youth's risk of joining a gang compared to youth with factors in only one risk domain. Reviewing the life histories of either alt-right or conventional street gang members, it becomes apparent that many individuals have risk factors across multiple domains (see Baron 1997; Johnson 2019; Reid & Valasik 2018; Simi 2006; Simi, Smith & Reeser 2008; Simi, Sporer & Bubolz 2016; Valasik & Reid 2019). Since risk factors can be, and often are, multidimensional, this means that successful intervention and prevention programs and policies must also be multidimensional (see Thornberry, Kearley, Gottfredson, Slothower & Fader 2018).

There are several ways to approach risk-factor research in relation to studying gangs. Most often it is discussed in terms of the "pushes" and "pulls" that put youth at risk for gang membership (for an overview see Howell & Griffiths 2018). For pushes, which have received more attention by gang scholars, research primarily focuses on the individual-, family-, social-, and community-level factors driving youth away from prosocial groups and toward antisocial groups like gangs. Of these four categories, social factors (i.e., peer influence), while extremely important at predicting delinquency (see Craig, Vitaro, Gagnon & Tremblay 2002; Lahey et al. 1999; Thornberry et al. 2003; Watkins & Taylor 2016), remains the domain least studied. Research examining what characteristics make a gang more attractive, thereby pulling youth toward gang membership, when compared to research on push factors, is also insufficient. The gang literature generally blends the individual-, family-, social-, and community-level risk factors, for both pushes and pulls, making it challenging to clearly demarcate how these varying levels explicitly influence gang membership. For this chapter we focus our analysis on these four levels of risk (i.e., individual, family, social, and community) by looking at each category separately.

The early years of ineffective policies and practices in dealing with conventional street gangs led to a need to understand risk factors in terms of how race/ethnicity, gender, and community impact how, when, and why youth join these groups. For alt-right gangs, recent studies have revealed the serious gaps in the gang literature, underscoring the need for generalizable findings about the risk factors influencing membership (see Johnson 2019; Reid & Valasik 2018; Simi et al. 2008; Valasik & Reid 2018a, 2018b, 2019). Currently, the risk factor research of alt-right gang members is hampered in the same way that early gang research was hampered (see Pyrooz & Mitchell 2015). Lack of consistent definitions, hard to reach populations, difficulties and inconsistencies with official data, and the overemphasis of very few studies (e.g., Hamm 1993; Klein 1995) have all negatively impacted research on these youth and therefore the ability to intervene effectively.

This chapter outlines the research that has been done on the risk factors and group dynamics associated with alt-right gangs. In some instances, this requires extrapolating from studies that have aggregated these youth into the larger white power movement. While the current body of literature is still growing, this review examines the overlap between alt-right gangs and conventional street gangs so that future research on both groups will be more thoughtful and inclusive of groups that fall into the definition of a street gang but also include white power identifiers. This inclusiveness will not only allow for a better understanding of how alt-right gangs are already being captured in traditional gang research, but also how to design research studies that properly target alt-right gangs outside of the larger WPM.

THE DIFFICULTY WITH RISK FACTORS

While extensive effort has been put into understanding the risk factors for conventional street gang membership, as mentioned in chapter 1, the vast majority of these studies have either explicitly or implicitly removed white power youth from their analyses. Due to these limitations, this chapter has two main goals. First, the aim is to review the limited research on risk factors for membership in alt-right gangs while providing a more nuanced look at risk factors through the framework outlined above. Second, some of the key issues impacting the broader understanding of risk factors are examined with a view toward framing future research on alt-right gangs from the lessons learned in the existing gang literature. To meet these goals, this chapter reviews the disconnects between perceived risk factors and those empirically supported.

Many of the broader issues that plague research on racist skinheads (and now alt-right gangs) are also apparent when reviewing the literature on risk factors for membership in these groups. As Blee (2002: 4) observes, the focus on "the organized facade of racism—the structure, leadership, and propaganda issued by racist groups—creates a strong impression of uniformity, which may be undermined by an examination of *individual* racists" (emphasis in original). This chapter builds upon Blee's statement to demonstrate that the focus on the perceived uniformity of skinhead youth has limited the inquiry into risk factors for membership (see also chapter 2).

The risk-factor literature on alt-right gangs, primarily racist skinhead youth, is as fraught with stereotypes as early gang research. The desire to understand the youth who join alt-right gangs as a homogeneous group, and the focus on uniformity to describe skinhead youth has greatly impaired inquiry into risk factors for membership. For example, studies have repeatedly described racist skinheads as being high school educated, abstaining from drugs, holding blue-collar employment, and having a stable home life (Baron 1997; Fangen 1998; Hamm 1993; Hicks

2004). Yet more recent and rigorous research contradicts or adds variability to this statement (Klein 2009; Pilkington et al. 2010; Pollard 2016; Simi & Futrell 2015; Simi et al. 2008; Simi, Sporer & Bubolz 2016; Waldner, Martin & Capeder 2006). The repeated citing of these advance findings perpetuates the mythology of the working-class orientation that is associated with racist skinheads and limits inquiry into the various risk factors for membership in alt-right gangs (Pollard 2016). The unsupported belief that these youth are from more stable and economically advantaged homes (i.e., working-class families) than members of conventional street gangs has led to the assumption that the risk factors for joining alt-right gangs must be different from risk factors for members of other conventional street gangs.

"ENTER THE MILK ZONE": RACE AND ALT-RIGHT GANGS

It is important to think about the role of race in the discussion of risk factors and of researchers' willingness to maintain the stance that alt-right gangs and their members are distinctly different from conventional street gangs and their membership. What is the image that pops into your head when you picture a street gang member? For most individuals, it is going to be a young male of color, and not a young white male (see chapter 2). The myth that gang membership is limited to minorities has had a lasting effect on how people view white gang membership (Curry 2000; Esbensen & Osgood 1999; Esbensen, Peterson, Taylor & Freng 2010; Esbensen & Winfree 1998; Freng & Winfree 2004; Howell & Griffiths 2018). This myth restricts the lens through which people define gang membership. Is a racist skinhead a gang member or simply a member of a subculture with an ideology that the general public does not approve of? While this may seem like a small distinction, when it comes to how researchers study these groups and how agencies like local law enforcement track them, it matters a great deal. If a police officer stops and talks to a young black male and enters his group name into a gang database, this is a vastly different outcome than if an officer stops a young white male and the youth identifies as a member of an alt-right group. In the latter case, the officer refrains from entering the individual into the gang database or, even worse, gives that group preferential treatment, as has been documented in relationships between Portland Policing Bureau officers and members of Patriot Prayer, a far-right group led by Joey Gibson that associates with Proud Boys, an alt-right gang (see Bernstein 2019a, 2019b; Neiwert 2019; Ortiz 2019; Wilson 2018b).

There is an even more telling example. Over 35 years ago, there was another group with a collective "street" identity. The group had chapters across the country, endorsed nationalism and street toughness, advocated a political message and were easily recognized by a unique uniform. As described in chapter 1, the characteristics that distinguish this group are analogous to Proud Boys, or any other alt-right gang. That group, however, was the Black Panther Party (see Bloom & Martin 2016). As history shows, when law enforcement at the local and/or federal level is seriously concerned about a group, it will use overtly oppressive actions to disrupt and disband the group, as observed with the Black Panthers (Ward 2018).

Alt-right gangs strive to maintain the perception that they are qualitatively different from conventional street gangs and their membership by portraying themselves as superior to such groups. Two approaches are commonly used to achieve this goal. First, they characterize themselves as benign fraternal organizations. Gavin McInnes, the founder of Proud Boys (see the focus box in chapter 1) regularly refers to the group as a community that celebrates manhood, "like the Elks Lodge, like Masons or whatever" (Rogan 2017). While this sounds innocuous, historically such exclusionary, fraternal organizations were established in reaction to increasing progressiveness and the feminization of society, which made men feel like they were losing their status and authority (see Kimmel 1996, 2013). Furthermore, Proud Boys members are often encouraged to and do actively participate in criminal acts of violence (Coaston 2018b; DeCook 2018; First Vigil 2019; Hermansson et al. 2020; SPLC 2019a). If a group of Black or Latino males acted the same way, police would easily categorize it as being gang-related violence. The second approach used by alt-right gangs to distinguish themselves from conventional street gangs is by appropriating and propagandizing, via internet memes and social media, scientific research on genetics to claim the evolutionary superiority of Caucasians (Harmon 2018; Saini 2019). An example of this tactic is the use of evidence that a genetic trait allowing lactose to be more readily digestible is more common in the white population than other groups (Freeman 2017; Harmon 2018) Thus, milk, "an ice cold glass of pure racism," has been adopted by the alt-right as an ironic symbol used to indicate their racial superiority over other street groups and marking them as something inherently different (Gambert & Linné 2018; Harmon 2018; Hermansson et al. 2020). Such manipulation of scientific research through caustic internet memes allows alt-right gangs to propagandize and mainstream their racist and hateful messages quickly across social media platforms (Collins & Roose 2018; DeCook 2018; Cristofaro 2018; Gambert & Linné 2018; Hawley 2019; Hermansson et al. 2020; Johnson 2019; Saini 2019).

Alt-right gang members' portrayal of their groups as something that should not be labeled a street gang has a tremendous amount of influence on how society, including law enforcement, interacts with these individuals. Law enforcement's discretion to include or exclude an alt-right gang member greatly impacts a number of potential future criminal justice decisions, as an individual with a gang label is greatly disadvantaged throughout the criminal justice system (Howell 2010; Klein 2009; Knox, Martin Tromanhauser, McCurrie & Laskey 1995). As seen in many urban centers (e.g., Portland, Oregon) these decisions to overload minorities in their gang database can lead to the gang database being shut down entirely (Bernstein 2017; Brosseau 2016; Dumke 2018a, 2018b; Flores 2017; Howell 2015; Howle 2016; PBS 2018a, 2018b). Many law enforcement agencies and researchers would argue that alt-right gang members are not intentionally excluded from gang databases based on their race; however, white youth who are members of conventional street gangs composed primarily of individuals of color *are* considered to be gang members. It is extremely important to be aware of how judgments about who is labeled a gang member affect decisions, data, and overall public policy.

INDIVIDUAL-LEVEL RISK FACTORS

While much of the racist skinhead literature is qualitative in methodology, some themes about risk factors have emerged. When examining the pushes into racist skinhead/alt-right gang membership, the more supported literature has found that the age range for youth involved in racist skinhead gangs ranges from adolescence to early adulthood (i.e., 12 to 25 across samples) (ADL 1995; Baron 1997; Klein 2009; Simi et al. 2008).[6] This age range is consistent with what researchers have found with conventional street gang membership (Curry 2000; Freng et al. 2012; Hughes 2013; Klein & Maxson 2006; Pyrooz 2014; Pyrooz & Sweeten 2015), and it comes with a number of characteristics that separate it from older age groups. This is the most crime-prone age group (Farrington, Ttofi & Coid 2009; Hirschi & Gottfredson 1983) as well as the one most likely to be victimized (Taylor et al. 2008; Watkins & Melde 2018; Wu & Pyrooz 2016). This age group is also more impulsive (Farrington et al. 2009; Hirschi & Gottfredson 1983) and risk seeking (Gottfredson & Hirschi 1990; Grasmick Tittle, Bursik & Arneklev 1993) than older age groups. As such, age is an important risk factor for both alt-right gang membership and street gang membership, since youth in this age group are undergoing important behavioral and cognitive changes, forming and evolving their personal identities, while shifting away from their families and toward their peer groups (Hennigan & Sloane 2013; Hennigan & Spanovic 2012; Klein & Crawford 1967; Vigil 1988b). These changes make youth more susceptible to gang membership, either conventional or alt-right. Moreover, as young people, they are more likely to be looking for a group that meets their psychological and social needs rather than one that aligns with their political or ideological beliefs (see Picciolini 2018).

While the research on alt-right gang youth is limited, much of the current scholarship contradicts many of the early stereotypes about these individuals

---

6. Given that research on racist skinheads has been ongoing for a number of years and represents one kind of Alt-Right gang, the term is used interchangeably with Alt-Right gang to reflect the broader research literature.

being from intact, working-class families who have chosen to be the youthful arm of the far-right. Much of the existing risk-factor literature focuses on what pushes youth away from prosocial connections and toward alt-right gang membership (Keane 1993). This includes being unemployed (Baron 1997; Fangen 1998; Kinsella 1994; Johnson 2019; Young & Craig 1997), abusing drugs and alcohol (Baron 1997; Johnson 2019; Wooden & Blazak 2001), and dropping out of high school (Baron 1997; Johnson 2019; Shashkin 2008). Racist skinheads often report discord with school and difficulty with teachers, suggesting that dropping out of school is an important risk factor for alt-right gang membership (Came 1989; Johnson 2019; King 1988; Kinsella 1994; Wooden & Blazak 2001). One racist skinhead youth highlighted the difficult relationship between himself and school: "Skipping and scrapping. I got kicked out of school 'cause I didn't go, and [for] fighting. Skipping and scrapping" (Baron 1997).

Many of the risk factors impacting alt-right gang membership is reflected in the broader conventional street gang literature. Table 3.1 provides a review comparing key risk factors across both alt-right and conventional street gangs. As the table shows, street gang members have also reported low academic achievement (Craig et al. 2002), low school attachment (Hill et al. 1999), drug use (Bjerregaard & Smith 1993; Hill et al. 1999; Thornberry et al. 2003), hanging out with delinquent peers (Bjerregaard & Lizotte 1995; Bjerregaard & Smith 1993; Hill et al. 1999), and externalizing behaviors (e.g., fighting, stealing, vandalism) (Craig et al. 2002; Hill et al. 1999).

Males are more at risk for membership in alt-right gangs than females (ADL 1995; Ezekiel 2002; Pollard 2016); however, as with the street gang literature, research on female membership remains understudied. An exception is the noteworthy work of Blee (2002, 2005, 2012, 2017) (see also Borgeson 2003; Castle 2012; Fangen 1997; Latif, Blee, DeMichele, Simi & Alexander 2019; Mattheis 2018). As the gang literature has underscored, female gang membership is often much more nuanced and comparable to male gang membership than had previously been thought (Alleyne & Pritchard 2016; Deuchar, Harding, McLean & Densley 2018; Hughes, Botchkovar & Short 2019; W. B. Miller 1973; J. Miller 2001; Moore 1991; Panfil & Peterson 2015; Peterson, Carson & Fowler 2018). While female gang members had traditionally been dismissed as not "real" gang members, but rather girlfriends or hangers-on, the current street gang literature has found that female gang members are highly active in the gang and require interventions that target their specific risk factors (see Howell & Griffiths 2018). For example, familial dysfunction/abuse is a key risk factor for female gang membership and needs to be specifically addressed when working with at-risk women (Fleischer 1998; Fox 2017; Joe & Chesney-Lind 1995; Moore 1991; Peterson & Panfil 2017). A clearer picture of female gang membership risk factors has emerged after more systematic study (for an overview see Panfil & Peterson 2015). It is feasible that as researchers

TABLE 3.1 Summary of Research on the Risk Factors for Alt-Right Gangs,
and Traditional Street Gangs

Motives for Joining (Pushes)	Risk Factors for Alt-Right Gangs	Risk Factors for Traditional Street Gangs
Age (i.e., adolescence)	ADL 1995; Baron 1997; Bjørgo 2002; Blazak 2001	Pyrooz & Sweeten 2015; Thornberry et al. 1993, 2003
Ethnic/racial identity	Blazak 2001; Miller-Idriss 2018; Simi & Futrell 2015; Watts 2001	Adamson 2000; Brotherton & Barrios 2002; Chin 1996; Horowitz 1983; Howell 2015; Moore 1978; 1991; Padilla 1996; Schneider 1999; Smith 2002; Spergel 1995; Sullivan 1989; Tapia 2019; Vigil 1988a, 1988b, 2002
Education	Baron 1997; Miller-Idriss 2018; Miller-Idriss & Pilkington 2017; Pyrooz 2014; Shashkin 2008	Craig, Vitaro, Gagnon & Tremblay 2002; Hill et al. 1999; Nuño & Katz 2018
Employment	Fangen 1998; Kinsella 1994; Young & Craig 1997	Levitt & Venkatesh 2000; Stephenson 2015
Substance abuse	Baron 1997; Simi & Windisch 2018; Wooden & Blazak 2001	Bjerregaard & Smith 1993; Thornberry et al. 2003
Neighborhood disadvantage	Brake 1974; Clarke 1976; Moore 1994	Densley 2013; Klein & Maxson 2006; Moore 1991; Nuño & Katz 2018; Sullivan 1989; Thrasher 1927; Tita et al. 2005
Extremism	Simi & Windisch 2018; Hayes et al. 2018; Mills, Freilich & Chermak 2017	Curry 2011; Pyrooz et al. 2018; Valasik & Phillips 2017
Criminality	Baron 1997; Bjørgo 2002; Ezekiel 2002; Simi et al. 2008; Simi & Windisch 2018	Hill et al. 1999; Levitt & Venkatesh 2000; Short & Strodtbeck 1965; Stephenson 2015; Sullivan 1989

begin to systematically study female members of alt-right gangs, a similar picture of risk factors for membership will emerge—meaning that female alt-right gang members, like their street gang counterparts, are not just peripheral members but are part of the same spectrum of membership seen with male membership (see Belew 2018; Bowman & Stewart 2017; G. Gordon 2018; Hall 2018; Mattheis 2018; Proud Boys 2019). This also means that studying the risk factors for females must be taken more seriously to have their risks and needs addressed appropriately. The motivations for joining a street gang differ between females and males; however, craving a common social identity, gaining status, protection, and filling a void are common (Moore 1991). That void for males is a yearning for adventure, while females are often searching for an emotionally satisfying familial group (Klein & Maxson 2006; Moore 1991; Peterson & Panfil 2017).

ALT-RIGHT IN THE FAMILY

The role of intergenerational racism also needs to be discussed in terms of how it could be a risk factor for alt-right gang membership. As discussed in chapter 2, belief in a racist ideology is not a precursor for alt-right gang membership, and for some youth, exposure to this ideology comes after joining (Christensen 1994, Blee 1996, 2002, 2017; Blee & Yates 2015; Bjørgo 2002; Bjørgo, Carlsson & Haaland 2004; Picciolini 2018; Simi & Futrell 2015; Wendling 2018). Research finds that some youth come from racist households (think Tony Kaye's 1998 film *American History X*), while others are not exposed to racism in their homes (Blee & Burke 2014). As such, it is necessary to consider how growing up in a racist household may make youth more vulnerable to alt-right gang membership (see Saslow 2018).

When considering risk factors that stem from the family, research is focused on how a youth's family, such as family structure, parenting styles, and parental drug use or incarceration, impact gang joining. Within the family domain, racist skinhead youth regularly report residing in a single-parent household (ADL 1995; Baron 1997; Ezekiel 2002; Kinsella 1994; Siedler 2011), enduring domestic discord (ADL 1995; Baron 1997; Bjørgo 2002; Ezekiel 2002; Johnson 2019; Kinsella 1994) and experiencing neglect or abuse (Baron 1997; Came 1989; Johnson 2019; King 1988; Kinsella 1994). More recent studies have expanded the list of familial risk factors to include youths' unsupervised time (Shashkin 2008) and parental unemployment (Siedler 2011). "I just don't get along with my Mom. I tried to kill her. My Mom hated me because I remind her of my father, who is in jail for a couple of murders he committed" (Baron 1997). Just as there is a lot of overlap between members of alt-right and conventional street gangs when comparing the individual-level risk factors, a similar pattern is observed with family-level risk factors, such as familial poverty (Freng et al. 2012; Hill et al. 1999; Thornberry et al. 2003) and single-parent households (Hill et al. 1999; Thornberry et al. 2003). Miller-Idriss (2018: 28) points out that "growing up in an environment of parental nonattention, absences and lack of communication interact with a parental or family members' political orientations and attitudes in important ways." These are influential factors for individuals at risk of joining an alt-right gang.

COMMUNITY-LEVEL RISK FACTORS

Risk factors within the community have not been systematically studied for alt-right gang members. Some of this lack of data is due to how researchers consider these youth (e.g., racist skinheads) as part of a larger movement (i.e., online or part of a national group) and not spatially situated in a community (see Belew 2018; Blee 2018). As we have seen from street gang research, the community can play an important role in youths' exposure to gangs and their risk of gang membership (see Valasik & Tita 2018). Some researchers comment on the communities of the alt-right in a qualitative manner as they discuss a youth's life history. For example, racist skinheads are more likely to come from disorganized neighborhoods (Brake 1974; Clarke 1976; Keane 1993; Moore 1994), and "youth who are marginalized from traditional measures of economic success or who are experiencing economic crises or youth unemployment or underemployment" are at greater risk of joining an alt-right gang (Miller-Idriss 2018: 28; see Johnson 2019). This parallels neighborhood-level risk factors identified to influence street gang membership, which include poverty and disadvantage (Hill et al. 1999; Thornberry et al. 2003) and feeling unsafe in the local community (Hill et al. 1999).

PULLED INTO AN ALT-RIGHT GANG

When examining the motivations for joining an alt-right gang, or the "pulls," research on racist skinheads has documented patterns analogous to the broader street gang literature in a number of ways. For these youth, membership in a skinhead gang offers a "sense of strength, group belonging, and superiority" (ADL 1995: 5). Researchers have highlighted the presence of fear and violence in many of these youths' lives and a hope that membership in an alt-right gang might offer them safety or protection (Baron 1997; Bjørgo 2002; Ezekiel 2002; Picciolini 2018). Simi and colleagues (2008: 759) also find support that youth are joining for purposes of protection, with racist skinhead gangs providing "white kids with defense from other gangs" in Southern California. Furthermore, it is not uncommon for racist skinhead gangs to partake in an array of profit-oriented crimes. These include drug sales, identity theft, counterfeiting, burglary, and armed robbery, which provide members financial incentives for joining an alt-right gang (Simi et al. 2008). Again, these are common themes routinely found in the gang literature, with a street gang occupying multiple voids, such as providing a collective social identity (Hennigan & Spanovic 2012), protection (Short & Strodtbeck 1965), and even economic opportunities (Densley 2013; Levitt & Venkatesh 2000; Stephenson 2015; Sullivan 1989).

AN INVENTORY OF RISK FOR
ALT-RIGHT GANG MEMBERSHIP

This is not a comprehensive inventory of all the factors confronting youth at risk of joining a street gang; however, it highlights the substantial similarities in risk factors between conventional street gang members and racist skinheads that have been documented in the literature. (For an extensive review of risk factors influencing street gang membership, see Howell and Egley 2005.) Table 3.1 lists research studies for the comparison of these sets of individual risk factors. There is still a need for systematic quantitative research that includes alt-right gang youth. Having a more generalizable set of risk factors will allow the development of a broader understanding of the magnitude these risk factors have on influencing youth who join an alt-right gang.

Understanding the risk factors that facilitate membership into an alt-right gang is crucial for developing effective prevention and intervention programs and policies. As we have seen from prevention programs such as Gang Resistance Education and Training (GREAT), targeting a range of risk factors for youth during crucial age ranges can help reduce future gang membership (Esbensen & Osgood 1999; Esbensen, Osgood, Taylor, Peterson & Freng 2001; Esbensen, Peterson, Taylor, Freng, Osgood, et al. 2011; Esbensen et al. 2012; Peterson & Esbensen 2004). Unfortunately, the repetition of stereotypical and anecdotal risk factors for membership in alt-right gangs has hindered the growth of quantitative, generalizable research into the factors that impact the risk of joining these groups. The dearth of quantitative research available on alt-right gangs has only provided limited insights into the risk factors for racist skinhead membership. Without additional quantitative research the ability of researchers to propose policies/programs or know if current programs (e.g., GREAT) are viable is severely restricted.

ALT-RIGHT GANGS AS A GROUP

Applying the programming and policies currently used for street gang members to target alt-right gang members requires that the risk factors between the two groups be similar enough to allow for properly targeting analogous risk factors. It is also necessary that the groups at-risk youth are joining are equally similar, for the same reasons that gang prevention programs specifically target gang membership, rather than just delinquency more broadly. In order to apply the current types of gang programming to youth at risk for alt-right gang membership, overlap between the structure and function of both types of gangs must exist. This is not to say that they have to look exactly the same all the time. Gang structure actually exists on a continuum, ranging from very loosely organized groups of young people to organized groups with distinct age groups and structure. (For a greater review, see Ayling 2011; Densley 2013; Klein & Maxson 2006; Maxson & Klein 1995; Stephenson 2015; Valasik & Phillips 2017, 2018.) This range of gang organization is also likely to be present for alt-right gangs, as discussed in chapter 2; however, empirical research investigating this question is still lacking. What is important is that the structure and function of alt-right gangs be comparable to that of conventional street gangs and not a different type of extremist group, such as the KKK or a highly organized drug cartel. At the group-level, the existing research on street gangs and alt-right gangs is teased apart to compare and contrast the different structural and organizational characteristics of these types of groups.

GANG ORGANIZATION AND STRUCTURE

The organization and structure of alt-right gangs is difficult to address for a variety of reasons. As previously discussed, one of the overarching issues is that much of the research on racist skinheads has studied them as a subculture, focusing on these groups at a scale that is not conducive to the study of a localized group structure (Borgeson & Valeri 2018; Etter 1999; Hamm 1993). Another complication in understanding group structure of racist skinhead gangs and alt-right gangs is the ethnographic nature of the literature (Picciolini 2018; Pilkington et al. 2010; Stern 2019). While the ethnographic literature has provided insights into the structure (and the variation in structure) of several racist skinhead gangs, it limits our understanding of the group structure in a broader sense. The racist skinhead literature is sometimes additionally complicated by its inclusion within larger studies of the WPM (e.g., Blee 2018; Tenold 2018). Researchers will generally speak to a handful of individuals across a range of white power groups, so that alt-right gang members are included in studies that also examine white power groups such as the KKK or the Council of Conservative Citizens. As such, alt-right gangs are given an illusion of organization that has yet to be supported in the literature. It is only in this vein that we see group structure being discussed to highlight how racist skinheads lack the organizational structure, management, and discipline necessary to achieve political change (e.g., Tarasov 2008). The limited research that speaks to the structure of racist skinhead gangs has discussed the loose nature of these groups, often focusing on the lack of leadership or a vertical hierarchy (Baron 1997; Wooden & Blazak 2001). In fact, Simi (2006) found that the management of racist skinhead gangs includes a range of gang structures from poorly organized, independent groups to more traditional and organized patterns of gang structure. The ADL (1995) report is one of very few studies that discuss the size of racist skinhead gangs, stating a range in size from 10 to a few dozen members. Additionally, Klein (2001, 2009) recategorized racist skinheads as *specialty* street gangs, which focus their attention on a particular type of crime (e.g., violence) (see chapter 2). Klein and Maxson (2006) consider specialty gangs to be smaller, with less than 50 members, and to not have cliques or subgroups. Specialty gangs also have shorter life histories, being in existence for less than 10 years. The groups' age range is generally narrow, being less than 10 years but may be broader. Lastly, specialty gangs have a territorial component, with gang members either hanging out in particular places or restricting their criminal activity to certain locations.

In general, the group structure of street gangs has been a source of contention among scholars. Much of the existing gang research argues that conventional street gangs are socially disorganized confederations of loosely structured individuals or small groups of friends that "coalesce irregularly over issues that emerge and vanish from the street" (Decker & Curry 2002: 351). Yet this very lack of organization has permitted street gangs to have a flexibility that increases their resilience to interventions. Street gangs are regularly comprised of age-graded cliques that are derived from a youth's residence, academic years, friendship, and shared interests. These age-graded cliques are also facilitated by similarities in gender, ethnicity, and age (Klein & Maxson 2006; Moore 1991). As such, the overall cohesiveness of a street gang tends to be weak to moderate; however, the social ties within a clique are substantially closer and more tightly knit (Klein & Maxson 2006). Individual status within street gangs can be differentiated. For instance, Short and Strodtbeck (1965) indicate that roles can be established (e.g., war counselor) in conflict-oriented gangs. Yet the confederated arrangement of most street gangs greatly reduces the likelihood of any sole authority emerging and taking control of the group.

Conversely, street gangs have also been described as being hierarchically organized. Typically, hierarchically organized street gangs center their criminal pursuits on economic activities (e.g., drug sales, extortion) (Densley 2013; Levitt & Venkatesh 2000; Stephenson 2015). For instance, many gangs in Chicago, were descendants of political, grass-roots organizations established in the 1950s (e.g., Almighty Latin King/Queen Nation [ALKQN]) that already had an existing social structure (Brotherton & Barrios 2004; Hagedorn 2008). Structuring the activities of a street gang into a vertical hierarchy greatly facilitates the "corporatization" of the group, which allows an entrepreneurial gang to concentrate on economic goals (Densley 2013; Stephenson 2015). Street gangs, however, remain a localized phenomenon that develop, adapt, and evolve within a particular environment (Ayling 2011; Valasik & Tita 2018). Densley (2013: 43) contends that street gangs exist on a spectrum, and synthesizes these two divergent depictions, suggesting that street gangs grow naturally from their emergence as a "neighborhood group to delinquent collectives to full-scale criminal enterprises to providers of extra-legal governance." This interpretation makes perfect sense given that street gangs have been observed throughout the gang literature as both disorganized and structured criminal enterprises. Thus, the observed differences in the literature on the organizational configuration of a street gang are due to the gang's current position on this evolutionary spectrum when the scholar is undertaking the investigation.

As mentioned above, it is critical for researchers to undertake a more systematic study of alt-right gang structure. Street gang research provides important insights and methodologies for examining group structure that should be utilized in the study of alt-right gangs. Whether researchers focus on law enforcement, street workers, or the youth themselves, it is essential that data are collected on a broader range of groups across a number of jurisdictions. This information will allow for a direct comparison between alt-right gangs and conventional street gangs on a number of structural characteristics, since our knowledge of racist skinhead gangs is extremely limited. Without such research, it is difficult, if not impossible, to adapt or implement conventional street gang programs or policies for group-level interventions on alt-right gangs. Gang programs that focus on the group level (e.g., Project Ceasefire) require some understanding of the structural characteristics of the groups being targeted. (For an overview see Braga, Papachristos & Hureau 2014; Braga, Weisburd & Turchan 2019; Braga, Zimmerman, et al. 2019; Roman Link, Hyatt, Bhati & Forney 2018.) Without a better understanding of group structure, group-level intervention or suppression efforts may not perform as suggested by the gang literature and may have unintended consequences or outcomes.

THE ROLE OF CUMULATIVE RISK

Across each of these domains—individual, family, and community—one can see how even with the minimal research on alt-right gang members, the risk factors mirror those that have been regularly documented throughout the life course of individuals that join street gangs (Curry et al. 2014; Fox 2017; Klein & Maxson 2006; Miller 2001; Moore 1991; Pyrooz & Sweeten 2015). This further suggests that "substantial overlap" in the life courses of white supremacists and street gang members actually exists (Simi et al. 2016: 540). This overlap is important, since it demonstrates that there are potentially already programs and policies in place to help at-risk youth avoid the consequences associated with alt-right gang membership. Future research should continue to systematically study risk factors across each of these domains to see if and how risk factors may vary across groups (see Howell & Griffiths 2018). More nuanced studies of gang risk factors have uncovered different gender and racial/ethnic patterns that should be expanded to include alt-right gang members so that prevention, intervention, and suppression activities can be appropriately modified for increased effectiveness.

4

IDENTITY AND IDEOLOGY

Music, Culture, and "Hitler Stuff"

In my life I've met a few steady proper skinhead crews.
But in '92 there was a crew that banged, a wild untamed skin-
   head gang.
I was young but I knew better, they claimed "white power" and
   they fought whoever.
These skinheads were out for blood.
Thought they were invincible. Casino in Mount Pocono.
They ruined Airport Music Hall. A time bomb ready to blow.
July 15 1992 they murdered a homeless dude.
Beaten and stabbed to death.
Lynch turned state's evidence.
Ritchie Krutch lost his tooth. Kicked in the face by skinhead boot.
Neil Rappley lost his life. Stabbed to death by skinhead knife.
To all the skinheads old & new, don't end up in a bonehead crew.
Respect the culture, respect your roots.
Be a steady proper skinhead crew!

WISDOM IN CHAINS (2015, A NON-RACIST HARDCORE
BAND), "SKINHEAD GANG"

We [PENI] were a group of fucken white boys that formed together to pro-
tect each other, gang style. It wasn't nothing fucken political at all. Some of
the members might have been more political . . . but generally we were only
interested in being gangsters.

SIMI, SMITH & REESER (2008: 766)

INTRODUCTION

Throughout life, individuals join and leave groups, from informal friendship groups to organized institutions. For youth, group membership plays an important role in identity development and personal growth. This is especially true as youth begin to build relationships to friendship groups outside of their families. While the prosocial benefits of group membership are extensive, the negative impact of membership in delinquent peer groups can be long lasting and serious (Pyrooz, Sweeten & Piquero 2013; Sweeten, Pyrooz & Piquero 2013). For example, youth who join a street gang commit more crimes on average than youth who are in another type of delinquent peer group (Decker 1996; Decker & Van Winkle 1996; Klein 1971; Melde & Esbensen 2011, 2013). One important element of designating group membership is the ability to discern the in-group from the out-group (see Papachristos 2005). These delineations can range from informal cues, such as inside jokes, hand signs, coded language, clothing choices, or tattoos, to more formal cues, such as rosters or group contracts (see Gambetta 2009).

Learning to decipher these informal cues is a process that occurs over time, with members eventually being able to easily discern insiders from outsiders. For example, consider a school fraternity. There are formal cues such as clothing that designate membership, but even without a fraternity shirt on, members can identify each other through other cues, such as hand signs, internal group slang, or other fashion choices. So even if an outsider wore a fraternity shirt, it would still be difficult to "pass" as an insider of that fraternity because joining a fraternity is not a quick process. The same is true of a gang. One cannot just walk in and automatically become a member; rather, there is a time period where one learns (both formally and informally) what it means to be a member, and then, oftentimes, the new member must undergo some sort of initiation. These rituals help build a group identity and delineate the in-group from the out-group. The fact that these initiation processes build group identity among members has fascinated scholars for some time (see Hagedorn 1998; Kimmel 2008). The conventional street gang literature has repeatedly discussed how the use of violence during initiation helps normalize violence and solidify group identity (Moore 1978, 1991; Vigil 1996). The same is true for alt-right gangs. Wooden and Blazak (2001) found that racist skinhead gangs regularly utilize the ritual act of "jumping in" new members. Gavin McInness, founder of Proud Boys, has routinely stated that initiation into a Proud Boys clique requires being beaten in and getting tattooed (ABC News 2018; NBC Left Field 2018; Rogan 2017).

This chapter examines the range of ways that youth who join alt-right gangs are able to learn in-group behaviors and ideology and how to display them. We first overview the range of ideologies adopted by alt-right gangs, since they are not universally or equally subscribed to by these groups. We then review the evolution of white power music and its role in helping diffuse white power rhetoric, along with social and behavioral norms, to a broad, international audience. Music and other media (e.g., television, the internet, social media, etc.) bring awareness of white power terminology and ideologies to populations previously unaware of them. Music also plays an important role in shaping much of the fashion that is associated with white power youth (see Borgeson & Valeri 2005, 2018; Miller-Idriss 2017, 2018). This chapter also discusses the different fashions and tattoos that help designate alt-right gang youth. While some of these cues are unique to a distinct group (e.g., a particular sign or tattoo), the general use of common identifiers, such as swastika tattoos, is not group specific (see Pilkington et al. 2010). The first part of learning to be a gang member, whether alt-right or conventional, is being able to "talk the talk." Some of the language and rhetoric associated with gang membership is not unique to being a gang member. For example, mainstream media have helped spread the basics of gang culture such that it is possible to feign gang membership to the uninitiated (Dunbar & Kubrin 2018; Esbensen & Tusinski 2007; Gravel, Wong & Simpson 2018; Gushue, Lee, Gravel & Wong 2018; Hallsworth & Young 2008; Howell 2007; Howell & Griffiths 2018). Parents, for example, may have concerns that their children are gang members because they listen to "gangsta" rap and wear a particular color or brand of clothing, despite no other indicators of gang involvement being present. It is for this reason that we consider these types of signs, symbols, and ideologies as descriptors rather than definers of alt-right gang membership. Not every alt-right gang member will adopt all of the in-group indicators, and some out-group members will use some of the more mainstream indicators (see Miller-Idriss 2017, 2018). Research has highlighted key identifiers of these youth groups, such as basic ideological beliefs, a clothing style, the role of white power music, and the use of particular signs/symbols (i.e., tattoos, swastikas, SS bolts, 88) (ADL 1995; Fangen 1998; Forbes & Stampton 2015; Hermansson et al. 2020; Miller-Idriss 2017, 2018; Moore 1993; Pollard 2016; Sarabia & Shriver 2004; Simi & Futrell 2015).[7] However, it is important to note that the blatant use of these visible symbols has begun to wane, as some members have begun to normalize with mainstream society (Cooter 2006; Hermansson et al. 2020; Jan 2017; Mettler 2016; Miller-Idriss 2017, 2018; Simi & Futrell 2015). This trend is also reflected within broader street gang culture as the use of blatant signs/symbols of membership (i.e., flying colors) has also evolved into more subtle cues to avoid law enforcement identification (see Garot 2010; Struyk 2006).

IDEOLOGY AND RHETORIC OF ALT-RIGHT GANGS

There is no "universal" ideology uniting or organizing every white power group; instead, different alt-right gangs adopt whichever elements suit their point of view. The alt-right remains a confederated movement, composed of a variety of factions generally held together by opposing feminism, globalism, immigration, multiculturalism, establishment politics, and political correctness (Hawley 2017,

7. For a more complete list of skinhead symbology see SPLC (2012).

2019; Hermansson et al. 2020; Lyons 2018; Main 2018; Marcotte 2018; May & Feldman 2018; Nagle 2017; Neiwert 2017; Waring 2019; Wendling 2018). Similarly, there is not one set of beliefs that a street gang adopts, and the political interests and activities of these groups are also likely to vary. Again, the ideology and political activities of these groups exist on a spectrum and are therefore considered descriptors of these groups, not definers (see chapters 1 and 2). As can be seen from this chapter's title, the off-hand use of the phrase "Hitler stuff" by an incarcerated youth highlights the lack of a clear ideological focus.[8] Considering ideology as a descriptor allows researchers to move away from examining each group as a unique entity with a distinctive ideology (Reid & Valasik 2018). When thinking about alt-right ideology, there are three questions to consider. The first is the most basic question: What are the different ideological themes that are adopted by alt-right gangs? The second focuses on the impact that ideology actually has on alt-right gang behavior compared to the mythology attached to these gangs. Third, if ideology and political rhetoric are critical to alt-right gang identity, is it really unique to these groups in a way that makes them distinctively different from conventional street gangs?

The ideologies referenced by alt-right gangs are often varied, and sometimes contradictory, with some centered on the very basic ideas of white power, anti-minority/anti-immigrant rhetoric, while others subscribe to more complicated mythologies and religious beliefs, such as Odinism, paganism, the World Church of the Creator, or National Socialism (see Berry 2017; Gardell 2003; Pollard 2016; Simi & Futrell 2015; Zeskind 2009). Many of these ideologies or beliefs are not limited to alt-right gangs, but exist in the larger WPM (Simi & Futrell 2015; Zeskind 2009). When considering the role ideology plays in alt-right gang membership, there is a range of how integral white power beliefs are to either the group's or an individual member's identity. As van Gemert and colleagues (2008: 8) point out when discussing neo-Nazis and racist skinheads in Europe, "These groups may or may not be linked to political organizations. In some countries juvenile gangs exist that merely use extremist symbols to add to their identity." In the United States, the image of the white power foot soldier is often countered with other evidence highlighting that alt-right gangs (i.e., racist skinheads) lack both the defined goals and shared beliefs that might make them well-organized, right-wing revolutionaries (Crothers 2019; Hamm 1993; McAuliffe 2019; Suall & Lowe 1988; Wooden & Blazak 2001). For instance, Pollard (2016) attests that the classic tradition of strict racial hierarchies of Nazism have largely been abandoned with the influx of people of Slavic ancestry joining alt-right gangs throughout America and Eastern Europe (see also Picciolini 2018). Furthermore, the influence of American

8. This term was used by a white power gang youth incarcerated in California's Division of Juvenile Justice during interviews (see Maxson et al. 2012; Valasik & Reid 2019).

white supremacy has shifted the focus of alt-right gangs away from ethnicity and toward skin color to achieve white racial purity, allowing for non-Aryan members to participate in these groups or for members to have relationships with nonwhite individuals (see Saini 2019; Simi & Futrell 2015; Mudde 2005; Picciolini 2018; Wooden & Blazak 2001). Waldner and colleagues (2006) find further ideological contradictions with gay racialist skinheads that are active in the alt-right movement (see also Borgeson & Valeri 2018; Koulouris 2018; Lyons 2018; Stern 2019).

As for delineating ideology as a unique feature in the membership of alt-right youth, existing research suggests that ideology is already integrated in the social fabric of street gangs. Gang scholars have demonstrated that race/ethnic-based pride and/or political ideology is not solely limited to white youth. The marginalization of black and Latinx youth has motivated many street gangs to incorporate a political ideology aimed at fighting for political power and producing social change in their neglected communities (Barrios 2003; Brotherton & Barrios 2004; Cureton 2011; Francisco & Martinez 2003; Helmreich 1973; Hughes & Short 2013; Montejano 2010; Oropeza 2005; Short 1974; Short & Moland 1976). Street gangs have also focused on religious or spiritual principles. The Almighty Latin Kings and Queens Nation (ALKQN) created a spirituality of liberation to resist American society's dehumanizing, objectifying, and criminalizing the group (Barrios 2003; Brotherton & Barrios 2004). Liberation spirituality directly contributed to the gang's social identity and established a process of acculturation for recruits (Brotherton & Barrios 2004). Other gangs may not have a true ideology but are formed with the intention of offering youth pride in their heritage. For example, the formation of Mara Salvatrucha (MS-13) in the city of Los Angeles has long been associated with Salvadorian pride and identity (Bruneau, Dammert & Skinner 2011; Cruz 2010; Ward 2013; Wolf 2012). Furthermore, Vigil (1996: 151) notes how gang initiation for Chicano gangs in Los Angeles "affirms one's ethnic identification . . . showing they are 'Chicano'" (see also Moore 1978, 1991; Tapia 2019; Vigil 1996). Research has also shown that street gangs adhere to a "code of the street," which can be thought of as a secular ideology, disseminated and mainstreamed through popular culture and "gangsta" and trap rap (see Anderson 1999; Dunbar, Kubrin & Scurich 2016; Harkness 2013; Kubrin 2005, 2006; Kubrin & Nielson 2014; Lauger & Densley 2018; McFarland 2008; Storrod & Densley 2017; Urbanik & Haggerty 2018; Van Hellemont & Densley 2019; Weitzer & Kubrin 2009). Typical tropes include money, women, drugs, guns, and criminal activity. Anderson (1999) portrays the "street code" as a set of rituals, norms, and beliefs that provides order to social interactions between individuals, particularly the use of violence, in distressed communities that lack resources and opportunities (see Harding 2014; Kubrin & Wadsworth 2003; Kubrin & Weitzer; Matsuda, Melde, Taylor, Freng & Esbensen 2013; Mitchell, Fahmy, Pyrooz & Decker 2017; Simon & Burns 1997). Just like political or religious ideologies, devotion to the "code of the street" presents a powerful set of norms and behaviors that adherents follow to achieve a greater reputation and status within their gang, among rival groups, and throughout the local community. It also aids in providing a social identity.

Overall, the points raised here highlight the fact that ideology should not be a factor in deciding to exclude alt-right gangs from the larger studies on youth gangs (e.g., Pyrooz et al. 2018; Simi 2006; Simi et al. 2008; Valasik & Reid 2019). As discussed, subscribing to an ideology is neither required in any meaningful way nor a phenomenon unique to alt-right gangs that places youth outside of the street gang spectrum. Focusing on the race-based orientation of alt-right gangs minimizes or ignores the role of ideology and racial/ethnic pride in the formation, maintenance, and membership of many conventional street gangs.

WHITE POWER MUSIC

Music plays a number of important roles in alt-right gang culture. Listening to white power music is not limited to alt-right gang members any more than "gangsta" or trap rap is strictly for street gang members. The music woven through both of these groups subtly educates youth about the social norms, behavioral expectations, and group dynamics that are normative within these groups. Since music is embedded in a larger subculture, this can also include fashion or other aesthetic expectations (see Bullock & Kerry 2017; Cotter 1999; DeCook 2018; Dyck 2017; Futrell, Simi & Gottschalk 2006; Love 2016, 2017; Miller-Idriss 2017, 2018; Picciolini 2018; Pieslak 2015; Putnam & Littlejohn 2007; Simi & Futrell 2015; Windisch & Simi 2017). According to Ed Wolbank, former director of the Northern Hammerskins and member of the white power band Bound for Glory, music is the key element in introducing white power political ideology: "Music is number 1. It's the best way to reach people. Through music people start getting into the scene, then you can start educating them. Politics through music" (ADL 2019). That being said, youth do not go to music shows or concerts to learn about white power ideology. Despite buying Resistance Records, William Pierce, the leader of the National Alliance, even noted that "kids are not interested in ideology as much as they are in resistance music" (Pieslack 2015: 62). Even those that research white power music note: "the diversity of musicians (Open Season, Chaos 88, Definite Hate, and hundreds of international white-power bands and solo artists), the multitude of events (Aryan Fest, NordicFest [now defunct], Hammerfest, European-American Heritage Festival), and numerous record companies (Tightrope Records, Antipathy Records, NSM88 Records, Resistance Records [now defunct], Final Stand Records). In short, there is too much musical activity in the movement for any single all-purpose perspective" (Pieslack 2015: 54).

Even if music did not play a critical role in the indoctrination or radicalization of alt-right gang youth, it does build community and help define in-groups from out-groups. As one of the women in Blee's (2002: 162) study noted, "There's a whole other genre of music out there that no one hears about, and it's real power-ful, especially at that awkward stage where no one exactly knows who they are. It gives you an identity." As articles and books on the white power music scene highlight, not knowing show etiquette (i.e., how to dance in the pit), the fashion, the bands or even how to locate a show's venue all aid in designating who does not belong or is inexperienced. For these reasons, the key elements of the evo-lution of the white power music scene that has been adopted by alt-right gang members will be outlined below. It is not an exhaustive discussion of this music or the cultural implications of this music scene, since there are a number of authors who have focused on this in depth (see Dyck 2017; Love 2016; Teitelbaum 2017a; Windisch & Simi 2017 for a broader review). However, it necessary to provide an overview of the white power music scene because music is one of the key cultural elements of the alt-right gang culture (see Bullock & Kerry 2017; DeCook 2018; Gogarty 2017; Love 2017; Stern 2019).

Before the current iteration of the alt-right, the youth of the WPM were pri-marily groups of racist skinheads that emerged from the skinhead music and fash-ion scene (Dyck 2017; Love 2016; Pollard 2016; Windisch & Simi 2017). This scene originally included both racist and non-racist skinheads, with a divide transpiring after the scene's development, resulting in some shared stylistic characteristics (see Borgeson & Valeri 2018). The original skinhead music scene started in the 1970s in the United Kingdom. It was a reaction to the upward mobility embraced by the larger mod subculture and grounded itself in promoting a working-class ethic (Brake 1974; Brown 2004; Cotter 1999; Dyck 2017; Hebdige 1979; Moore 1993; Pollard 2016; Worley 2013). One of the founding elements in this music was its appreciation of black music, especially American soul music and Jamaican ska. In the late 1970s and early 1980s, the original hard mod/skinhead scene evolved under the influence of punk rock and the political leanings of this subculture (Forbes & Stampton 2015; Goodrick-Clarke 2002; Worley & Copsey 2016). In this context, Oi! music grew to include not only skinheads but also punks and other working-class youth rebelling against the commercialization of punk rock (Brown 2004; Dyck 2017; Forbes & Stampton 2015; Hamm 1993; Love 2016; Pollard 2016; Sarabia & Shriver 2003; Wood 1999).

The political inclinations of this scene led to the split between racist and non-racist skinheads, with racist skinheads embracing far-right politics (Borgeson & Valeri 2018; Love 2016; Pieslak 2015; Pollard 2016; Wood 1999). This split led to a number of altercations, with racist and non-racist skinheads regularly clash-ing at shows and other public encounters. The music of the racist skinheads included the expected themes of support for the working class but also pushed hypermasculinity and a range of far-right themes (i.e., racism, xenophobia, anti-Semitism, anti-feminism). These early racist skinhead Oi! bands, particularly the charismatic British band Skrewdriver, became principal conveyors of white power ideals. The National Front, a far-right political party in Great Britain, utilized them to advocate for the termination of nonwhite immigration, the repatriation of immigrants residing in the United Kingdom, exiting the larger European community, and reintroducing capital punishment (Dyck 2017; Forbes & Stampton 2015; Goodrick-Clarke 2002; Love 2016; Pollard 2016). Other white power bands patterned themselves after Skrewdriver across Europe, North and South America, and Australia, echoing the band's white power messages in their lyrics and further spreading white power rhetoric (Brown 2004; Dyck 2017; Forbes & Stampton 2015; Pollard 2016; Teitelbaum 2017a). While punk and hardcore genres get most of the attention, white power messages have also been found in "rockabilly" (a 1950s-style mix of rhythm and blues), country and western music, folk, heavy metal, rap, and synthwave (Crew 2003; Futrell et al. 2006; Love 2012, 2016; Messner, Jipson, Becker & Byers 2007; Putnam & Littlejohn 2007; Shekhovtsov 2012; Teitelbaum 2017b; Windisch & Simi 2017). Today "fashwave," a variety of electronic instrumental music by artists like Cybernazi and Xurious, appeals to younger generations by incorporating synthwave's aesthetic style of the 1980s, offering familiar themes from millennials' childhood but adding a fascist element in songs and music videos (Bullock & Kerry 2017; DeCook 2018; Gogarty 2017; Hann 2016; Hermansson et al. 2020; Kelley 2017; Love 2017; Smith 2018). Some bands have even pushed into the rap/hip-hop scene, although these genres of music are traditionally considered by white power groups to be nonwhite (Dyck 2017; Goodrick-Clarke 2002; Holt 2007; Love 2017; Putnam & Littlejohn 2007; Teitelbaum 2017a, 2017b). On Stormfront, a popular white power website and online forum, even those who voice the opinion that rap is "too black" to appreciate or enjoy admit that it may appeal more to youth. Overall, the diversity of white power music and its youthful orientation has greatly facilitated the spread of these messages (DeCook 2018; Gogarty 2017; Love 2016, 2017).

The spread of the racist skinhead subculture to the United States marks an important turning point in the production and subsequent distribution of white power music. America's lenient hate speech laws allow for white power groups to operate in the recording industry without legal repercussions unless they directly incite a specific act of criminal violence against an individual (Cotter 1999; Dyck 2017; Love 2012, 2016; Shekhovtsov 2011; Simi & Futrell 2015). Many of the activities associated with the white power music scene, such as recording, producing, holding shows/concerts/festivals, or even band rehearsals, if held in other countries (e.g., Germany) would be shut down, and the participants involved could be prosecuted (Pieslack 2015). For example, in 2003 the lead singer of the neo-Nazi band Landser, Michael Regener, was sentenced to over three years in prison for his lyrics celebrating Nazism (Shekhovtsov 2013). That is not to say that law enforcement in the United States does not try to shut down white power music festivals,

still get panelture

but it cannot be done for lyric content. In his book on radical music, Pieslack (2015) discusses the 2012 St. Paddy's Hammerskin concert and highlights the secrecy that was needed to prevent it being shut down or infiltrated (see also Tenold 2018): "To maintain secrecy the CHS [Confederate Hammerskins] posted a contact phone number on their discussion forum the evening before St. Paddy's Day 2012. Unless one had an inside connection or was well established in the scene, concertgoers had to call the number, identify themselves, and provide background information in order for the wary man answering the calls to reveal the exact location. Past events, such as Hammerfest 2007 in Portland, Oregon, had been shut down by police and protesters, so the need for secrecy was imperative." Live music continues to be an element of this scene, since it provides a large opportunity for socialization. For example, Blood and Honour (B&H), a major player in white power music, organizes a number of concerts and events across Europe, including Summerfest in Sweden, a Day of Honour in Hungary, the Summer Solstice in France, Defend Europe in Bulgaria, 15 Years in Slovenia, the Ian Stuart Donaldson (ISD) Memorial in Britain, and many others. These events pull in people from around the world (May 2018).

The white power music scene has evolved and expanded through internet message boards and online distribution (see chapter 6). This has made white power music more accessible to a wide range of youth who previously would have been introduced to the music in a much more localized manner (Dyck 2017; Feischmidt & Pulay 2016; Futrell et al. 2006; Lennings, Amon, Brummert & Lennings 2010; Lewis 2018; Schafer 2002; Simi & Futrell 2006, 2015). Currently, the Stormfront website has entire message boards dedicated to discussing white power music. To illustrate the extensive spread of white power subculture through music, over 300 white power bands are active across 30 European countries, approximately 100 bands reside in the United States, where the white power music scene is a multimillion-dollar industry (SPLC 2001).

As Pieslack (2015: 195) states, "Music, perhaps more so than other cultural idioms, becomes intimately involved in the processes of recruitment, social bonding, ideological reinforcement, and motivation for action within these groups." For alt-right gang members, the music, and the scene that comes with it, helps outline social mores. Violence and hypermasculinity are two characteristics highly visible within this scene. Shows are punctuated with slam dancing in the pit, fights often break out, and advertising flyers (see figure 4.1) and lyrics underscore the tough-guy mentality (Futrell et al. 2006; Kimmel 2008; Pilkington 2010; Simi & Futrell 2015; Windisch & Simi 2017; Wood 1999). It is also critical to note that themes and expectations around violence and hypermasculinity are not limited to this particular music scene. Many non-racist punk and hardcore shows have very similar dynamics, and other, even more popular music scenes (gangsta rap/hip-hop, hard rock, and metal) have embraced violence as part of their subcultural and musical identity (see Kubrin 2005, 2006; Kubrin & Nielson 2014; Harkness 2013).

FIGURE 4.1. Hammerfest show flyer.

From its inception with Oi! in 1970s Britain, white power music has also been a recruitment tool, appealing to a younger audience to replace the aging population of far-right racists (Cooter 2006, 2011; Cotter 1999; Futrell & Simi 2004; Langer 2003; Simi & Futrell 2015). In an effort to become more mainstream, white power music has evolved to incorporate popular trends, with the hope of indoctrinating larger audiences of non-racists into the white power movement. This strategy is particularly salient today with fashwave, trendy electronic instrumental music that sounds like a John Carpenter movie soundtrack from the 1980s (i.e., synthwave) or an episode of Netflix's *Stranger Things* (DeCook 2018; Gogarty 2017; Hann 2016; Kelley 2017; Love 2017; Smith 2018). The integration of white power music into mainstream society further allows for their racist values and use of violence against nonwhites to become commonplace to the point that, rather than being offended or disgusted, people become indifferent. In fact, Valasik and colleagues (forthcoming) find that white college students, compared to black college students, are less offended by the lyrics of white power music than by either rap or heavy metal lyrics, and that it is likely the pervasiveness of coded-language, dog whistles, and incendiary rhetoric that leaves white millennials unperturbed by the racist messages being disseminated by white power music.

While the music of these groups cannot be banned for its content at the governmental level, music providers continue to exclude these bands from their platforms. For example, since 2014, iTunes has begun removing bands that the Southern Poverty Law Center (SPLC) has labeled as hate music (Hogan 2017). Other music platforms such as YouTube, Spotify, and Google Play have said that they are against hate music and will remove it based on user notifications, although plenty of it can still be found on these sites (Hogan 2017). Different venues and festivals have also worked to cancel gigs booked by white power bands (e.g., Riot Room, Cobra Lounge, and Bar XIII) or block members of groups like Proud Boys from being admitted into shows (see Joe Hardcore's response to members of Proud Boys wanting to attend his This Is Hardcore festival, posted on Facebook November 12, 2017).

WHITE POWER CLOTHING

Fashion and clothing have played an important role in discerning who is in a group and who is outside of a group, particularly for gangs (Conti & Cooper 2018; Decker & Van Winkle 1996; Garot 2010; Garot & Katz 2003; Miller-Idriss 2017, 2018; O'Neal 1997). While some of the clothes have subcultural implications, such as street fashions for conventional street gangs or Oi!/hardcore/punk fashion that is now associated with alt-right gangs, members within these gangs know the nuances that distinguish wannabes or peripheral individuals from "true" members. As we consider the fashion associated with current alt-right gangs, it is important to trace the roots of the symbolic meaning behind the clothing (see Miller-Idriss 2017, 2018). For the last 50 years, white power fashion has evolved alongside the music scene. Many consider the first uniquely skinhead fashion to have been the "hard mods." Hard mods mixed elements of mod fashion, such as clean cut, quality suiting, with the authority-defying rude-boy fashion of cool, young Jamaican immigrants (Brake 1974; Brown 2004; Cotter 1999; Dyck 2017; Hebdige 1979; Moore 1993; Pollard 2016). As hard mods shifted into what we recognize as traditional skinheads, the subculture adopted a fashion idealizing the industrial worker: a shaved or close-cut hairstyle, denim work pants, braces (suspenders), tattoos, and Dr (Doc) Marten steel-toed boots.[9] As Brown (2004: 159) notes, "Against the 'coming man' of the late-1960s—the middle-class, peace-loving, long-haired

---

9. See SPLC (2006) for review of traditional skinhead tattoos.

student—the skinhead—short-haired, violent, and working-class—became rebel par excellence" and the fashion reflected this. More specifically, racist skinhead culture has included Fred Perry or Ben Sherman shirts, band shirts, Doc Marten boots, Levi's jeans, bomber jackets, and shaved heads. Again, these clothes are not limited to racist skinheads, and can also be seen worn by traditional, non-racist or Skinheads Against Racial Prejudice (SHARP), Gay skins, or other punk rock youth (Borgeson & Valeri 2018; Roy 2008; Sarabia & Shriver 2004; Ventsel 2008). That being said, there are subtle identifiers distinguishing racist skinheads from other skins, such as red or white shoelaces and shirts with white power band logos (e.g., Skrewdriver, H8Machine, Brutal Attack). Racist tattoos such as swastikas, iron crosses, 88, and SS bolts are also key distinguishers between racist and other skins (Baron 1997; Simi & Futrell 2006, 2015; Pilkington et al. 2010; Pollard 2016; Sarabia & Shriver 2004; Valeri, Sweazy & Borgeson 2017).

Clothing is used as a simple identifier to designate in- and out-group individuals in a few ways. Although the internet could help an individual pass the initial inspection, there could be local differences not as well known. For example, Sarabia and Shriver's (2004) racist skinheads from Southern California wore black shoelaces, which clearly differentiated them from the more traditional white laces worn by most racist skinheads. In addition, there are more subtle cues that distinguish racist and non-racist skins (e.g., particular brands, color choices, and tattoos). Going back to the original racist/non-racist scene split, the non-racist SHARP skins used fashion to revolt against what they considered a negative political trend in the scene. As Brown (2004: 159) observes, in response to the more extreme fashion associated with far-right skins, the other "skins began to stress the cultivation of the 'original' look, making fashion, like music, a litmus test for authenticity. Violators of the proper codes were not skinheads, but 'bald punks,' a category to which racists—who, in the eyes of purists, failed completely to understand what the subculture was about—were likely to belong. The connection between right-wing politics and 'inauthentic' modes of dress was personified in the figure of the 'bone head,' a glue-sniffing, bald-headed supporter of the extreme right, sporting facial tattoos, a union-jack T-shirt, and 'the highest boots possible.'"

In the current iteration of alt-right gangs, one sees a mixture of the more old-school racist skinhead fashion and a newer, more subtle fashion aesthetic. Proud Boys, for example, utilize a number of the racist skinhead traditions—perhaps due in part to the fact that many youth who belong to local alt-right gangs also affiliate with Proud Boys—including a black Fred Perry polo shirt with yellow piping and close cropped hair (see figure 4.2) (Beery 2017; Cauterucci 2017; Hermansson et al. 2020; Jan 2017; Mettler 2016; SPLC 2019; Stern 2019; Swenson 2017). As we have seen with conventional street gang members, subtlety is now a better way to avoid censure and law enforcement detection. It is rarer to see youth displaying blatant gang colors today. Instead, street gang youth use brands (clothes, shoes),

FIGURE 4.2. Proud Boys members' blatant display of membership by wearing their gang colors (photo by David Neiwert).

sports teams, or other subtle cues to designate membership while still providing some plausible deniability to law enforcement (see Conti & Cooper 2018). For instance, in the Los Angeles Police Department's Hollenbeck Community Policing Area, street gangs readily adopt mainstream symbols with El Sereño using the Superman symbol as an identifier of gang membership, while Big Hazard, uses the Biohazard symbol (see Valasik 2014). Similarly, the blatant use of traditional white power symbols has also been declining, with more members conforming to a conventional, more normalized appearance (Cooter 2006; Hermansson et al. 2020; Miller-Idriss 2017, 2018; Simi & Futrell 2015). While there is a history of white power groups appropriating clothing brands without the consent of the brand (e.g., Fred Perry or Ben Sherman polo shirts, Doc Marten boots, Alpha Industries Bomber Jacket) (Cooter 2006; Hermansson et al. 2020; Miller-Idriss 2017, 2018; Simi & Futrell 2015), today something more disturbing is taking place. With this mainstreaming of alt-right gangs there has also been a commercialization of clothing brands (e.g., Thor Steinar, Erik and Sons, Ansgar Aryan), which are for all practical purposes identical to popular brands like Aeropostale or Abercrombie and Fitch but use coded white power symbols to intentionally market their apparel to members of alt-right gangs (see Miller-Idriss 2017, 2018). Miller-Idriss (2017) notes a similar trend for alt-right youth in Germany: "In the German context, where it's illegal to display a swastika, you can zip up your Lonsdale jacket, which displays the letters NSDA [the acronym for National Socialist German Worker's Party in German]. But if a police officer stops you, you can unzip it, and it's just 'Lonsdale.' So they initially co-opted these brands for whatever symbolic representation they determined was connected from this logo, and then somebody figured out there was a market to create their own brands and sell to their own market."

The purpose of highlighting the nuanced fashion of alt-right gangs is to underscore how these cultural identifiers help designate in- and out-group status. Fashion can also have serious consequences. For instance, in 2007, members of FSU (Friends Stand United/Fuck Shit Up), which is classified as a gang by several law enforcement entities, killed a man outside a hardcore music show for wearing a confederate flag shirt (Binelli 2007). FSU is not an alt-right gang; rather, it was originally meant to fight Nazis in the scene; this case shows the importance of fashion in designating who belongs to a group and who does not. The creation of these in-group distinctions helps build the group identity and feelings of solidarity that are important for youth joining these groups (see chapter 3).

CONCLUSION

This chapter provides an overview on how the ideology, music, and fashions of alt-right groups play a critical role in developing a group's identity. Group identity is necessary for gangs to exert control over members' social and behavioral conduct. As gang research has shown, the behavioral impacts of gang membership are more powerful than association with delinquent peers alone (Bjerregaard & Lizotte 1995; Bjerregaard & Smith 1993; Hill et al. 1999). It is known that these group dynamics amplify antisocial behavior; thus, an understanding of all of the indicators feeding into the development of this identity provides a more complete picture of the processes by which youth become involved in these gangs. Such indicators also underscore why we cannot use ideology, as suggested by Curry, Decker, and Pyrooz (2014); Hamm (1993); and Klein (1995), as the principal reason to exclude alt-right youth in gang studies. Today racist skinheads represent a substantial component of violent alt-right gang members. In America there has been a general growth in the number of alt-right groups since 2000, with sharp increases in "patriot" and militia groups following the election of President Obama in 2008 (Crothers 2019; Finn 2019; Lyons 2018; Neiwert 2017). According to the SPLC (2017) there are 78 documented racist skinheads groups in the United States, making up nearly 17% of the documented alt-right gangs. Internationally, alt-right groups are just as prevalent in Europe, and taking hold in Eastern Europe's Slavic countries (Fieltz & Thurston 2019; Pollard 2016; Waring 2019). Media and music play a critical role in helping bring these far-right ideologies and cultural signals to a broad audience. Chapter 6 will examine the larger impact of the internet on the growth of white power groups over the last 30 years.

It is important to remind the reader that the intersection of media, music, and the internet is not unique to the alt-right as a means of spreading their ideology and social norms. Jihadi extremist groups have also taken advantage of this nexus of communication (see Laqueur & Wall 2018; T. Morris 2017; Valasik & Phillips 2017, 2018). Furthermore, media and the internet have also impacted street gang culture, helping to spread gang ideology and culture to a broader audience (Esbensen & Tusinki 2007; Klein 2001; Maxson 1998). Before the internet became the primary source for youth to learn about gang culture, movies such as *Colors*, *Menace II Society*, and *New Jack City*, along with gangsta rap, all helped spread knowledge about gangs throughout the United States and across the globe (see Van Hellemont & Densley 2019). Youth who lacked any genuine gang affiliations were alarming parents and law enforcement professionals across the United States as they began adopting the fashion and language of conventional street gangs. As Papachristos (2005: 49) notes, "The increasing mobility of information via cyberspace, films, and music makes it easy for gangs, gang members, and gang wannabes to get information, adapt personalities, and distort gang behaviors. Most often, these images of gang life are not simply exaggerated; they're flat-out wrong."

Thus, the internet image of these groups does not necessarily reflect the reality (Van Hellemont & Densley 2019). It is the reality of alt-right gang membership that needs to be addressed, but the ideology, music, and fashion imagery all factor in to how youth see themselves and their groups.

5

ALT-RIGHT GANGS' USE OF SPACE

We never really claim territory, you know, we just think that wherever we are is our territory. That's how PEN1's always been. Why claim specific territory? We don't need to say this street or block is ours. It's all ours.

SIMI & FUTRELL (2015: 55)

Details are kept secret, the meetings usually consist of drinking, fighting, and reading aloud from Pat Buchanan's Death of the West.

GAVIN MCINNESS (2016)

INTRODUCTION

This chapter explores how alt-right gangs use space in the real world. The relationship between street gangs and how they emerge from, interact with, and use space has been a topic of interest since Thrasher's (1927) seminal work, *The Gang: A Study of 1,313 Gangs in Chicago.* The examination into how local geography influences street gangs' patterns of behavior has yielded valuable insights for both the broad sociological understanding of place (see Liebow 1967; Suttles 1968; Whyte 1943) and the community correlates of crime literature (Blasko, Roman & Taylor 2015; Brantingham, Tita, Short & Reid 2012; Ley & Cybriwsky 1974; Papachristos, Hureau & Braga 2013; Taniguchi, Ratcliffe & Taylor 2011; Valasik 2018). Valasik and Tita (2018: 843) highlight the fact that "the social relationships binding the members of a gang to the broader community are complex and sometimes competing." This is also true for alt-right gangs. In the limited literature on alt-right gangs and space, there is a lack of consensus about how these groups orient themselves. For instance, much of the prevailing gang literature would consider alt-right gangs, particularly racist skinheads, to be less territorially confined than many conventional street gangs, since they are "inside . . . working on their written materials" (Klein 1995: 22). But even if an alt-right gang emerges from an online collective, its members do not solely reside in the digital realm (Castle &

Parsons 2019). Many of the activities these members participate in transpire in the physical world and can adversely affect their communities. The most recent and infamous example is that of the Unite the Right rally in Charlottesville, Virginia, August 11–12, 2017, and its violent aftermath (Atkinson 2018; Hawley 2017, 2019; McAuliffe 2019; McCoy 2018). Futrell and Simi (2017: 76) point out that "white supremacist beliefs have not changed," with the current manifestation of alt-right gangs being just the most recent iteration of white power youth groups. Racist skinheads, for example, have a sordid history of being not only active on the streets but also online (Belew 2018; Berlet & Vysotsky 2006; Dobratz & Shanks-Meile 2007; Gerstenfeld & Grant 2004; Kaplan, Weinberg & Oleson 2003; Langer 2003; Lyons 2018; Tenold 2018). Furthermore, alt-right gang members transport their whiteness with them into any physical space that they occupy and behave as if they have "natural dominion" over that space (Simi & Futrell 2015: 55). With this mentality, alt-right gang members have less of a need to carve out and maintain a particular territorial boundary. For white youth today, territory is less of a necessity than it is for conventional street gangs (see Klein & Maxson 2006). Even for conventional gangs, the role of territory is shifting as "cyber banging" grows (Peterson & Densley 2017).

This chapter proceeds with a brief overview highlighting the territoriality of conventional street gangs and our knowledge about how street gangs use space. We then discuss the territoriality of alt-right gangs and *Aryan free spaces* or "settings where white power members meet with one another, openly express their extremist beliefs, and coordinate their activities" (Simi & Futrell 2015: 4). Aryan free spaces exist in both the physical and digital worlds (see Simi & Futrell 2006), but this chapter will focus on the former and conclude by comparing and contrasting Aryan free spaces to conventional street gangs' set spaces—localized, geographically distinct areas (street corner, park, alley, etc.) within a gang's territory where members gather (Blasko et al. 2015; Taniguchi et al. 2011; Tita et al. 2005; Valasik 2018). Chapter 6 extends this discussion by examining alt-right gangs' use of virtual spaces.

TERRITORIALITY OF CONVENTIONAL STREET GANGS

Territoriality is generally described as a spatial strategy used by an individual or a group to exert control over specific space(s) and the resources that are contained within its confines (Lyman & Scott 1967; Sack 1983). Thus, territoriality is thought of as a process employed to protect the occupied space of an individual or group (Newman 1972). Dominance over an area is exhibited when that claimed space is defended, reifying local relationships of power, and authority is exerted over community residents and resources (Dyson-Hudson & Smith 1978; Sack 1983; Van Valkenburg & Osborne 2012). These territorial behaviors are common among conventional street gangs as they seek to influence the actions of local individuals (e.g., neighborhood residents, rival gang members) within their claimed territories (Brantingham, Valasik & Tita 2019; Padilla 1996; Popkin, Gwiasda, Olson, Rosenbaum & Buron 2000). A gang's territorial home is constructed not only by the built environment (e.g., railways, highways, roadways, buildings), but also by establishing symbolic barriers, such as through the use of graffiti, to create an area of influence (see Adamson 2000; Ley & Cybriwsky 1974; Phillips 1999, 2016; Schneider 1999). A fledgling gang marks public spaces to claim its home turf, a place that instills a sense of security and allows them to be unrestrained in their behaviors (see Valasik & Tita 2018). Within a claimed turf, "gang leaders hold sway like barons of old, watchful of invaders and ready to swoop down upon the lands of rivals and carry off booty or prisoners or to inflict punishment upon their enemies" (Thrasher 1927: 6). The creation of a gang's turf is just the first step, because the space will require constant upkeep. It is this regular maintenance, such as placing graffiti on boundaries and important locations within a group's space, that transmits a message to other gangs, specifically rivals, that interlopers are unwelcome and place themselves at risk in the area (Bloch 2019a, 2019b; Ley & Cybriwsky 1974; Phillips 1999, 2016). It is crucial for gangs to continually reify their territories, typically through direct competition with rivals, intra-gang rituals, and cognitive maps (see Brantingham et al. 2012, 2019; Garot 2010; Grannis 2009; Vigil 2009). As such, gang territoriality is a "learned behavior with intergenerational adherence to historical boundaries and rules of engagement" (Pickering, Kintrea & Bannister 2012).

Thrasher (1927: 26) attests that conventional street gangs evolved from informal neighborhood youth "play groups." Living in the same neighborhood provides youth a collective identity to muster around. In general, urban youth are much less mobile than adults. They rely on walking or biking as their modes of transportation. It is in these "walking arenas" that youth interact and socialize with local inhabitants. Grannis (2009) argues that these walking areas coincide with residential street networks that guide residents' perceptions of their neighborhood and act as the organizers of social interaction, either constraining or facilitating relationships. Grannis (2009) insists that discontinuous residential streets actually produce non-permeable barriers between ethnic groups and can contribute to the social patterning of gang formation and the creation of rivalries between these groups (see also Brantingham et al. 2012; Moore 1991). By not routinely venturing through these neighboring communities, youth remain uninformed about the people, places, and activities that transpire outside of their particular gang's turf, creating a "fog of war."

Today, as gang members have greater levels of mobility through private or public transportation, it is not uncommon for them to be less entrenched in their gang's claimed territory and may reside and travel substantial distances outside of their gang's claimed turf (Densley, McLean, Deuchar & Harding 2018; McLean, Deuchar, Harding & Densley 2019; Miller 1966; Moore, Vigil & Garcia 1983; Storrod & Densley, 2017; Valasik & Tita 2018; Valasik, Gravel, Tita, Brantingham & Griffiths forthcoming; Whittaker et al. 2020). This process of commuting to turf (see Gatz & Klein 1993; Klein 1995) has been well documented among Chicano street gangs in Los Angeles (see Moore 1978, 1991; Moore et al. 1983; Vigil 2007); surfer gangs (Duane 2019; Kaffine 2009; Usher & Kerstetter 2015); and throughout urban centers in Europe, Russia, Australia, and New Zealand (see Valasik & Tita 2018). Still other conventional street gangs demonstrate more nomadic mobility patterns that are not constrained by a claimed turf. For instance, Vietnamese street gangs do not hold in high regard maintaining a claimed territory and instead travel extensively to participate in criminal activities (Ong 2003; Vigil 2002; Vigil & Yun 2002). As Vigil (2002: 113) points out, "Vietnamese gangs are certainly street gangs but their street is often an interstate highway."

GANG SET SPACE

The importance of space for social groups, including gangs, has been routinely observed throughout the anthropological, sociological, and criminological literatures, indicating that multiple group members "hang out" together at particular public locations (Blasko et al. 2015; Cartwright & Howard 1966; Fraser 2013; Jansyn 1966; Kinnes 2012; Klein 1971, 1995; Ley & Cybriwsky 1974; Liebow 1967; Miller 1966; Monod 1967; Moore 1978; Moravcová 2012; Pickering et al. 2012; Sullivan 1989; Suttles 1968, 1972; Taniguchi et al. 2011; Thrasher 1927; Tita, Cohen & Engberg 2005; Ward 2013; Whyte 1955). Investigating the spatial dynamics of street gangs in the city of Pittsburgh, Tita and colleagues (2005) introduced the concept of gang *set space*, defined generally as a localized, geographically distinct area where gang members congregate within their territory. It is in these set spaces where members loiter in their gang's turf, with these hangouts being the "group's life space" (Klein 1995: 79). Just like any other social group, these hubs provide a sanctuary for the group and allow members to feel protected. Members routinely "hang around, brag a lot, eat again, drink, hang around some more" and spend the majority of their daily activities in their gang's set space (Klein 1995: 11). A gang member thus is "fairly attached to a definite locality and wanders only occasionally beyond its frontiers" (Thrasher 1927: 166). A gang's set space becomes so established within a neighborhood that local inhabitants, particularly youth, quickly figure out how to navigate in order to avoid confrontations with the local gang or neighboring rivals (Garot 2010; Tita et al. 2005).

A consistent and compelling characteristic about the location of a street gang's set space is the lack of social control, either formal or informal, within this locale. For example, a powerful indicator of the presence of a gang set space in an area is the percent of vacant housing present (Sullivan 1989; Tita 1999). Vacant and blighted properties are often indicative of local residents' physical and psychological abandonment of a neighborhood, serving as a visible signal of the community's limited ability to supervise, surveil, and sanction antisocial behavior, including violence, within an area (see Valasik, Brault & Martinez 2018). It is not surprising that unsupervised groups of youth spend the majority of their days hanging out in these forgotten areas that disregard official supervision and laws. Studies have also suggested that law enforcement is not as attentive to areas within a neighborhood where vacant and blighted properties are prevalent (Branas et al. 2018; Mills 1990).

Social control is lacking not only in places where abandoned and blighted buildings are concentrated, but also in locations with greater levels of population density. Tita (1999) discovered that densely populated areas are actually more likely to have gang set spaces. Such a finding may seem contradictory. How is it possible for areas that are densely populated to have a concentration of abandoned or blighted properties and be attractive spaces for conventional street gangs? Just because an area has greater numbers of abandoned or blighted properties does not mean that place is a "ghost town." Often the housing units that remain occupied in a deteriorating area, such as a public housing high-rise, hold a large number of residents but are surrounded by a lot of derelict buildings (see Popkin et al. 2000; Sullivan 1989; Urbanik, Thompson & Bucerius 2017). Furthermore, places with high population densities may actually be more appealing, as people milling around may better camouflage the activities of loitering gang members from law enforcement. Besides being able to conceal antisocial behavior, areas that have lots of pedestrian traffic may also facilitate the economic livelihood of street gang members (e.g., drug-dealing). Regardless of a location's level of commotion, areas with a low level of social control are advantageous to develop into the set space of a street gang.

Valasik and Tita (2018) highlight that the physical environment plays an important role in how gang members use space, directly impacting not only where members are likely to hang out but also where gang-related violence is likely to transpire. For example, Papachristos (2009) articulates that gang-related homicides have an inherent structure to them, in which gang members base "missions" around retaliatory attacks, traveling to locales that are well known to be where rivals live or spend a good portion of their day (see Fremon 2008; Papachristos et al. 2013; Vigil 2007). As such, it is not surprising that areas most vulnerable to experiencing a gang-related homicide have greater concentrations of gang set spaces and gang member residences (Valasik 2018).

Given conventional street gangs' relationship to space, many control strategies used by law enforcement are based upon the assumption that the majority of gang member activities transpire within a specific geographic space, usually a gang's turf (Grogger 2005; Muñiz 2014, 2015; O'Deane 2012; Ridgeway, Grogger, Moyer

& MacDonald 2018). One such anti-gang strategy that has become prevalent over the last 25 years throughout the United States, United Kingdom, and Australia has been the civil gang injunction (CGI) or analogous dispersal orders (Ayling 2011; Bichler, Norris, Dmello & Randle 2019; Carr, Slothower & Parkinson 2017; Crofts 2011; Densley 2013; O'Deane 2012; Walsh 2003). Essentially, a CGI is a civil restraining order that restricts enjoined gang members from participating in a range of activities within a demarcated area, commonly referred to as a "safety zone." Typical CGI expectations include illegal activities, such as possession of drugs/firearms/graffiti paraphernalia, but also behaviors that would be considered legal, such as associating with fellow gang members. What makes CGIs such an innovative and popular anti-gang strategy is the hybridization of criminal, civil, and administrative law used to bring a lawsuit that sues the targeted gang as an unincorporated criminal organization (Maxson, Hennigan & Sloane 2005). While the lawsuit brought against a gang is a civil matter, the sanctions used to enforce a CGI violation are criminal. As prosecutors have a great deal of discretion in how they direct their cases, the legal hybridity of CGIs provides greater flexibility to prosecutors so they can pursue gang members in either civil or criminal court. Even though harsher penalties exist in criminal court, civil courts are expedient and lack the robust due-process protections of defendants in criminal cases (e.g., not requiring legal representation for a defendant, substantially lower burdens of proof, and lacking the constitutional rigor of a criminal trial) (Beckett & Herbert 2010; Muñiz 2014; 2015).

Given that CGIs are designed to influence the routine activities and behaviors of enjoined gang members, it would be expected that these enjoined gang members would refrain from hanging out in known set space locations that local residents, rival gang members, and law enforcement officers are familiar with (see Valasik, Reid & Phillips 2016; Valasik & Torres forthcoming). Investigating a CGI's influence on gang members' patterns of association, Valasik (2014) finds that enjoined gang members are less likely to be observed loitering in their gang's set space following CGI enjoinment. While a CGI is able to disrupt enjoined gang members' patterns of association, it does not actually displace gang activities into adjacent areas outside of the CGI's safety zone. In fact, CGIs actually decrease the likelihood that gang members will travel outside of their claimed turf (Valasik 2014) (see also Valasik et al. forthcoming). Enjoined gang members' lack of displacement into adjacent neighborhoods is consistent with Grogger's (2002) findings, further suggesting that CGIs do not move gang members or gang-related crime around the corner. Valasik (2014), however, did find that enjoined gang members reorient where they associate with each other, shifting from public to private spaces (e.g., private residences, driveways, backyards), a pattern also consistent with other studies (see Bichler et al. 2019; Hennigan & Sloane 2013). Enjoined gangs' movement toward spending increasing amounts of time in private spaces demonstrates that street gangs do not have to be solely street oriented and can remain a functional group in spite of a diminished physical presence in public.

TERRITORIALITY AND ALT-RIGHT GANGS

Just like defining characteristics and other issues in gang research, there has been a lack of consensus about the territoriality of alt-right gangs. As pointed out in earlier chapters, much of the early research investigating racist skinhead gangs, relied on anecdotal evidence to portray these groups as being less territorially constrained than conventional street gangs (see Curry et al. 2014; Hamm 1993; Klein 1995). Guided by the stances of these academic bigwigs, the development of, and advocacy for, research to better develop our knowledge base on the relationship between alt-right gangs and space/territoriality have been greatly hindered. As such, only a handful of studies have explicitly examined this relationship (see Futrell & Simi 2004; Simi 2006, 2009; Simi & Futrell 2015; Simi et al. 2008). In fact, the very nature of alt-right gangs would lead people to believe that they have an interesting relationship with space. Alt-right gangs generally believe that members have a "natural dominion" over any space they are occupying (Simi & Futrell 2015: 55). This very sentiment was reiterated during conversations with the Southern Poverty Law Center (SPLC) who asserted that the need for physical space is less necessary when one can take their whiteness with them (personal communication, 2017). That being said, this does not mean alt-right gangs do not maintain a claimed turf or try to control space. Research has highlighted that conventional street gangs exist on a spectrum of mobility and territoriality patterns (see Gatz & Klein 1993; Klein 1995; Moore et al. 1983; Valasik et al. forthcoming; Valasik & Tita 2018). Alt-right gangs are no different. Simi and colleagues (2008: 766) highlight how Public Enemy Number One (PEN1), an alt-right gang, is street-oriented, focusing its antisocial behaviors in particular neighborhoods, keeping their racism "territorial and localized." Through the creation and maintenance of this territory, the gang is able to send a message to others, particularly rivals, that outsiders are denied access to this area. Simi's (2006: 155) interviews with racist skinheads in Southern California highlight that alt-right gangs define "their violence as a means of protecting themselves from aggressive non-skinhead groups" and that these violent altercations, which could be between rival street gangs composed of white and nonwhite members, regularly result from interpersonal disputes and are retaliatory in nature. This is a pattern routinely observed among conventional street gangs (see Brantingham et al. 2012, 2019; Lewis & Papachristos 2019; Papachristos et al. 2013; Tita & Radil 2011; Valasik & Tita 2018). Simi (2006: 155) also stresses that even though alt-right gangs would attack nonwhites and their groups if they "transgressed perceived boundaries," the racially motivated violence engaged in by alt-right gangs does not go "beyond the longstanding pattern of white gangs' defense of racial neighborhood boundaries" and oppositional use of violence is localized with "no clear political program for broad change" (see also Adamson 2000; Brown, Vigil & Taylor 2012; Cureton 2009; Howell 2015; Short & Strodtbeck 1965; Thrasher 1927). Prior studies further confirm that bias/hate crimes occur in which white offenders from predominantly white communities defend spaces they consider to be theirs from newly arrived nonwhite migrants (see Green, Glaser & Risch 1998; Green, Strolovitch & Wong 1998; Howell 2015; Howell & Griffiths 2018; McDevitt, Levin & Bennet 2002). Ironically, many alt-right gangs form to serve as a refuge from nonwhite groups migrating into a local community who are misperceived as being a threat to white inhabitants (Simi 2006, 2009). Howell and Griffiths (2018) point out that many conventional street gangs form for analogous reasons, except they serve as sanctuaries for youth of color being victimized by white youth (see also Howell 2015).

Creating and maintaining ownership over a claimed space, typically through graffiti tags, loitering, or assaulting transgressors, allows conventional street gangs to send a powerful message to other groups, particularly rivals, that access to the area is restricted. This attachment to space regularly translates into conventional street gangs naming themselves after the local streets, landmarks, and neighborhoods where they originate (Ley & Cybriwsky 1974; Monod 1967; Moore 1991; Philips 1999; Salagaev & Safin 2014; Thrasher 1927). For example, in Los Angeles, the Avenues gang exists in an area where all of the streets begin with the word "Avenue" followed by the street number (e.g., Avenue 43). They have appropriated these street names for their gang's name (Leap 2012; Rafael 2007). Similarly, the Rollin' 90s is just a specific clique of the Crips whose claimed territory occupies a series of streets between 90th Street and 100th Street in South Los Angeles (Alonso 2004; Brown et al. 2012). Alt-right gangs also name themselves after spaces that they have claimed (although more broadly, probably due to their perceived "natural dominion" over larger municipal areas), such as LaMirada Punk (LMP), Huntington Beach Skins, Chino Hills Skins, South Bay Skins, and Norwalk Skins (see Simi 2006, 2009). Overall, it is clear that space plays just as important a role in alt-right gangs' maintenance of collective identity and group solidarity as it does for conventional street gangs (Futrell & Simi 2004; Moore 1994; Simi 2006, 2009; Simi et al. 2008), despite the reservations of other researchers (e.g., Curry et al. 2014; Hamm 1993; Klein 1995; Moore 1993).

ARYAN FREE SPACES

Alt-right gang members regularly gather in what Simi and Futrell (2015: 4) term Aryan free spaces "where white power members meet with one another, openly express their extremist beliefs, and coordinate their activities" (see also Futrell & Simi 2004). It is within these environments where alt-right gang members' oppositional identity to prevailing cultural codes and social arrangements are nurtured (Futrell & Simi 2004). Aryan free spaces that exist in real-world locations are likely to exist in benign settings that fail to draw the attention of outsiders, including residences, local hangouts, bars, or crash-pads (Futrell & Simi 2004; Simi & Futrell 2015). For instance, Proud Boys groups regularly meet and loiter at local bars where they are well-known patrons and feel safe and insulated from outsiders (see Antoine 2018; Disser 2016; Hall 2018; McInnes 2017; Proud Boys 2019; Rogan 2017; Wicentowski 2018). These Aryan free spaces are analogous to conventional street gangs' set spaces, being localized, geographically distinct areas where members routinely gather. Just as the set space of a conventional street gang becomes the "group's life space" within their turf (Klein 1995: 79), Aryan free spaces provide members with an indisputable space with a distinct zone of influence. It is within these refuges that alt-right gang members hang around and feel protected (Klein 1995; Futrell & Simi 2004; Simi & Futrell 2015). For both conventional and alt-right gang members, the establishment of a "home territory," turning a space into a place provides members a sanctuary where their actions can be unrestrained and they feel safe from outsiders (Lyman & Scott 1967: 240). Furthermore, a conventional street gang "becomes fairly attached to a definite locality and wanders only occasionally beyond its frontiers" (Thrasher 1927: 166). Simi and Futrell (2015) observe analogous patterns by alt-right gang members regularly frequenting known white power bars, semi-permanent crash-pads, and recurrent house parties. As with the turf of conventional street gangs (see Garot 2010; Tita et al. 2005), the Aryan free spaces used by boisterous alt-right gangs eventually become recognized by local residents in the community and are either avoided or picketed (Simi & Futrell 2015). Regardless of where conventional street gang members establish their set space or alt-right gang members their free space, the consistent feature among both is the overall lack of social control by either informal or formal agents, which allows members to engage in inappropriate or predatory behaviors that can be detrimental to local residents. Such behaviors have been well documented by members of alt-right gangs, such as Proud Boys and racist skinhead cliques throughout the United States (Cosgrove 2018; Disser 2016; Hall 2018; Hobbs 2017; Randle 2018; Steward 2018; Wohlfeil 2018).

One type of Aryan free space that is unique to alt-right gangs, and more so to the broader WPM, are large gatherings of members at music festivals, concerts, and conventions (see ADL 2017; Aho 1990; Balch 2006; Dobratz & Shanks-Meile 1995; Drabble 2007; Dyck 2017; Futrell & Simi 2004; Futrell et al. 2006; Ridgeway 1995; Saslow 2018; Simi & Futrell 2006; Suall & Lowe 1988; Wright 2009). These unique Aryan free spaces allow for large numbers of the alt-right to attend such gatherings unencumbered by society's judgments. For instance, Wright (2009: 109) observed that attendees at an Aryan Nations World Congress held at Hayden Lake, Idaho, "appear giddy with the excitement of showing off once secret, forbidden Nazi attire for the first time in a public setting. Best of all, no one need feel shame for who they are." This expression of social identity is analogous to those made at other more mainstream conventions, such as comic-cons, filled with attendees that are far less maladjusted to society but just as passionate (Gunnels 2009). While planned Aryan communities remain atypical (e.g., Hayden Lake, Elohim City), white power music festivals (e.g., Hammerfest, Nordic Fest, Rocky Mountain Heritage Festival) have become much more of a prominent fixture and are able to bring together alt-right gang members from many different locations, facilitating communication and fostering social ties between these detached groups (Aho 1990; Dobratz & Shanks-Meile 1995; Dyck 2017; Futrell & Simi 2004; Hamm 2001; Simi & Futrell 2015; Tenold 2018; Windisch & Simi 2017; Wright 2009). As the notoriety of planned Aryan communities and prodigious white power concerts, conferences, and festivals develop over time, they become susceptible to law enforcement interventions, eventually limiting the public accessibility of these events, thereby tapering the net to enmesh potential skinhead recruits, eventually concluding their operations (Aho 1990; Dyck 2017; Freilich, Chermak & Caspi 2009; Futrell & Simi 2004; Lough 2018; Saslow 2018; Simi & Futrell 2015; Tenold 2018; VICE 2018).

What remains unknown is how these large gatherings actually influence the day-to-day activities or identities of alt-right gang members. For instance, if studies show that alt-right gang members' criminal activity is localized in nature, or that members are from impoverished communities, then what is the motivation pulling them to travel potentially large distances to attend white power conferences or festivals? While large conferences, rallies, and gatherings provide an interesting glimpse into the WPM, it remains unclear, in a vein similar to cosplayers attending a comic convention, just how many attendees shed these displayed identities after leaving these venues and reenter society. For alt-right gangs, members' identities are not situational, as these individuals "possess a white supremacist orientation and are also simultaneously organized around profit-oriented criminal activity" (Simi et al. 2008: 756). That being said, in the last few years alt-right gang members have been observed attending multiple "free speech" rallies (e.g., Berkeley, Portland) and/or public demonstrations in response to the removal of Civil War statues (e.g., Charlottesville, New Orleans) across the United States (see Atkinson 2018; Bacon & Warren 2017; Bamiro 2018; Crothers 2019; Hawley 2017, 2019; McAuliffe 2019; Nagle 2017; Philips 2015; PBS 2018a; Wendling 2018). At these public exhibitions, alt-right gangs are routinely observed maintaining their cafeteria-style offending patterns, which include harassment, theft, assault, hate-related crimes, weapon possession, and even murder (Duggan 2018; First Vigil 2019; Heim 2018; Martinez 2018; Shallwani & Weill 2018; Thompson et al. 2018). The overt nature of alt-right gangs' anti-social behavior, along with the frequency and seriousness of their criminal actions showcases just how unconcerned alt-right gangs are about violating society's norms or even its laws. In the United States, the incendiary rhetoric of President Trump at rallies and on Twitter, with his coded language and dog whistles has facilitated an atmosphere that is accepting of the increased boldness of alt-right gangs in their use of street violence (Strickland 2018; Burke 2018; Lopez 2017; Reid & Valasik 2018; Roose & Winston 2018; Valasik & Reid 2019).

VIRTUAL ARYAN FREE SPACES

Given the online origins of the alt-right, it is not surprising that some alt-right gang members' access to, and use of, virtual Aryan free spaces on the internet is more salient than the physical Aryan free spaces. As noted in chapter 2, despite alt-right gangs emerging from online collectives, members of alt-right gangs still engage in activities that can adversely impact local neighborhoods and their residents in the material world (see Castle & Parsons 2019). While chapter 6 will more thoroughly discuss the evolution of alt-right digital communications, including the internet, message/image boards, and social media, this section focuses on how virtual Aryan free spaces mirror physical Aryan free spaces to maintain and advance the alt-right gang subculture (Berger 2018; Bessant 2018; Blee & Creasap 2010; Daniels 2009a, 2009b, 2018; DeCook 2018; Dyck 2017; Futrell & Simi 2006; Hermansson et al. 2020; Perry & Scrivens 2019; Pollard 2018; Reid et al. 2020; Saslow 2018; Scrivens, Davies & Frank 2018; Simi & Futrell 2015; Valeri, Sweazy & Borgeson 2017; Zannettou et al. 2018a, 2018b). Today, there is a lot of variation in the types of virtual Aryan free spaces that exist across the globe. These digital spaces include online sites where members of alt-right gangs can plan activities and get-togethers, listen to music, play games, chat, post social media, and even educate children (Back 2002; Bogerts & Fielitz 2019; Burris, Smith & Strahm 2000; Castle & Parsons 2019; Chroust 2000; Corb 2011; Costello & Hawdon 2018; Daniels 2009a, 2009b; Futrell & Simi 2006; Hermansson et al. 2020; T. Morris 2017; Saslow 2018; Simi & Futrell 2015; Tynes, Rose & Markoe 2013).

Launched in 1995, the internet forum Stormfront provides a powerful example of the immense potential of alt-right gangs to extend themselves (Perry 2001; Saslow 2018; SPLC 2014, 2017). Stormfront has been considered the most popular forum for "white nationalists" in the Western world, with over 320,000 registered members as of February 2017, around 1,800 logins on a daily basis (SPLC 2017). Furthermore, members of Stormfront are disproportionately involved in hate-related crimes and mass killings, with almost 100 homicides between 2009 and 2014 (SPLC 2014). Also, after bias/hate-related events occur and are publicized, such as Anders Breivik's mass attack in Norway, online traffic to Stormfront surges, further illustrating the significance and scale of this online presence (SPLC 2014). It is not only in niche online communities like Stormfront, Gab, 4chan, Telegram, and The Daily Stormer that alt-right gang members are able to connect members with each other, but also through mainstream digital platforms and social media like Twitter, Snapchat, Discord, Facebook, Pinterest, Instagram, and Tumblr (Donovan et al. 2019; Fielitz & Thurston 2019; Finklestein, Zannettou, Bradlyn & Blackburn 2018; Hermansson et al. 2020; O'Brien 2017; Owen 2019; Perry & Scrivens 2019; Philips et al. 2018; Pollard 2018; Scrivens et al. 2018; Simi & Futrell 2015; Winter 2019; Zannettou et al. 2018a, 2018b).

While the alt-right originally manifested and evolved through the digital realm of social media and the internet more broadly, over the last few years a variety of alt-right gangs have emerged in the public sphere. As the frequency of public exhibitions, demonstrations, and "free speech" rallies have increased, so have incidents of crime and violence (see First Vigil 2019; KPIX 2017; Neiwert 2019; VICE 2017). The seriousness of these offenses (i.e., assault, harassment, larceny, hate-related crimes, and murder) illustrates that alt-right gangs are more than maladjusted online trolls. In fact, stepping out of the digital realm and into the real world has given alt-right gangs the ability to develop stronger connections with other far-right groups in the broader WPM (e.g., patriot movement, manosphere, white supremacists, etc.). Instead, of being relegated to online forums typing away their insecurities and misperceptions, alt-right gangs are tweeting on the streets and triggering violence in the wake of their digital footprint.

CONCLUSION

While Aryan free spaces can vary in size and location (digital versus physical), their overall function remains the same. These spaces provide a forum for alt-right gang members to participate in rituals, espouse group norms and values, cultivate social ties, and develop their social identities. In many regards, how alt-right gangs use space to provide a sanctuary for members to affirm their social identities and not feel judged by society is analogous to what has been observed in conventional street gangs (see Futrell & Simi 2004; Klein 1995; Simi & Futrell 2015; Tita et al. 2005). A notable disparity between Aryan free spaces and gang set spaces is that alt-right gangs are more likely to conceal their loitering in spaces that are more private and away from the public's gaze (i.e., house parties, crashpads, bars). These findings, however, have been potentially biased by focusing on the racist and hidden activities of alt-right gang members in the literature. Despite the focus on the hidden nature of the WPM, a number of researchers have highlighted the very public nature of alt-right gangs' activity (Atkinson 2018; DeCook 2018; Ezekiel 1996; Moore 1994; Perry, Hofman & Scrivens 2018; Reitman 2018). In fact, Baron (1997), Hamm (1993), and Ezekiel (1996) all recruited racist skinhead youth for their studies from public places, including street corners. In some ways the idea that alt-rights gangs adopt a particular style of dress that is aimed at providing clear identification of their identity but then hide it from the public sphere to avoid being scrutinized for being a group member seems counterintuitive. The use of space and presence of turf is a necessary area of inquiry for future research as policies are put into place for dealing with alt-right gangs. If police choose to intervene and inhibit alt-right gangs from congregating, certain place-based interventions may still be viable tactics (e.g., nuisance abatement); however, alt-right gangs use of private property for their gatherings requires approaches that are more flexible. Furthermore, alt-right gang members' online presence is much more substantial than that of conventional street gangs and should not be ignored by law enforcement.

Perry and Scrivens (2018: 172) declare that white power groups, including alt-right gangs, "are situationally located; they have a spatial element that is often overlooked, although just as often implied by the language of 'border,' 'boundaries,' 'transgressions,' or 'territory' RWE [Right Wing Extremist] groups are concerned with policing the appropriate 'spaces for races'"(see also Perry & Blazak 2010). Thus, even if alt-right gangs have an expansive online presence, they still engage in real-world activities that cause harm to individuals within their local communities (Castle & Parsons 2019). As Futrell and Simi (2018) warn, the alt-right is only the most recent iteration of white power gangs, with more traditional racist skinhead gangs being active in the United States for at least the last three decades and throughout the United Kingdom and Europe since the 1960s. Despite several lawsuits and criminal legal proceedings (e.g., *Berhanu v. Metzger*) facilitating the decline of planned Aryan communities and pushing racist skinhead gangs to find solace deeper and deeper in the bowels of the internet, these gangs never completely left the real world (Belew 2018; Berlet & Vysotsky 2006; Dobratz & Shanks-Meile 2007; Gerstenfeld & Grant 2004; Kaplan et al. 2003; Langer 2003; Lyons 2018; Tenold 2018). Instead, they have maintained their antisocial behavior and penchant for violence, as seen throughout rallies and demonstrations over the last few years (Atkinson 2018; Crothers, 2019; Hawley 2017, 2019; Nagle 2017; Philips 2015; Wendling 2018).

6

THE LEADERLESS RESISTANCE
OF ONLINE MEMES AND HATE

I believe that the internet will begin a chain reaction of racial enlightenment that will shake the world by the speed of its intellectual conquest.

DAVID DUKE, FORMER KU KLUX KLAN GRAND WIZARD
(1998, QUOTED IN DANIELS, 2018)

O.T.S. [Old Town Skins] members come together, often via cell-phone calls, to prey on their victims generally in the downtown area and subways. Dark-skinned victims are preferred, but the homeless, gays, and occasional Jews also are hassled or attacked.

MALCOLM W. KLEIN (2009: 142)

INTRODUCTION

White power groups' use of digital technologies, particularly the internet, is not a new or novel phenomenon (see Belew 2018; Berlet & Mason 2015; Daniels 2009a, 2009b, 2013, 2018; Donovan et al. 2019; Hawley 2019; Kimmel 2013, 2018; Michael 2012; T. Morris 2017; Schafer 2002; Simi & Futrell 2006, 2015; Simpson & Druxes 2015). Broadly, the WPM has been at the forefront of utilizing digital technologies to build up social connections among individuals and groups, maintain norms, and spread their racist rhetoric. In 1984, Louis Beam, a prominent neo-Nazi created Liberty.net, a clandestine Aryan Nations website (Amster 2009; Belew 2018; Berlet & Mason 2015; T. Morris 2017; Winter 2019). Liberty.net provided white power sympathizers access to message boards, recruitment materials, lists of potential targets, pen pals to write to, and personal ads accessible only via codeword (Belew 2018; T. Morris 2017). The creation of Liberty.net by Louis Beam made him one of the first to utilize computers and digital technology as tools to share ideas and organize individuals (Belew 2018; Berlet & Mason 2015; T. Morris 2017).

The adoption of the internet by members of white power groups to communicate with each other was in accord with Louis Beam's ([1983] 1992) strategy of "leaderless resistance" (see also Belew 2018; Berlet & Mason 2015; Berntzen & Sandberg 2014; Dobratz & Waldner 2012; Gardell 2018; Joosse 2017; Kaplan 1997; Levin 2002; Michael 2012; McCleery & Edwards 2019; T. Morris 2017; Winter 2019). In response to years of law enforcement infiltration (Cunningham, 2003; Dobratz & Waldner 2012; Jones 2015; Reitman 2018), Beam ([1983] 1992) argues that the large, centralized white power organizations (e.g., KKK, Aryan Nations) should be abandoned in favor of smaller groups or cells that are better at avoiding disruption and detection by law enforcement (see also Belew 2018; Michael 2012; T. Morris 2017). Through online message boards, like Liberty.net, white power groups and their membership could utilize the internet asymmetrically to maintain communication while not being spatially proximate to each other, spread their white power rhetoric with minimal resources, and recruit new members (Beam [1983]1992); Belew 2018; Berlet & Mason 2015; Michael 2012; T. Morris 2017; Simi & Futrell 2015). The adoption of "leaderless resistance" as a strategy has greatly contributed to the proliferation of white power websites internationally (Belew 2018; Burris et al. 2000; Daniels 2009a, 2009b, 2018; T. Morris 2017; Simi & Futrell 2015). In addition to providing communication between white power members/groups, these virtual spaces also are also a resource for members to post on social media, plan activities, educate children, listen to music or podcasts and play games (Amster 2009; Bogerts & Fielitz 2019; Burris et al. 2000; Daniels 2009a, 2009b, 2018; Futrell & Simi 2004; Hawley 2019; Hermansson et al. 2020; T. Morris 2017; Saslow 2018; Sela-Shayovitz 2012; Simi & Futrell 2015; Simi, Futrell & Bubolz 2016; Tynes et al. 2013).

A compelling example of just how large scale the adoption of the internet has been is the white power website Stormfront, launched in 1995 (Bowman-Grieve 2009; Koster & Houtman 2008; Perry 2001; Perry & Scrivens 2019; Saslow 2018). With over 300,000 registered users and approximately 1,800 daily logins, Stormfront is the most popular forum for white power members (SPLC 2014, 2017). Websites like Stormfront, The Daily Stormer, and The Right Stuff are representative of virtual Aryan free spaces where white power advocates are able to discuss their beliefs and share their points of view away from the prying eyes of outsiders (Futrell & Simi 2004; Hawley 2019; Hermansson et al. 2020; Hodge & Hallgrimsdottir 2019; O'Brien 2017; Perry 2001; Saslow 2018; Simi & Futrell 2006, 2015). These virtual Aryan free spaces allowed the alt-right to organize, albeit loosely, through a diverse array of online interactions between online trolls, misogynists, white power advocates, conspiracy theorists, militia members, and political dissenters (see introduction). Over time, however, the alt-right expanded into mainstream digital platforms such as Twitter, Snapchat, Periscope, Facebook, Pinterest, Instagram, Tumblr, and YouTube to increase the reach of their messages to populations outside the echo chambers of these virtual Aryan free spaces (see Berger 2018; Bessant 2018; Costello, Barrett-Fox, Bernatzky, Hawdon & Mendes 2018; Donovan et al. 2019; Ellinas 2018; Finklestein et al. 2018; Hawley

2019; Hermansson et al. 2020; Hodge & Hallgrimsdottir 2019; Klein 2019; Lewis 2018; Massanari 2018; Mattheis 2018; Nagle 2017; Phillips 2015; Pollard 2018; Simi & Futrell 2015; Yogeeswaran, Nash, Sahioun & Sainudiin 2018; Winter 2019). Yet many of these digital platforms require an individual to create an account to become a registered user, which could be traced back to that user or allow an account to be removed if the terms and conditions set forth by the content provider (e.g., Twitter, Facebook, YouTube) are violated. If an alt-right user or group is de-platformed, there are two potential alternatives to continue spreading white power rhetoric without reprisals. One is to use anonymous imageboard online forums, such as the /pol/ discussion boards on either 4chan or 8kun, or rely on social media platforms like Gab or Voat that are "free speech" advocates and have loose restrictions on what material is not permitted to be published (see Costello, Barrett-Fox, Bernatzky, Hawdon & Mendes 2018; Daniels 2018; DeCook 2018; Donovan et al. 2019; Finklestein et al. 2018; Hermansson et al. 2020; Kelly 2018; Lima et al. 2018; Lyons 2018; Nagle 2017; Phillips et al. 2018; Pollard 2018; Reid et al. 2020; Reitman 2018; Stern 2019; VICE 2019; Zannettou et al. 2018a, 2018b). Furthermore, after hate-related events involving white power protagonists (e.g., the Tree of Life Synagogue shooting in Pittsburgh, Pennsylvania, the Al Noor Mosque shootings in Christchurch, New Zealand, the Chabad Temple shooting in Poway, California, or Anders Breivik's mass murder in Norway), there is often a surge of online activity in these virtual Aryan free spaces, further highlighting the scale and significance of the alt-right online (see Barrouquere 2019; Bogost 2019; Hankes 2019; Hankes, Janik & Hayden 2019; SPLC 2014).

The remainder of this chapter focuses on the role that digital technology plays in shaping the manifestation and spread of the WPM broadly, and alt-right gangs specifically (Berger 2018; Bessant 2018; Blee & Creasap 2010; Bliuc, Faulkner, Jakubowicz & McGarty 2018; Burris et al. 2000; Daniels 2009a, 2009b, 2018; De-Cook 2018; Dyck 2017; Hawley 2017, 2019; Hermansson et al. 2020; Love 2017; Lyons 2017; Main 2018; McVeigh 2009; T. Morris 2017; Nagle 2017; Neiwert 2017; Perry & Scrivens 2019; Pollard 2018; Scrivens & Perry 2020; Scrivens et al. 2018; Simi & Futrell 2006, 2015; Valeri et al. 2017; Waring 2019; Wendling 2018; Yogeeswaran et al. 2018; Zannettou et al. 2018a, 2018b). This chapter traces the evolution and adaptation of alt-right gangs from solely being organized in either a physical space or digital space to wholeheartedly embracing an amalgamation of both realms (DeCook 2018; Fieltiz & Thurston 2019; Futrell & Simi 2017; Hawley 2019; Lyons 2018; Michael 2012; T. Morris 2017; Reid et al. 2020; Simi & Futrell 2015; Stern 2019; Waring 2019; Wendling 2018). The proliferation of virtual Aryan free spaces has allowed alt-right gang members to interact with the global WPM, allowing for the planning of activities (e.g., rallies, demonstrations, attacks), listening to and sharing white power music, playing racist video games (e.g., Ethnic Cleansing), chatting, indoctrinating youth, and distributing propaganda (ADL

2020; Coaston 2019; Daniels 2018; DeCook 2018; Druxes 2015; Froio & Ganesh 2019; Hermansson et al. 2020; Jackson & Gable 2011; Klein 2019; Simi & Futrell 2015). This chapter also discusses the progression from cloaked websites (see Daniels 2009a, 2009b, 2018) to the use of memes (Bogats & Fielitz 2019; DeCook 2018; Hawley 2019; Hodge & Hallgrimsdottir 2019; Nagle 2017; Phillips 2015) and today's emergence of "fake news" (Berger 2018; Crothers 2019; Daniels 2018; Darmstadt, Prinz & Saal 2019; Lima et al. 2018; Marantz 2019; Marcotte 2018; Pollard 2018; Samuels 2019; Wendling 2018). Next, the rise of "free speech" rallies, public demonstrations, and protests against the removal of confederate monuments from public lands by alt-right gangs is explored as facilitating the interdependence of using virtual spaces and manifesting in the physical world (see also Fielitz & Thurston 2019). This leads to a discussion of how alt-right gang members use digital technologies compared to members of conventional street gangs.

VIRTUAL ARYAN FREE SPACES REVISITED

Aryan Free Spaces

As discussed in chapter 5, virtual Aryan free spaces are places in the digital world where alt-right gang members are able to maintain and advance the general subculture of the broader WPM (Adams & Roscigno 2005; Back 2002; Blee & Creasap 2010; Bliuc et al. 2018; Caren, Jowers & Gaby 2012; Crothers 2019; Daniels 2009a, 2009b; Futrell & Simi 2004; Simi & Futrell 2006, 2015) and alt-right gangs specifically (Daniels 2018; DeCook 2018; Hawley 2019; Klein 2019; Lyons 2018; Nagle 2017; Pollard 2018; Reitman 2018; Simi & Futrell 2006, 2015; Scrivens et al. 2018; Stern 2019). The widespread adoption of digital technologies, particularly the internet, was based on the belief that the proliferation of a cyber-utopia would allow for a greater exchange of information between individuals; however, some unintended consequences have arisen (see Daniels 2009a, 2009b, 2018; Nagle 2017; Phillips 2015). The promise of the internet and the reality of today's internet do not often align with each other. One unanticipated ramification has been development of the internet's dark underbelly, including "The Dark Web," or content that mainstream search engines cannot easily access (Corb & Grozelle 2014; Donovan et al. 2019; Weimann 2015). It is in these hidden areas of the internet where virtual Aryan free spaces have provided a place for the WPM's "dark ideas" to prosper and metastasize over the last three decades (T. Morris 2017: vii). As Crothers (2019: 152) stresses, "These platforms, among others, have made it possible for people who would otherwise have had a difficult time finding like-minded allies to come together and promote their ideas." Map 6.1 highlights the widespread usage of two of these virtual Aryan free spaces across the United States, namely, The Daily Stormer and Iron March. While being only a subsample of core users on either of these "Alt-Tech" platforms, the spatial data reveals that nearly every state across the country is impacted by the WPM (see also Owen 2018; Owen & Hume 2019).

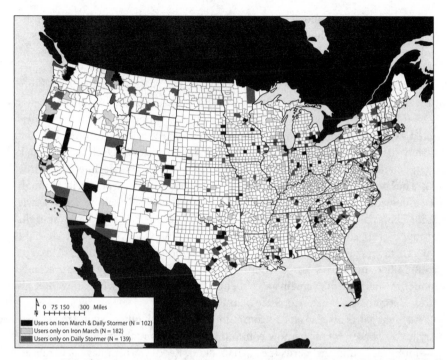

MAP 6.1. United States counties with members posting in message boards on *The Daily Stormer* and/or *Iron March* (data retrieved February 7, 2018, from Fashmaps.com and November 6, 2019, from https://archive.org/details/iron_march_201911_backup).

Additionally, about 25% of counties (*N* = 102) with users visiting these Aryan free spaces actually post on both The Daily Stormer and Iron March. This appears to support Donovan and colleagues' (2019: 53) parallel ports assertion that "the simultaneous use of multiple platform companies' products coupled with lesser-known communication tools as their movement's infrastructure ensured that if one line of communication were shut down, the event could still carry on." Therefore, it is important that the strategies used to combat alt-right gangs are both flexible and systematic to address both the localized actions of alt-right gangs, but also the WPM's more global point of view. It is important to keep in mind that even though Alt-Tech platforms, such as The Daily Stormer, Iron March, or Gab may be organized as parallel ports, functioning independently of each other, "they must be plugged into other internet services such as service providers, domain registrars, and cloud services." Thus, policy makers and consumers can target these businesses to regulate the content being distributed, impose sanctions, or even de-platform violators that spread hate/bias-content (Donovan et al. 2019: 62).

Just as digital technologies have developed and evolved over the course of the last three decades, so have virtual Aryan free spaces. While many of these technological adaptations have benefited the broader WPM (e.g., greater global influence, real-time communication, increased anonymity), some have had a more negative impact. For instance, the internet has increased the reach and ubiquity of white power music throughout the world, yet the downside of this has been a tremendous loss in revenue for white power record companies. These companies acted as financial conduits, where profits from record sales were funneled to a variety of white power groups (see Corte & Edwards 2008; Dyck 2017; Pieslak 2015; Schafer 2002; Windisch & Simi 2017). To counter this decline in revenue there has been a need to monetize websites. This has been done primarily through revenue-generating advertisements (ADL 2017; Daniels & Lalone 2012; Lewis 2018; Ellinas 2018; Hermansson et al. 2020) and commercialization of far-right products (e.g., clothing, books, digital music, online videos) aimed at alt-right gang members or individuals aligned with the WPM (ADL 2017; Cohen-Almagor 2018; Miller-Idriss 2018, 2019; Proud Boys 2019). Yet the inability to appreciably monetize social media remains a challenge for the alt-right (see Donovan et al. 2019; Hermansson et al. 2020; Saslow 2018).

Alt-right gangs are also able to communicate with each other beyond the virtual Aryan free spaces. Members now communicate through mainstream social media platforms and on imageboards (i.e., 4chan, 8kun, Reddit), which have generalized topical forums but also forums with more distinct content. For instance, 4chan or 8kun's /pol/ board features "politically incorrect" material, and is a haven for the alt-right (Finklestein et al., 2018; Hawley 2019; O'Brien, 2017; Philips et al., 2018; Pollard, 2018; Simi & Futrell, 2015; Tuters 2019; Wendling 2018; Zannettou et al., 2018a, 2018b).

ALT-RIGHT LULZ: FROM CLOAKED WEBSITES TO "FAKE NEWS"

A "'cloaked site,' is a sort of precursor to today's 'fake news'" and "is a form of propaganda, intentionally disguising authorship in order to conceal a political agenda" (Daniels 2018: 63). "Fake news" shares the same principal goal of propaganda, bending the truth for a political benefit, "but goes far beyond propaganda in its spread and potential effects" (Paxton 2018: 339). But what exactly is a cloaked website? Cloaked websites used by the WPM are designed not so much as a recruitment tool as to erode "the cultural value of racial equality," which includes denying the truths about the end of slavery and the Civil War, the Holocaust, and the civil rights era (Daniels 2009a: 119). With digital technologies, particularly the internet, the validity of sources and expertise becomes blurred, as the ability to create professional-looking web pages with minimal resources greatly limits an individual's ability to ascertain a site's legitimacy (Daniels 2009a, 2009b). As subsequent generations are further and further removed from people with experiential knowledge of past events, the risk that a white power cloaked website will be believed becomes greater, undermining racial and ethnic equality while "rearticulating an essentialist notion of white racial purity and along with it, a sense of entitled privilege based on that whiteness" (Daniels 2009a: 134). For instance, World War II ended nearly 75 years ago, and the lack of Americans' and Europeans' knowledge about the Holocaust makes the recent increases in anti-Semitic attitudes concerning and disheartening (Hermansson et al. 2020; Miller-Idriss 2019). Especially for youth, "who are often fluent in digital media, but not in critical-media literacy, or who do not have an understanding of racial inequality, the cloaked white supremacist sites do pose a serious threat to how they understand the history of civil rights in this country, how they view civil rights in the present, and how they value racial equality and human rights in a global society" (Daniels 2009a: 192).

Gamergate and the Origins of Alt-Right Trolling

Gamergate began as a contention about ethics in video game journalism. A text-based video game, developed by a woman, received positive reviews from a video game website/blog that many in the gaming community did not agree with (see Hawley 2019; Marcotte 2018; Nagle 2017; Salter 2017). What ensued was backlash from online gamers, who are predominantly male. A number of women working in the video game industry, or those critical of the existing sexism in the video game industry, were targeted in a large-scale harassment campaign under the Twitter hashtag #Gamergate (see Massanari 2018; Nagle 2017; Hawley 2017, 2019; Hermansson et al. 2020; Lyons 2018; Salter 2017; Wendling 2018). The repercussions of Gamergate for the alt-right were two-fold. First, alt-lite provocateurs like Milo Yiannopoulos and Mike Cernovich gained notoriety and a reputation in the manosphere and alt-right communities as voices that could begin to bridge the gap between the extreme and mainstream (Donovan et al. 2019; Hawley 2019; Marcotte 2018). Second, Gamergate "strongly influenced the alt-right's own online activism" with "significant overlap and interchange between the manosphere and the alt-right" (Lyons 2018: 68). Furthermore, "the mainstreaming of the ideology and tactics of the 'alt-right'" can be traced back to Gamergate for its genesis (Massanari 2018: 2). Learning from Gamergate and the manosphere trolls, "Alt-right harassment often emphasized sexual violence and the humiliation of women and girls, even when men were the supposed target," such as the attacks on *National Review* writer and critic of the alt-right and Donald Trump, David French, as well as his wife and their adopted daughter (Lyons 2018: 79). Given that "[t]rolling behaviors are gendered male, are raced as white, and are dependent upon a certain degree of economic privilege," it is no surprise that the members of the alt-right and manosphere shared common cause to protect white males from being disenfranchised by uppity women (Phillips 2015: 42) (see also Hermansson et al. 2020; Marcotte 2018).

The Lulz of Alt-Right Memes

Briefly, *lulz* can be defined as an online troll's "amusement at other people's distress." It basically celebrates "the anguish of the laughed-at victim" (Phillips 2015: 27). Online trolls get even more pleasure from their victim's rage than from tears (see May & Feldman 2018; Phillips 2015). Phillips (2015: 32) also reveals that lulz can be magnetic, lending "cohesion to an otherwise faceless collective" as "[t]rolls may not know who their comrades are in real life; in fact, they may never interact with the group of people again, but through lulz they are united." Additionally, as online trolls share their lulz content it becomes generative among the larger troll community and has the potential to transform into a meme as it "gestures toward and/or taps into a previously shared experience and is subsequently integrated into the collective subcultural fabric" (Phillips 2015: 31) (see Bogerts & Fielitz 2019; Hermansson et al. 2020; May & Feldman 2019). The original definition of a meme was described by Dawkins (1976: 249) as a "unit of cultural transmission" for the circulation of ideas (see also Jefferies 2018; Phillips 2015). In the online realm, memes are considered to be "(a) a group of digital items sharing a common characteristic of content, form and/or stance; (b) that are created with awareness of each other; and (c) were circulated, imitated, and transformed via the Internet by many users" (Shifman 2014: 41). As such, "memes only make sense in relation to other memes, and allow participants to speak clearly and coherently to other members of the collective while baffling those outside the affinity network" (Phillips 2015: 22) (see Hermansson et al. 2020; Tuters 2019).

Alt-right gangs utilize "memes as signifiers to strengthen their own sense of an 'in-group' and collective identity" but also to socialize new members (DeCook 2018: 489; Hodge & Hallgrimsdottir 2019). Strategically employing memes that are able to shift the Overton window (see chapter 2) for alt-right gangs, "the thinking goes: if today we can get 'normies' talking about Pepe the Frog, then tomorrow we can get them to ask the other questions on our agenda: 'Are Jews people?' or 'What about black on white crime?'" (Daniels 2018: 64). Thus, alt-right gangs use memes to "visually represent their ideas of the social world, or what they hope is to be, and imposes upon others who come across their content and accept their message" (DeCook 2018: 489). Recall the example in chapter 2 of the "Take Back Our Future" meme endorsed by Proud Boys members. Alt-right gangs employ memes to mask offensive, disturbing, and racist material in a joking or ironic manner in order to alter how people think about society or history. The goal is that whoever sees the meme will remember the "humor" that is associated with the image and not actually think about the horror of it (Bogerts & Fielitz 2019; Hawley

2019; Hermansson et al. 2020; Marcotte 2018; May & Feldman 2019; Tuters 2019). Probably the most successful alt-right meme to date was the "It's okay to be white" meme, which advanced the idea that white people "are a besieged group, and that they do not need to be ashamed of their race" (Hawley 2019: 112) (see also ADL 2017; Hayden 2017). The goal, like any meme, is to provoke a public reaction. The success of this alt-right meme was due to the distribution of flyers across college campuses with "It's okay to be white" written on them. Given that alt-righters created and disseminated the flyers, many felt that they should be denounced, feeding the false notion "that whites are an aggrieved minority, despised by the nation's elites" and in fact, it is not okay to be white (Hawley 2019: 13). The alt-right's use of Reddit, 4chan and 8kun as meme factories where they assemble, modify, and calibrate a meme to spread quickly from virtual Aryan free spaces into mainstream social media platforms to be endorsed by prominent conservatives, including President Donald Trump, is staggering and alarming (see Cohen 2019; Collins & Roose 2018; Hodge & Hallgrimsdottir 2019; Yogeeswarann et al. 2018).

Twitter

Alt-right gangs have come to rely upon mainstream social media platforms, like Twitter and YouTube, to reach the general public (see Bliuc et al. 2018). In fact, Twitter has "become a major avenue through which hate groups spread their ideologies with larger sections of the population" (Yogeeswaran et al. 2018: 2) (see also Forio & Ganesh 2019; Hale, 2012; Hermansson et al. 2020). Klein (2019: 301) contends that "Twitter has become a domain ideally suited for cultivating these fragmented and hyperpolarized communities and an unintended incubator for political extremism," a space ripe for "political factions to clash and for rivalries to amplify." Alt-right gangs' use of Twitter has allowed groups like Proud Boys "to circulate a call for battle, [and] other forms of rhetoric—such as mockery, nationalism, and appeals to defense—were equally as effective in priming the community for a state of combat while not crossing the line into fighting words or, worse, something that could get one's account removed from Twitter" (Klein 2019: 298).

Klein's (2019: 300) study highlights the importance of Twitter providing "a digital record that captures the day-to-day viewpoints of its users in their own words," which can be used as a litmus for alt-right gangs that claim they are not racist or support the broader white power narrative. For instance, Woods (2017: 1) was able to document that despite Proud Boys founder Gavin McInnes's attempts to disavow his racist beliefs, he has regularly pontificated his concerns about "white genocide"—a white power shtick that was originated by Derek Black on Stormfront message boards (see Saslow 2018)—and has tweeted in all caps "10 THINGS I HATE ABOUT THE GODDAMN MOTHERFUCKING JEWS!" with a video link attached. Yet, even if these racist tweets are meant to be ironic or provocative, the results are the same; recall Ken White's (2018) rule about goats pointed out in the introduction regarding the spreading of racist hate and white power propaganda.

From "Cloaked Sites" to "Fake News"

The origins of "fake news" can be traced back to the dismantling of the Fairness Doctrine in 1987. The Fairness Doctrine, created in 1949, required television and radio stations to cover multiple sides of an issue by providing countering viewpoints, thereby, having a reasonable degree of objectivity in covering the news (see Crothers 2019). Repealing the Fairness Doctrine removed the need to have credentialed journalists seriously analyze and assess the newsworthiness of events before reporting on them. This directly facilitated the launch of Fox News nearly a decade later as "a platform on which conservatives could present their programs" and "their critiques of liberal points of view" (Crothers 2019: 112). Partisan news programming took root on AM radio with talk shows by Rush Limbaugh and Glenn Beck. It shifted to the internet as digital technologies became user friendly and more ubiquitous, since a broadcast license was unneeded, eventually evolving into online programs (e.g., Alex Jones's *Infowars*) and podcasts (e.g., *The Daily Shoah* [*TDS*]) (see Crothers 2019; Hawley 2019; Hermansson et al. 2020; Marantz 2019; Marcotte 2018; Paxton 2018; Stern 2019).

The degradation of objective news media into partisan far-right fanboys, radical or extremist, means that waiting to spin facts is no longer necessary, since "alternative facts" can be concocted and disseminated online without any need for vetting. As Paxton (2018: 338) points out, "It is not just that facts have become less influential than appeals to emotion and belief; if there are facts and alternative facts, the very existence of truth [defined as agreement with reality] appears to be denied." Such extreme attitudes have even seeped into mainstream conservatism, with Newt Gingrich saying to Alisyn Camerota on CNN at the 2016 Republican National Convention that the FBI's violent crime statistics are incorrect since "the liberals have a whole set of statistics, which theoretically may be right but . . . as a political candidate I will go with how people feel" (CNN 2016). This behavior runs counter to Daniel Patrick Moynihan's famous adage that "everyone is entitled to his own opinion, but not his own facts." As we have seen today, any unpopular or damaging news can just be labeled "fake" if it "undermines or challenges one's political point of view . . . and thus should be ignored rather than respected" (Crothers 2019: 116; Marcotte 2018). Furthermore, alt-right gangs are fearful "that experts will be listened to and that alt-right ideological dogma and policy positions that do not accord with scientific or other expert-based facts will be rejected by the public" (Waring & Paxton 2018: 66). Thus, the shared meaning of social facts that define reality are no longer shared by all of society (Esposito 2019; Finn 2019; Marcotte 2019; Neiwert 2017). Instead, we have the creation of what Neiwert (2017: 33) calls "Alt-America, [which] is an alternative universe that has a powerful resemblance to our own, except that it's a completely different America, the nation its residents have concocted and reconfigured in their imaginations." While Alt-Americans live beside us, their perception of the United States places them in an entirely different universe (see Finn 2019; Neiwert 2017). For Alt-America's beating heart "is the ancient drum-beat of white identity politics, a fear of nonwhite people who speak foreign languages and follow alien creeds" (Neiwert 2017: 36). Within "Alt-America" the mainstream media is presented by alt-right gangs "not only as 'fake' but also 'brainwashed,' 'dangerous,' and 'aligned with the enemy.' And the deeper ideological menace behind it all, the American left, is characterized as a 'radical' and 'unpatriotic' insurgency and 'violent'" (Klein 2019: 306). It feels like two dichotomous Americas exist. Survival requires one to navigate between them, reminiscent of Anderson's (1999) code switching between "decent" and "street" behavior depending upon the context.

The Alt-Lite

The group that predominantly facilitates the existence of "the upside down" today is the alt-lite. Think of the alt-lite as a racist, libertarian uncle who uses a lot of inappropriate language and backs up all of his examples with anecdotes instead of empirical evidence. The alt-lite are considered the "acceptable faces" of the broader alt-right movement, remaining in a peripheral orbit around the extreme core, with fluidity existing between it and the hardcore racism of the alt-right (Marantz 2019; Hermansson et al. 2020; Wendling 2018). The alt-lite can be thought of as the intersection of online trolls and the WPM. Provocateurs of the alt-lite include Steve Bannon, Milo Yiannopoulos, Alex Jones (host of *Infowars*), Mike Cernovich (a primary promoter of the Pizzagate conspiracy), Lauren Southern, Tucker Carlson, and Ann Coulter (Hawley 2018, 2019; Hermansson et al. 2020; Laqueur & Wall 2018; Lyons 2018; Main 2018; Marantz 2019; Marcotte 2018; Stern 2019; Wendling, 2018). As it plays down the extreme rhetoric of the alt-right, the alt-lite is able to draw a large following from mainstream society into the movement by presenting racist ideas, such as anti-immigration and Islamophobia, in a more palatable and appealing form (DeCook 2018; Hawley 2019; Hermansson et al. 2020; Lyons 2018; Marantz 2019; Marcotte 2018; Stern 2019; Wendling 2018). That said, a tension exists between the alt-lite and alt-right, with each trying to use the other to increase their influence. The alt-right tolerates the "moderate" voices of the alt-lite with the hope that they will introduce more people to the identity politics of the alt-right (Hawley 2019; Hermansson et al. 2020; Stern 2019; Wendling 2018). For instance, Fox News commentator Tucker Carlson explicitly suggested that white supremacy in the United States "is a lie. . . . It is actually not a real problem in America. . . . The combined membership of every white supremacist organization in this country would fit into a college football stadium. . . . It is a hoax. . . . It is a conspiracy theory used to divide the country and keep a hold on power" (CNN 2019). Yet this notion pushed by Carlson is just one example of how the alt-lite provocateurs "portray the far right as victims of censorship and political correctness" and getting their audiences to view the alt-right "in a sympathetic light without having to defend the content of their ideas" (Marcotte 2018: 122–123). Conversely, the alt-lite uses a less blatant ethno-nationalism and anti-Semitism that they can transform into a more mainstream and influential political force (Hawley 2019; Marantz 2019; Stern 2019). While the alt-right "want to split off from the United States or destroy it altogether," the alt-lite "want white people and white culture to be openly dominant in the United States once again" (Lyons 2018: 220). Overall, if the alt-right wants to continue building upon the 6% (11 million) of Caucasian Americans (see Hawley 2018) that already support their rhetoric, then they need the more "moderate" alt-lite, with their "alternative facts," to grow their membership and influence.

Gab as an Echo Chamber of Hate

Following the violence at Charlottesville, many social media platforms began taking harsher approaches (i.e., de-platforming) to hate-filled content by the alt-right (Donovan et al. 2019). This resulted in many in the alt-right searching for new social media platforms to serve their needs (see Donovan et al. 2019; Hermansson et al. 2020; Marcotte 2018). The answer was Gab, which Andrew Torba established in August 2016, a social media platform akin to Twitter but heralded as an alternative that promises "free speech, individual liberty and the free flow of information online" (Gab 2019a). As such, Gab has an extremely lax moderation policy, allowing lots of obscene content to be posted and only prohibiting illegal pornography (e.g., underage, revenge, etc.), doxing of a fellow user's personal information, and the promotion of terrorist acts (Gab 2019b). Gab is constructed as a hybrid of both Twitter and Reddit (Donovan et al. 2019; Hermansson et al. 2020). As with Twitter, users can post 300-character messages, referred to as "gabs." Additionally, users have the ability to vote on posts, up or down, which determines the popularity of a post, similar to Reddit (see Zannettou et al 2018a, 2018b). In reality, "Gab resides on the border of mainstream social networks like Twitter and fringe Web communities like 4chan's Politically Incorrect (/pol/) board" (Zannettou et al. 2018a: 6). The word cloud depicted in figure 6.1, constructed by examining over 43 million gabs (including posts, replies, and reshares) by approximately 450,000 users between August 2016 and October 2018, shows the most common keywords (e.g., hashtags) found on Gab (see Phillips et al. 2018; Reid et al. 2020. This Gab word cloud looks eerily similar to Berger's (2018: 24) Twitter word cloud of the most commonly used words by alt-righters on this more mainstream platform. The biggest differences are the increased appearances of conspiratorial words like *QAnon, pizzagate,* and *fakenews.*

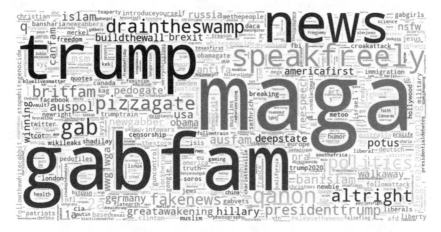

FIGURE 6.1. The most commonly used words on Gab (from Phillips et al. 2018).

Despite advertising themselves as a haven for free speech, most people that utilize mainstream social media platforms do not use Gab. Those attracted to Gab include a vast array of alt-righters, including gang members, traditional white power advocates, alt-lite purveyors, conspiracy theorists, and other fringe groups (e.g., militia/patriot members, trolls, incels) (Donovan et al. 2019; Marcotte 2019). Many of these alt-right users have been banned or removed from the more mainstream social media platforms (i.e., de-platformed, see section below) and have no other place to go. Alt-right gangs have also made themselves present on Gab, with Proud Boys members actively communicating with each other and the larger community. Comparing user content shared by Proud Boys members to the larger Gab community, there is substantial overlap between the two groups (see figure 6.2). Many of the same terms appear in both word clouds; there is really just a shift in the frequency of their use. For instance, Proud Boys consistently use terms like *Trump*, *MAGA*, and *white* (see Reid et al. 2020). This suggests that Proud Boys members' attitudes do not differ that much from the overall Gab community, or that Proud Boys members are self-moderating their public persona to downplay their white power motivations and racism.

Yet Gab also attracts individuals even more extreme than alt-right gangs. The content of these far-right extremists' posts is not self-moderated in any way. The Tree of Life Synagogue shooter in Pittsburgh, Pennsylvania, was a Gab user, and Phillips and colleagues (2018) examine posts the shooter contributed. They found that despite similarities between his posts and the larger Gab community, there was a distinct orientation. As figure 6.3 illustrates, the two most commonly used terms by the shooter were *kike* and *Jew*, and were often connected to words like *degenerate* and *vile*, along with a variety of other anti-Semitic references (Phillips

FIGURE 6.2. The words most commonly used by Proud Boys on Gab (from Reid et al. 2020).

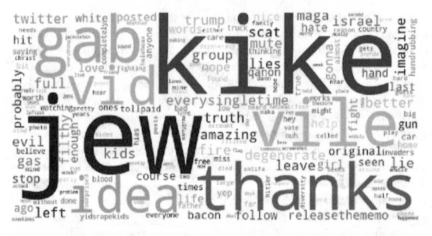

FIGURE 6.3. The words most often used by the Tree of Life Synagogue shooter on Gab (from Phillips et al. 2018).

et al. 2018). "For example, he frequently used the hashtag '#everysingletime,' referring to an alt-right Jewish conspiracy theory in which Jews are behind orchestrated efforts to attack white culture and values" (Phillips et al. 2018). Yet, even though the focus was on anti-Semitic ideations, the shooter did venture into other topics, generally focused on alt-right talking points such as "white genocide" and conspiracy theories.

It is important to note that activity on Gab is responsive to real-world events, particularly those involving the alt-right and President Donald Trump (see Phillips et al. 2018; Zannettou et al. 2018a). It is this feature about Gab that may be exploited by law enforcement or policy makers in dealing with alt-right gangs and the larger far-right threat (see Donovan et al. 2019; Hermansson et al. 2020).

OFFLINE PROGRESSION AND DE-PLATFORMING
"Free Speech" Rallies, Demonstrations, and Protests

In the lead-up to the 2016 U.S. presidential election, members of the alt-right began to become involved in the real world, with some alt-right gangs emerging and absorbing racist skinhead gang members. Alt-right gang members would routinely mobilize at public political demonstrations, protests (particularly for the removal of Confederate monuments), and "free speech" rallies, routinely held in liberal or progressive urban centers (e.g., Berkeley, Charlottesville, New York, Portland, etc.) (see KPIX 2017; McAuliffe 2019; Neiwert 2019; Stern 2019; VICE 2017). As the frequency of these public exhibitions continued to increase, prominent alt-right figureheads planned a rally to take place in Charlottesville, Virginia, to protest the removal of a statue of Robert E. Lee. Dubbed "Unite the Right," the rally "was meant to be a pivotal moment for the alt-right, signifying that it was moving off the internet and into public spaces in the real world" (Hawley 2019: 139). It turned out to be the largest gathering of individuals sympathetic to the WPM in over a decade, bringing together not only groups within the alt-right, but also a variety of groups in the larger WPM (e.g., neo-Nazis, neo-Confederates, the KKK) (Crothers 2019; Hawley 2019; McAuliffe 2019; Tenold 2018). However, the tragic death of counterprotester Heather Heyer, along with jarring images of white males brandishing burning tiki torches and clashing violently with counterprotesters and bystanders, as well as the level of vitriol by rally attendees, did not produce the response from mainstream America that the alt-right was hoping for (First Vigil 2019; PBS 2018a, 2018b; VICE 2017). Instead, Unite the Right became a hot potato that no one among the alt-right wanted to touch. Jason Kessler (former Proud Boys member) organized the event, but following Charlottesville he was chastised by alt-right figureheads, including Gavin McInnes (former Proud Boys patriarch), who banned him from Proud Boys (Barnes 2017; Lind 2017). While Charlottesville hampered the alt-right's manifestation in the public sphere, it did not end their progression from online to offline activities. Particularly in Portland, Oregon, but across the United States there have been a number of "free speech" rallies that have allowed many alt-right groups to develop stronger ties with other far-right groups but have also left local residents bloodied and battered, as these events tend to end in violence (Kavanaugh 2018; Marcotte 2018; Palmer 2019; Valasik & Reid 2018a). Alt-right gangs regularly converge around crises fabricated by other far-right groups to defend society from social justice warriors and governmental overreach (e.g., the removal of Confederate monuments).

De-Platforming

In the aftermath of the Unite the Right Rally in Charlottesville (August 11–12, 2017), there was a substantial increase in tech companies reassessing the services they were willing to provide to individuals and groups associated with the alt-right and the WPM more generally (Donovan et al. 2019; Hawley 2019; Klein 2019). This process of de-platforming denied the use of online venues to the alt-right to hamper the spread of their racist messages and to prevent their access to online services such as PayPal or the Amazon affiliate program, essential tools used to generate revenue (Donovan et al. 2019; Hawley 2019; Hermansson et al. 2020). One of the more substantial blows to the alt-right was GoDaddy's dropping of the domain for The Daily Stormer on August 13, 2017. The site was in limbo, jumping domain registrars over the next six months, resulting in a good portion of its membership being lost (Hawley 2019; O'Brien 2017). With alt-right gangs continuing to be a menace across the country, and as alt-right and alt-lite figureheads continue to espouse hateful rhetoric, much of the tech industry has continued to de-platform individuals of the far right that engage in or promote violence (Beauchamp 2019). For instance, before the second annual Unite the Right Rally in 2018, Twitter suspended the accounts of Proud Boy members from its platform for being a "violent extremist group" and violating its user agreement (Klein 2019). As such, the censoring by private tech companies is not the only anxiety for alt-right gang members. Being doxed, or making public an individual's private information or identity, has become a growing concern (Hawley 2019; Miller 2018; Tenold 2018; Wendling 2018). Ironically, the alt-right learned this tactic from online trolls and utilized it for their own purposes, such as doxing members of Antifa (Hawley 2019; Marcotte 2018; Phillips 2015; Wendling 2018). As Crothers (2019: 179) points out, in a post-Charlottesville world, "even online, then, it becomes increasingly difficult for alt-righters to protect their anonymity as they promote alt-right political activity" (see also Hermansson et al. 2020; Wilson 2018). Even alt-right mainstay Chris Cantwell (a.k.a. the "crying Nazi") is seriously concerned that the internet's anonymity no longer benefits the alt-right, which needs "secure communications and ability to do business." He further notes that "of course it doesn't matter how secure your protocols are if you don't know who you are talking to, and so we need to start meeting each other in person and developing networks of trust" (VICE 2018). Similar to Proud Boys ritual gatherings to hang out and drink (Cosgrove 2018; Feuer 2018; Hall 2018; Proud Boys 2019; Stern 2019), Cantwell's suggestion to engage in face-to-face communication, meeting in the real world instead of on an internet chat room, imageboard, or social media platform is just another example of how alt-right gangs are resembling conventional street gangs more.

CONCLUSION

The internet often serves as both a "mechanism of harassment" and as a "force multiplier" for far-right groups, including alt-right gangs (Daniels 2009: 80). Furthermore, alt-right gangs' ability to harness social media has the "particular potential to gain more recruits, to make acceptable the previously unacceptable, and therefore to allow the alt-right to develop and broadcast ideas that are further and further away from the democratic mainstream" (Paxton 2018: 358). "Such websites, persons, and social media have combined to create an alt-right subculture shared among many Americans" (Crothers 2019: 154). The politics of digital technology is of a cyberlibertarian bent; it "shields harassers under the guise of 'free speech' while offering little in the way of protection to those of us who are being targeted" (Massanari 2018: 2). Social media platforms and their algorithms do not have a neutral design; they benefit particular political and economic positions while being a detriment to others (Gillespie 2010; Massanari 2018). For instance, in reference to the 2016 presidential election, America saw a "whitelash," a white voting block backlash that was "algorithmically amplified, sped up, and circulated through networks to other White ethno-nationalist movements around the world, ignored all the while by a tech industry that 'doesn't see race' in the tools it creates" (Daniels 2018: 65). This amplification was fueled by "fake news" that alt-right gangs endorsed and pressed into the mainstream through digital technologies, particularly social media platforms. Alt-right gangs are "dependent on the sociotechnical affordances of social media platforms, both as a channel of coordination and as a tool of harassment," and this makes these digital technologies their Achilles heel, which could be exploited by law enforcement (see chapter 8) (Massanari, 2018: 6). Lastly, analogous to conventional street gang studies on the influence of social media, Bliuc and colleagues (2018: 86) point out that what happens online for white power sympathizers does have repercussions offline, with studies showing that "individuals use online channels to validate their beliefs and achieve a sense of belonging to (virtual) communities of like-minded supporters of racism." This is particularly concerning given that individuals have engaged in offline violence, as seen in Norway (Berntzen & Sandberg 2014; Enstad 2017; Hemmingby & Bjørgo 2018), Quebec (Perry & Scrivens 2019), Pittsburgh, Pennsylvania (Phillips et al. 2018), Christchurch, New Zealand (Coaston 2019), and San Diego, California (Beauchamp 2019).

7

CRIMINALITY AND VIOLENCE

Violence doesn't feel good, justified violence feels great, and fighting solves everything.

GAVIN MCINNESS (2017)

We were a street gang and that's how we viewed ourselves.... We banded together to protect each other and we did our fighting in the streets.

SIMI, SMITH & REESER (2008: 766)

INTRODUCTION

While it can be shocking and upsetting to see youth wearing white power symbols, screaming slurs, and marching through campus, the real concern around membership in alt-right gangs is the relationship between gang membership and crime, especially violence. This concern is the same as with members of conventional gangs. The reason law enforcement, policy makers, and local communities are concerned about street gangs is not because youth are hanging out in groups, but because crime and violence coexist with these groups. It is participation in a range of criminal activities that separates these groups from non-criminal social groups (e.g., Boy Scouts, sports teams, etc.) that some attempt to equate them with. The focus on ideology-motivated crimes perpetrated by alt-right gangs has constricted much of the research on the criminality of these youth to fit this particular narrow narrative. As researchers have noted, alt-right gang members engage in crime that is unassociated with any political ideology (Baron 1997; Berlet & Vysotsky 2006; Blee 2002; Borgeson & Valeri 2005, 2018; Pollard 2016; Sarabia & Shriver 2004; Simi & Futrell 2015; Simi et al. 2008; Teitelbaum 2017). When considering the criminality of juveniles and young adults, it is shortsighted to focus on only bias/hate crimes when prevention, intervention, and suppression efforts would be most effective as these youth begin to gain the attention of school officials or law enforcement for a range of delinquent activities.

In order to more fully examine the criminality and violence of alt-right gangs, this chapter will provide an overview of the relationship between alt-right gang members and their criminal activities. While there is often a desire to frame criminal activity as an instrumental act (e.g., stealing for money), for groups like gangs, crime can also serve a symbolic purpose. Like their street gang counterparts, alt-right gangs participate in both symbolic and instrumental violence and criminality (ADL 1995; Arnold 2010; Baron 1997; Caspi, Freilich & Chermak 2012; DeCook 2018; Massanari 2018; Moore 1994; Pilkington et al. 2010; Pollard 2018). Yet most prior research on the patterns of violence and criminality by alt-right gangs has been oriented around the group's ideology (see chapter 4), despite bias/hate crimes being relatively rare events compared to other crime types. While not wanting to minimize bias/hate-based crimes, which are discussed in this chapter, focusing solely on these types of crimes ignores the more routine participation in criminality, which likely has a greater impact on residents' daily lives and the overall safety of their community. Alt-right gangs have been shown to participate in a range of criminal activity in much of the same type of "cafeteria-style offending" that has been observed by street gangs (Klein 1995: 68), including drug selling (Simi 2006), identity theft (Freilich et al. 2009; Simi 2006; Simi et al. 2008) and property crime (ADL 1995; Baron 1997; Ezekiel 2002; Simi 2006). It is also important to note that scholars have found no evidence suggesting that profits from these crimes are used to fund larger far-right political endeavors (Simi 2006). This chapter closes by describing in detail how alt-right gangs use symbolic and instrumental violence to benefit their groups.

GANG-RELATED CRIME OR CRIME
BY A GANG MEMBER

Before delving too deeply into the discussion of the criminality associated with alt-right gang members, it is worth noting that quantifying gang-related crime is not always straightforward. Gang-related crimes can be defined differently depending on what definition a researcher or law enforcement agency is using. For example, if an alt-right gang member reports that they sell drugs to buy a new Fred Perry shirt, is that a gang-related crime? What if they spray-paint a swastika or their gang's name on a building? Is that a gang-related crime? How does one decide? Definitionally, gang-related crimes or acts of violence are described as being either a motive- or member-based criminal act. Acts directly relating to gang-related activities (e.g., recruitment, retaliation, territoriality) satisfy the motive-based definition (Klein & Maxson 1989; Maxson 1998; Maxson, Gordon & Klein 1985; Maxson & Klein 1990, 1996, 2002; Rosenfeld, Bray & Egley 1999). Conversely, in a crime where any participant, whether suspect or victim, is associated with a gang, the incident is considered to be a gang-related crime under an affiliated- or member-based definition (Klein & Maxson 1989; Maxson 1998; Maxson et al. 1985; Maxson & Klein 1990, 1996; Rosenfeld et al. 1999). Using a member-based definition errs on the side of including criminal incidents that could be driven completely by a motive (e.g., a domestic dispute) that is unrelated to an individual's status as a gang member: "After all, gang members can and do act of their own accord" (Papachristos 2009: 86). In contrast, utilizing a motive-based definition samples "too heavily on the dependent variable by capturing only those cases in which a group motive was determined" (Papachristos 2009: 86). When considering the criminality of alt-right gangs the focus on ideologically oriented crimes driven by a very particular motivation has restricted the number of gang-related crimes counted. As mentioned above, focusing on ideological crimes limits our understanding of the range of crimes alt-right gang members are involved in, both as part of their gang and as individuals. Moving forward, researchers and law enforcement need to consistently account for the range of crimes that alt-right gang members commit. Not doing so will continue to impede the nuanced understanding of gang-related crimes and hinder the development of more targeted prevention, intervention, and suppression strategies.

CRIMINAL ACTIVITY

As we consider alt-right gang members' participation in gang-related activity and violence, we need to keep in mind the definitional issues explicated in chapter 1. Our understanding of alt-right gang crime comes from targeted qualitative and/or quantitative studies that include school samples, law enforcement data, and correctional settings. Most prior research focuses on white power prison gangs, which is an older population (see Blazak 2009; Pelz, Marquart & Pelz 1991; Ross 2014). A comparable range of studies focusing on alt-right gang members does not exist. In some studies, alt-right youth are considered but cannot be separated from other gang youth in the sample. The focus on violence, especially bias/hate-based violence, has also impacted how drug market participation or nonviolent offending by these gang members is reported. In other words, while studies may discuss the criminality of alt-right gang members, there is a limited understanding of the full range of criminal activities these youth take part in. Only a few researchers have examined the criminality of these youth without overly focusing on ideologically driven crime (see Blazak 2001; Simi 2006, 2009; Simi et al. 2008; Valasik & Reid 2019). Being aware of these limitations, the range of crimes that alt-right gang members participate in is reviewed.

Using the description of "cafeteria-style offending," which refers to conventional street gang members' varied and often unplanned criminal activity, a similar pattern for alt-right gang members is observed. Alt-right gang youth have been shown to participate in a range of criminal activity. These crimes include drug selling (Simi 2006, 2009), identity theft (Freilich et al. 2009; Simi 2006; Simi et al. 2008), credit card fraud (Simi 2009), tax fraud (ADL 2006), and property-related offenses (ADL 1995; 2006; Baron 1997; Ezekiel 2002; Simi 2006, 2009). As a crime analyst assigned to racist skinheads in Portland, Oregon, Christensen (1994) discusses in his book the range of serious crimes these youth commit, including assault, arson, rape, and murder. More recently, members of Atomwaffen Division have also been arrested for child pornography, other sex offenses, and weapons offenses (First Vigil 2019; Weill 2019). We would expect the range and quantity of alt-right gangs' participation in nonviolent offending to be even higher than what is portrayed in the limited literature. During interviews with alt-right gang youth incarcerated with California's Division of Juvenile Justice (DJJ), when youth discussed the crimes they committed as part of the gang, none reported hate crimes or race-related violence, but rather participation in stealing, fighting, and drug use (Scott 2019; Valasik & Reid 2019). Furthermore, it is common for alt-right gangs to partake in an array of profit-oriented crimes (e.g., drug sales, identity theft, counterfeiting, burglary, armed robbery) that provide financial incentives for joining the group (Simi 2009; Simi et al. 2008). Recently, members of the New Aryan Empire (NAE) were charged in a RICO indictment with criminal activity ranging from drug trafficking, attempted murder, kidnapping, and gun violations in Arkansas (Department of Justice 2019). It is important to note that renowned researchers such as Simi (2006) have found no evidence to suggest that these gangs use criminal profits to fund larger political endeavors. Sarnecki's (2004: 188) research also supports this pattern in which alt-right gangs "seem to participate in all kinds of offenses of which a small proportion may be motivated by politics or perhaps rather by hate." Lastly, it should be noted that paying attention to violence, particularly bias/hate-motivated acts, has likely influenced how law enforcement reports alt-right gangs' nonviolent criminal offending and drug market participation. As such, the quantity and range of nonviolent offending is likely much greater than what is portrayed in the limited literature.

VIOLENT CRIME

The violence associated with alt-right gangs has been the focus of the majority of the studies on these groups. The late 1980s and the 1990s marked a peak in the first wave of racist skinhead violence before the current iteration of alt-right gangs. During this time period, racist skinheads murdered a black man and a police officer in Denver, in Texas a group of racist skinheads murdered a Vietnamese youth, two Aryan National Front skins murdered a black man, brothers who belonged to Aryan Nations Skinheads killed their parents, and a dozen skins stabbed a youth to death who ousted them from a party (Blazak 2001). As we consider this interracial violence, it is worth pausing to consider that interracial violence does not always equal a hate/bias crime. For alt-right gang members, the focus on ideology has led some to consider all interracial/ethnic violence as hate or bias based, but Christensen (1994) highlights that some of this interracial/interethnic violence is gang-related. For example, Christensen (1994) discusses violence between racist skinheads and Southeast Asian gang members, Bloods, Crips, and other black gang members and notes a police officer's comment that the skinhead's lifestyle had caught up with him when he was shot by a black gang member (see also Langer 2003; Simi 2006, 2009). Furthermore, hate/bias-related violence against people of color is not just an alt-right gang phenomenon, with black gangs attacking Latinx gangs and vice versa (see Kun & Pulido 2013). All of this is not to diminish the hate/bias crime that does occur, but rather to show that if we view all acts of violence from alt-right gang members solely through this ideological lens, then the larger, and possibly more remediable, picture is being lost (see Caspi et al. 2012). In Portland (and most likely other cities), whites are victimized by alt-right gang youth more often than out-group racial, ethnic, or religious groups are (Christensen 1994; see also Boggess 2012; Hipp, Tita & Boggess 2009; Martinez 2008, 2016, 2017).

One of the pivotal events that highlights the racist skinhead violence of this time period is the murder of Muguletta Seraw, an Ethiopian man in Portland. Three male and three female East Side White Pride members were involved in this murder after a violent brawl erupted on Geraldo Rivera's daytime talk show in 1988 (Carmody 1988). One of the racist skinhead men beat Seraw to death with a baseball bat before the others stomped upon the fallen man (Christensen 1994; Langer 2003). The fallout from this was huge, as lawyers from the Southern Poverty Law Center (SPLC) filed a civil lawsuit, *Berhanu* v. *Metzger*, asserting that both the Metzgers and White Aryan Resistance (WAR) were as responsible for the murder as the racist skinheads (SPLC 2019b). In October 1990, the victim's family was awarded $12.5 million in damages. This marked the beginning of the end for WAR, which resulted in moving their activities online (SPLC 2019b). For street-level violence, much of the focus shifted to traditional white power gangs that had become entangled in the correctional system. This includes, but is not limited to gangs like PEN1, Nazi Low Riders (NLR), Peckerwoods, and the Aryan Brotherhood of Texas who had a penchant for violence in the street and in correctional settings (see Blazak 2009; Pelz et al. 1991; Pyrooz & Decker 2019 Ross 2014; Simi et al. 2008).

The evolution and "reemergence" of white power youth gangs participating in street violence has begun to occur under the new umbrella of alt-right gangs. With them has come what we are considering the second wave of serious violence. More recently, free speech demonstrations by white supremacists in Charlottesville, Berkeley, and Portland have resulted in hate-related crimes, violence, and even murder (Atkinson 2018; Crothers 2019; Hawley 2019; Tenold 2018; VICE

2017; Wendling 2018). Groups like Rise Above Movement (R.A.M.) have openly discussed their participation in violence in California, and they were indicted for their participation in violence at Charlottesville (PBS 2018a; Reitman 2018). Members of Proud Boys, many of whom also have affiliations to local skinhead gangs, have been arrested for gang assault, weapons possession, and rioting (First Vigil 2019; Moynihan & Winston 2018). Proud Boys founder Gavin McInness has also stressed that violence is expected to rise in the ranks of the group (2017). Atomwaffen Division, a newer alt-right gang, has members participating in a range of violent crimes. Examples include a 17-year-old member murdering his parents, an 18-year-old member shooting his roommates, and a 20-year-old murdering an openly gay Jewish college student (Bromwich 2018; First Vigil 2019).

THE ROLE OF CONFLICT AND VIOLENCE

While it is easy to just say that alt-right gang members participate in violence as a way to demonstrate their adherence to white power ideology, that is only a portion of the how and why alt-right gang members engage in violence. As discussed in chapter 4, both alt-right gangs and conventional street gangs are focused on in- and out-group designations. For street gangs, these designations help identify rivals (although not always accurately) and potential enemies. For alt-right gangs, the out-group designation includes people that are not a part of "the life," such as immigrants, women, Jews, Muslims, or LGBTQ individuals (again not always identified properly). Conflict with out-group members plays a critical role in the formation and maintenance of group identity. In this way, conflict is the principal driver sustaining gang life. When considering violence and out-group designations, alt-right gang members have high levels of entitativity—perceiving rival group members as being unified and cohesive (Vasquez et al. 2015). "Entitativity makes all members of the offending group blameworthy," a perilous belief facilitating the spread of violence into the civilian population (Vasquez, Wenborne, Peers, Alleyne & Ellis 2015: 249). Much of bias/hate-based violence by alt-right gangs highlights the lack of discretion in participating in acts of violence against nonwhites (Mills et al. 2017). DeCook (2018: 12) observes this behavior with Proud Boys members' calls for violence against Antifa, viewing them "as the true enemy of the Christian, white ethnonationalist West because of their embrace of socialism and multiculturalism. By positioning them as the enemy, the solidification of an 'out-group' strengthens the 'in-group' identity" (see also Rogan 2017). Thus, any individual that is associated with or thought to be sympathetic to Antifa is treated as an enemy combatant by Proud Boys and attacked, regardless of provocation. Such behavior was observed in New York City with members of Proud Boys assaulting individuals protesting outside of the Metropolitan Republican Club following a speaking event by Proud Boys patriarch Gavin McInnes (Burley

2018; Dickson 2019; First Vigil 2019; Holt 2018). Among conventional street gangs this perspective of collective responsibility, that any group member can be held responsible for the actions of any other member, is pervasive and facilitates retaliatory violence (Densley 2013; Stephenson 2015). For instance, Leovy (2015: 206) relates a prime example of street gangs' high levels of entitativity in South Central Los Angeles: "A black assailant looking to kill a gang rival is looking, before anything else, for another black male . . . a presumed combatant, conscripted into a dismal existence 'outside the law' whether he wanted to be or not."

The extant research on conventional street gangs has shown a strong, positive relationship between gangs and violence, existing across places and over time (Howell & Griffiths 2018; Papachristos 2013; Pyrooz, Turanovic, Decker & Wu 2016; Valasik, Barton, Reid & Tita 2017). Starting with Thrasher's (1927) foundational work in Chicago, for nearly the last century research has revealed that conventional street gangs thrive in areas where social discord and disrespect, perceived or real, between groups is present (Howell 2015; Howell & Griffiths 2018; Papachristos 2009; Taniguchi, Ratcliffe & Taylor 2011). Two vital ingredients required for the establishment and preservation of a street gang are the threat of violence and actual conflict. Being a victim of violence or the perception/fear of becoming a victim facilitates the emergence of group bonds, promotes solidarity, and increases cohesion, reifying ties among members (Decker, Pyrooz, Sweeten & Moule 2014; Hagan 1993; Hennigan & Spanovic 2012; Pyrooz, Sweeten & Piquero 2013; Wood 2014). For example, the threat of being attacked by members of a rival group encourages at-risk youth to join a gang, either conventional or alt-right, for protection, while providing an outlet for violence that might not transpire if these youth were to remain unaffiliated (Hughes & Short 2014; Klein & Crawford 1967; Melde & Esbensen 2011; Papachristos 2009; Short & Strodtbeck 1965). Researchers have highlighted the presence of fear and violence in the lives of many of these alt-right gang youth and their hope that membership might offer them safety (Baron 1997; Ezekiel 2002). Simi and colleagues (2008: 759) also find support for the idea that youth are joining for purposes of protection, with racist skinhead gangs providing "white kids with defense from other gangs" in Southern California (see also Simi 2006, 2009).

Gang-related violence also has a myth-making quality. Incidents and tales are told, retold, and embellished, increasing a gang's street reputation/status and strengthening the group's identity while also spreading exaggerated accounts of the group's activities through social media or news outlets (Patton, Frey & Gaskell 2019; Esbensen et al. 2001; Felson 2006; Gravel, Allison, et al. 2018; Howell & Griffiths 2018). The process of socializing new members into a gang is also facilitated by experiences with violence, allowing for the gang's mythology to be shared and integrated into individuals' identities (Decker 1996; Hennigan & Spanovic 2012). As additional experiences are shared among gang members, they increasingly embrace and adhere to their group's norms and behaviors, which encourage violence as a means of resolving conflict (Anderson 1999; Decker 1996; Klein 1995; Short & Strodtbeck 1965). Studies routinely find that when compared to non-gang members, including associates of other delinquent groups, gang members have a greater likelihood of participating in criminal acts, engaging in inter-group violence, and carrying/possessing a firearm/weapon. They are also at an increased risk of being violently victimized (Battin, Hill, Abbott, Catalano & Hawkins 1998; Decker 1996; Melde & Esbensen 2013; Taylor et al. 2008; Wu & Pyrooz 2016).

Focusing on bias/hate-based violence has overshadowed findings by Baron (1997), Simi (2006, 2009), and Simi and colleagues (2008, 2015) that expound on alt-right gang youths' participation in localized violence and criminality. Emphasizing hate crimes ignores the more routinized participation in violence and criminality that impacts these youths' daily lives and the safety of local communities. Studies that focus specifically on racist skinhead youth, rather than the larger white power movement, discuss the cultural values that encourage violence (Baron 1997; Borgeson & Valeri 2005, 2018; Gil & Lopez 2017; Moore 1994; Picciolini 2018; Pilkington et al. 2010; Sarabia & Shriver 2004; Simi 2006, 2009; Simi & Futrell 2015; Simi et al. 2008; Valasik & Reid 2018a). Violence is used by racist skinheads as a public statement to bolster their group's status and reputation, reify boundaries, intimidate local residents, and assert their dominance over rivals, just like conventional street gangs (Brantingham et al. 2012, 2019; Nakamura, Tita & Krackhardt 2019; Papachristos et al. 2013). Retributive violence, for real or perceived slights, is supported by both the alt-right gang members' peers as well as other alt-right gangs (Baron 1997; DeCook 2018; Hawley 2018; Klein 2018; Lyons 2018). For example, violence is regularly called for by Proud Boys against perceived rivals, most notably Antifa (DeCook 2018). The concern about Antifa counterprotesting at alt-right events is so great that Proud Boys developed a paramilitary division, the FOAK (Fraternal Order of Alt-Knights), to provide extra "muscle" at "free speech" demonstrations and President Trump's political rallies to protect far-right activists (DeCook 2018; Finn 2019; Hawley 2019; SPLC 2019b). Unsurprisingly, many events alt-right gangs attend also end in violence (e.g., Berkeley, Charlottesville, New York City, Portland) (Atkinson 2018; DeCook 2018; Hawley, 2019; Klein 2018; Marcotte 2018; Wendling 2018). Map 7.1 illustrates just how widespread Proud Boys' public acts of violence, intimidation, harassment, and/or threats of violence are throughout the United States (Kutner 2019). Of the 64 incidents documented by either news or social media, about half (48%) culminated in violence. The vast majority of violent incidents (71%) transpired at "free speech" rallies or counterprotests, where Proud Boys members and opposition group members were not properly separated and corralled by law enforcement (figure 7.1). The remaining acts of violence include

FIGURE 7.1. Members of Proud Boys and other alt-right supporters reeling from a violent confrontation with counterprotesters (photo by David Neiwert).

confrontations between Proud Boys members and patrons or employees at pubs that escalated from targeted attacks (e.g., stabbing, hate/bias crime, vehicular assault, and murder) on particular individuals or groups (i.e., counterprotesters, Antifa). Lastly, there are a host of "liberal" cities that have experienced the majority (69%) of incidents involving Proud Boys, with Portland (15), Seattle (5), Washington, D.C. (4), and New York City (4) enduring the greatest amount (see map 7.1).

Similarly, chronic feuding between street gangs to redress prior grievances has been well documented in the street gang literature (Brantingham et al. 2012, 2019; Lewis & Papachristos 2019; Nakamura et al. 2019; Papachristos et al. 2013; Tita & Radil 2011; Vigil 1996). Disputes involving alt-right gangs are usually interpersonal in nature (Baron 1997; Simi 2006; Simi et al. 2008), often white-on-white or focused on other street youth (ADL 1995; Baron 1997; Hamm 1993; Simi et al. 2008). In fact, such confrontations have been observed between Proud Boys and Patriot

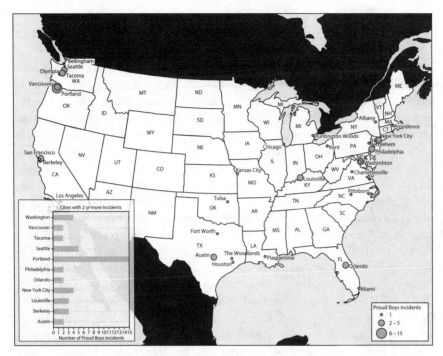

MAP 7.1. Documented incidents involving Proud Boys members in the United States from October 2016 to October 2019 (N = 64) (data retrieved November 1, 2019, from arcg.is/4OGLb; (see Kutner 2019).

Prayer, as the ties between both groups have unraveled and tempers have flared between the two alt-right gangs (see Humphrey 2019; Neiwert 2019). Scholars also discuss how racist skinhead violence mirrors conventional gang rivalries on the street (see Bjørgo 2016; Fangen 1998; Klein 2009; Shaskin 2008; Travis & Hardy 2012). Both Baron (1997) and Simi et al. (2008) discuss the group dynamics present when youth talk about their reasons for participating in violence and the need for retaliation against those who slight other members or the group. Participation in violence is believed to help affirm racist skinhead group identity and strengthen the group's symbolic solidarity (ADL 1995; Baron 1997; Moore 1994; Simi 2006, 2009). Wooden and Blazak (2001) found that racist skinhead gangs utilize the ritual act of "jumping in" new members. The street gang literature has repeatedly discussed how the use of violence during initiation helps normalize its use and solidifies group identity (Moore 1978, 1991; Vigil 1996). As observed with street gangs (Densley 2013; Levitt & Venkatesh 2000; Stephenson 2015), alt-right gangs also use instrumental violence in their other criminal undertakings, such as burglary, drug dealing, robbery, or territorial control (Simi 2006, 2009; Simi et al. 2008).

CONCLUSION

Alt-right gang members are involved in a range of criminal activities, from the most serious violence to more traditional delinquency often associated with youthful offenders. Alt-right gang members do not limit themselves to only ideology-based crimes, and the research examining these groups and their members must reflect this reality. These youth, like their street gang counterparts, participate in both symbolic and instrumental acts of violence and criminality (Densley 2013; Levitt & Venkatesh 2000; Moore 1994; Simi 2006, 2009; Simi et al. 2008; Stephenson 2015; Valasik & Reid 2019). The reasons motivating alt-right gang members to commit crimes varies. As such, developing programs and policies targeting only a particular subset of offenses such as bias/hate-crimes will not effectively reduce alt-right criminality. As with most youth in conventional street gangs, many members of alt-right gangs will age out as they become disillusioned about continuing to participate in gang life. Some, however, will continue on to more serious groups. The more effectively we can intervene while these youth are younger, the better the long-term outcomes for all (see Bjørgo 2002; Bubolz & Simi 2015; Horgan, Altier, Shortland & Taylor 2016; Picciolini 2018; Simi, Blee, DeMichele & Windisch 2017; Windisch, Simi, Ligon & McNeel 2016). As observed in the literature, gangs fill multiple voids in a youth's life, including protection (Short & Strodtbeck 1965), social identity (Hennigan & Spanovic 2012), and economic opportunities (Densley 2013; Levitt & Venkatesh 2000; Stephenson 2015). Crime and violence may seem irrational, but for youth involved in alt-right or conventional street gangs, these antisocial acts play important roles in what it means to be part of the group.

8

THE ALT-REICH IN THE TWENTY-FIRST CENTURY

Dealing with "The Upside Down"

Just remember, what you're seeing and what you're reading is not what's happening.

PRESIDENT DONALD TRUMP (JUNE 24, 2018)

INTRODUCTION

This chapter's title references "The Upside Down" from the Netflix series *Stranger Things*. "The Upside Down" is a parallel dimension to our own world whose physical landscape is identical, containing the same places; however, the environment is dark, cold, and cloaked in an omnipresent fog (see also chapter 6). There is no human life present, and a toxic biological material is pouring out from "The Upside Down" threatening to transform our world into its replica. This analogous, yet perverted, reality exists in how some alt-right gang members are envisioning the world and the laws guiding it (see Finn 2019; Neiwert 2017; Stern 2019). As one considers all that this book discusses in relation to alt-right gangs, it is necessary to note that there are important areas where additional research is needed. This includes the role of the current political climate on the development of these far-right groups, since neither alt-right gangs nor conventional street gangs form in a vacuum. The role of women in alt-right gangs needs to be thoroughly researched and not dismissed as if women are peripheral in these gangs. Both alt-right gang researchers, and conventional gang scholars, need to better understand how online activity translates into real-world action. Not every online threat, call to arms, or crime has a real-world consequence, but some do, and researchers need to better understand how and why some actions move between these spaces (see Fielitz & Thurston 2019; Reid et al. 2020). We conclude by highlighting how decades of omitting white power groups from street gang research has left policy makers at a disadvantage in developing strategies to prevent or intervene in these groups. As nationalism and xenophobia become more and more mainstream throughout the United States and across Europe, it is imperative to understand the radicalization and public appearance of alt-right gangs (Ahmed 2020; VICE 2017; Waring 2019). This book provides some arguments demonstrating that alt-right gang members are no more "fringe" or exceptional than the average gang member, countering the continuing exclusion of alt-right gangs and their members from gang scholarship based on ideological concerns (for a recent example see Pyrooz et al. 2017). In light of the common characteristics and risk factors for both youth involved in alt-right gangs and street gang youth, this book provides a starting point for researchers and policy makers to adapt and deploy effective programs to intervene with alt-right youth (Johnson 2019; Reid & Valasik 2018; Reid et al. 2020; Valasik & Reid 2018a, 2019). The conclusion also reviews potential strategies that have been shown to be effective with street gangs that could be adapted and utilized on alt-right gang members. Reinvigorating scholarship into these far-right groups is essential, since membership in an alt-right gang, like conventional street gangs, can produce negative short- and long-term consequences on youth and their local communities.

IN THE EPOCH OF TRUMP!

Despite public scrutiny and the fracturing among alt-right sympathizers following the "Unite the Right" rally in Charlottesville in August 2017, the alt-right's favored digital platforms (e.g., 4chan, 8kun, Reddit, Gab, etc.) did not see a decline in their use the way some people expected. Instead, since Charlottesville there has been a growing boldness by alt-right gangs (e.g., racist skinheads, Proud Boys, Atomwaffen Division, R.A.M., etc.) and far-right extremists, seen in such actions as the Tree of Life Synagogue shooting in Pittsburgh, Pennsylvania; the Al Noor Mosque shootings in Christchurch, New Zealand; and the Chabad Temple shooting in Poway, California (Al Jezeera 2018; Barrouquere 2019; Bogost 2019; Burke 2018; Hankes 2019; Hermansson et al. 2020; Lopez 2017; McAuliffe 2019; Roose & Winston 2018; Valasik & Reid 2018a). McVeigh and Estep (2019: 225) warn that "white nationalism is most consequential when it enters the mainstream—so mainstream, in this case, that it captured the White House." In fact, President Trump's incendiary rhetoric of coded language and dog whistles and his apologetic stance toward alt-right street violence has created an environment that is conducive to alt-right gangs' mobilization (see Haney-Lopez 2014). A perceived loss of status/ privilege/authority by whites, particularly by males, has driven about 6% of Americans to explicitly support the rhetoric of the alt-right (see Hawley 2018). However, many more white Americans feel that the current political and economic conditions are cheating them out of what they are entitled to (see Hochschild 2016; Kimmel 2013; McAuliffe 2019; Norris 2018; Stern 2019).

"Dubbed the 'Trump Effect,' this resurgent white supremacy is real and violent: in the weeks following Trump's win, hate crimes in the US surged to a level not seen since the days immediately after 9/11" (Perry & Scrivens 2018: 184) (see also Perry & Scrivens 2020). The fourth quarter of 2016 was the "worst fourth quarter for hate crime since 2008" and November 2016 was the "worst November going back to 1992, when the systematic national record keeping began" (Levin & Reitzel 2018: 15). In 2018, despite the overall decline in violent crime across the country, violence against persons motivated by hate or bias reached a 16-year high in the United States, with substantial increases in aggravated assault, simple assault, and intimidation compared with even 2017's elevated number of incidents (Levin & Nakashima 2019).

It is clear that a relationship between the alt-right and the Trump administration exists (see Crothers 2019; Finn 2019; Hawley 2017, 2019; Lyons 2018; Main 2018; McVeigh & Estep 2019; May & Feldman 2019; F. Morris 2017; Mudde 2018, 2019; Neiwert 2017; Paxton 2018; Perry & Scrivens 2020; Saslow 2018; Tenold 2018; Tuters 2019). What exactly that relationship is remains unclear, but it has been mutually beneficial, providing a propagandist platform that the alt-right can exploit for their own advantage (see Crothers 2019; Finn 2019; Hawley 2017, 2019; Hermansson et al. 2020; Lyons 2018; Main 2018; McVeigh & Estep 2019; Mudde 2018; Neiwert 2017; Paxton 2018; Saslow 2018; Tenold 2018). For instance, alt-right gangs loathe establishment politics and "were delighted to see him [Trump] attack mainstream Republicans and conservative institutions" (Hawley 2019: 179). President Trump's reactive labeling as "fake news" any opposing facts and viewpoints has allowed alt-right gangs and the broader alt-right movement to popularize through alternative media platforms some sympathetic voices (the alt-lite) that have traditionally been ignored in mainstream news reporting (see chapters 6 and 8) (Crothers 2019; Hawley 2019; Hermansson et al. 2020; Marantz 2019; Marcotte 2018; McVeigh & Estep 2019).

Guiding alt-right political ideology is what Finn (2019: 5) calls the "Alt-Constitution," refiguring the U.S. Constitution so that it "is a vision of American political life that emphasizes absolute rights and unassailable liberties (especially for speech and guns); states' rights and a corresponding suspicion of the federal government; racial classifications recognized and legitimated by law; and privilege for white Christians" (see also Whitman 2017). Under the Trump administration more candidates with overt white power beliefs or ties to white power groups have run for political office as Republican candidates (e.g., Corey Stewart, a neo-Confederate in Virginia; Arthur Jones, a neo-Nazi in Illinois; Paul Nehlen, a white supremacist in Wisconsin; John Fitzgerald, a Holocaust denier in California), making their mark on the political discourse (Crothers 2019; McAuliffe 2019). "As part of the official political apparatus, such extremists have the appearance of legitimate actors with valid interpretations of the state of economic and cultural relations throughout the country" (Perry & Scrivens 2018: 178). For these alt-right sympathizers the Alt-Constitution provides a "comprehensive worldview, self-contained, and impervious to other ways of thinking" (Finn 2019: 9).

As Lyons (2018: 216) warns, "In this period of uncertainty, far rightists will have more opening to promote their supremacist visions and either draw more people into oppositional politics or at least widen the space for intensified scape-goating and oppression within the existing system." As such, "the conditions that led to the rise of the alt-right have not gone away" but are likely to remain for the foreseeable future, particularly if Americans continue to support the ideations of the alt-right (Crothers 2019: 180). The political shift allows for easier recruitment into these gangs, as youth are already exposed to portions of this rhetoric and less indoctrination has to occur within the gang.

WOMEN IN ALT-RIGHT GANGS

Stereotypes and misogyny have plagued the study of women in conventional street gangs, traditional racist skinhead gangs, and present-day alt-right gangs. While a few researchers, especially Blee (2002, 2003, 2012, 2017), have worked to show the realities of women who join the WPM (see also Borgeson 2003; Castle 2012; Fangen 1997; Hermansson et al. 2020; Latif et al. 2019; Mattheis 2018), more often women are described as hang-arounds, girlfriends, or scene sluts (among the nicer terms), with minimal autonomy. Within the street gang literature, re-search by feminist criminologists has provided a much more complete and multi-faceted view of female youth involved in gang life. Until gang researchers like Miller (2001), Chesney-Lind and Hagedorn (1999), and more recently Peterson and Panfil (2017) and Hughes et al. (2019) began to focus on the experiences of women gang members, women were often not considered "real" gang members by researchers or police. These studies forced researchers to shift away from the stereotyped narratives of women members being relegated to the fringes of gang life (see Brown 1977; Campbell 1984; Miller 1973; Quicker 1983). Luckily, research focusing on women in street gangs has allowed for a clearer understanding of both the true number of women members and the gender differences across risk factors, behavioral outcomes, and victimization. Recent studies have highlighted that there are women in most street gangs, comprising as much as 30%–50% of membership (depending on the sample) (Curry 2000; Gover, Jennings & Tewks-bury 2009; Miller & Brunson 2000).

Female gang membership is often more nuanced and comparable to male gang membership than had previously been thought (Alleyne & Pritchard 2016; Deuchar, Harding, McLean & Densley 2018; Hughes, Botchkovar & Short 2019; Miller 1973; Miller 2001; Moore 1991; Panfil & Peterson 2015; Peterson, 2012; Peter-son, Carson & Fowler 2018). Given the predominantly male orientation of gangs

(Joe & Chesney-Lind 1995; Griffiths & Howell 2018), it is not surprising that there is a power imbalance between female and male members (Bjerregaard & Smith 1993; Griffiths & Howell 2018; Hayward & Honegger 2014; Peterson et al. 2004). Women street gang members tend to be younger than male members when they join, typically in early adolescence, and they often desist earlier (Bell 2009; Joe & Chesney-Lind 1995). When it comes to criminality, women members are less likely to be involved in the most serious violence, such as drive-by shootings, both by choice and because of gendered expectations or rules put in place by male members (Brown 1977; Esbensen, Peterson, Taylor & Freng 2010; Miller & Brunson 2000). Female members are also more likely than males to be victims of sexual violence (Dorais & Corriveau 2009; Miller 2001; Miller & Brunson 2000). Experiences and expectations for female street gang members often ensue from the sex composition of the gang, as more male-dominated gangs tend to increase young women's experiences with criminal activity and victimization (Esbensen et al. 2010; Peterson, Miller & Esbensen 2001; St. Cyr & Decker 2003). Rather than considering women members analogous to male members, prevention and intervention programs aimed at reducing female membership need to address the specific issues women in gangs face (see Howell & Griffiths 2018).

As noted by Anahita (2006: 146), most of the analysis "of feminine identity and women's participation in the white power movement has been framed from male participants' points of view." While we might expect males to be more at risk for membership in alt-right gangs than females (ADL 1995; Ezekiel 2002; Pollard 2016), as more studies systematically focus on female alt-right gang members, they may be shown to play a more serious role in these groups than previously thought. The expectation is that female alt-right gang members, like their street gang counterparts, are not just peripheral members but exist on the same spectrum of membership as seen with males (see Belew 2018; Bowman & Stewart 2017; G. Gordon 2018; Hall 2018; Mattheis 2018; Proud Boys 2019). For instance, Proud Boys have female cliques (i.e., Proud Boys' Girls) like the women's groups of the KKK, as a support for the men's organization (DeCook 2018; Proud Boys 2019; Zadrozny & Siemaszko 2018). Furthermore, the study of the risk factors for women in alt-right gangs must be taken seriously to make sure their risks and needs are appropriately addressed. The few studies discussing women in alt-right gangs highlight that some women reject the idea that they should be sidelined because of their gender (Blee 2002, 2004) and actively participate in criminal activity, including violence (Christensen 1994). An ADL (1988) report noted that half of the members of Portland's East Side White Pride gang were women and that the Skinhead Army of Milwaukee gang was actively recruiting young women members. Prior research on the online activity of racist skinheads underscores the more heteronormative and hypermasculine orientation of interactions, as "virtual skinheads largely shut women out of frontline activist roles, and mostly relegate women to subservient, helpmeet status" (Anahita 2006: 155). More recent work by Scrivens, Bowman-Grieve, and colleagues (2018) takes a much more nuanced approach to the study of women in the WPM through women-centric message boards on Stormfront. This technique provides a better means of understanding how women construct their identities in these spaces, including their feelings about misogyny present in the Stormfront community and larger alt-right movement (see Darby 2017; Hermansson et al. 2020; Mattheis 2018). Future research needs to reconcile the realities of alt-right female gang members with the stereotypes perceived about these women. As we have seen with conventional street gangs, women are most likely not relegated to these side roles in the way that male members may describe or believe. Until there is a recognition that these women are not just girlfriends, wives, or hangers-on, prevention, intervention, and suppression efforts will fall short of effectiveness.

ONLINE ANGER TO REAL-WORLD VIOLENCE

Another important avenue for future research is understanding the transmission of online activity into real-world action (see Fieltiz & Thurston 2019; Reid et al. 2020). While there has been a more recent push to examine and explain the behavior of right wing extremists broadly online, and a call from researchers to better understand the online behavior of individuals (e.g., the Tree of Life Synagogue shooter) who commit mass violence, these pathways between online activity and real-world actions remain a black box. For every individual that goes online and announces an intention of going to "do something" for the white race, only a fraction of those individuals actually commit a crime. For larger events, the online-to-offline link is clearer. These are events like the "Unite the Right" rally, which "was meant to be a pivotal moment for the alt-right, signifying that it was moving off the Internet and into public spaces in the real world" (Hawley 2019: 139), and a number of "free speech" rallies have allowed alt-right groups to develop stronger in-person opportunities to participate in violence. Such events have offered an opportunity to look at how these groups organize online and how that translates into real-world activity, yet they constitute just a fraction of the more numerous smaller interactions moving between on- and offline spaces. A better understanding of what types of online action move into the real world (e.g., interpersonal disputes or criminal activity) will allow more direct action to intervene, intercept, or suppress criminal activity.

For conventional street gangs, more effort has been spent in trying to understand the online-to-offline link in the day-to-day interactions between gang members. Research on the online behaviors exhibited by conventional street gang members has focused on the symbolic nature of gang members' posts, referred to colloquially as "cyberbanging" (see Densley 2013; Décary-Hétu & Morselli 2011;

Irwin-Rogers, Densley & Pinkney 2018; Morselli & Décary-Hétu, 2013; Moule et al. 2014, 2017; Patton et al. 2013, 2019; Pyrooz et al. 2015; Sela-Shayovitz 2012; Storrod & Densley 2017; Stuart 2019; Urbanik & Haggerty 2018). A similar pattern of "cyberbanging" may exist with alt-right gangs, where members are posting online to not only spread their images and build reputation, but also to delegitimize a rival group (e.g., Antifa), promote acts of physical violence, and digitally tag space (see DeCook 2018; Klein 2019). As with alt-right gangs, conventional street gangs in the twenty-first century value digital technology, particularly social media, and its use and influence on the lives and activity patterns of gang members should not be minimized (see Densley 2013; Moule, Decker & Pyrooz 2017; Moule, Pyrooz & Decker 2014; Patton et al. 2019; Pyrooz, Decker & Moule 2015; Storrod & Densley 2017; Stuart 2019; Urbanik & Haggerty 2018). It remains unclear if members from alt-right and conventional street gangs behave similarly online, but without studying both the smaller, more localized online-to-offline behaviors for both groups, effective interventions will be lacking.

CURRENT LACK OF POLICY

Following the Oklahoma City bombing in 1995, federal law enforcement began to investigate white power groups more aggressively; however, this increase was short lived, as there was a shift to jihadi extremism following the events on September 11, 2001 (Crothers 2019). Because most of the attacks perpetrated by the far right "are decentralized, the level of violence is not high enough to generate the same panic"; thus, the level of scrutiny by law enforcement has been scant (Laqueur & Wall 2018: 173). Even the first far-right suicide bombing in the United States, taking place in Panaca, Nevada, in July 2016, went unnoticed by the vast majority of society, including law enforcement (Sottile 2019). As such, law enforcement has tended to underestimate the threat posed by alt-right gangs and do not adequately train to deal with this growing phenomenon (see Chermak, Freilich & Shemtob 2009; Chermak, Freilich & Simone 2010; Kundnani 2012; Lehr 2013; McAuliffe 2019; Perry & Scrivens 2018, 2019). In essence, law enforcement created a "blind spot" for themselves by discounting white power/alt-right groups for the last two decades (Kundnani 2012; Lehr 2013; Myre 2019; Perry & Scrivens 2018) and a bright ray of hope for the alt-right's desire for expansion (figure 8.1).

Ward (2018: 168) stresses that there is a long history of white supremacy policing in America including "racist ideologies, violence, and other political actions of law enforcement authorities, and underpolicing of White supremacist threats by legal authorities." It is not surprising, considering the happenings at the "Unite the Right" rally in Charlottesville, that "Antifa branded local police forces as sympathetic to the 'alt-right' and even as protecting groups like the Ku Klux Klan: 'Cops and Klan go hand in hand'" (Klein 2019: 313). Similar concerns have been

FIGURE 8.1. Since not enough systematic research of alt-right gangs is being conducted to develop prevention, intervention, and suppression initiatives, Proud Boys' future is so bright they have to wear shades (photo by David Neiwert).

raised in Portland, Oregon, ranging from law enforcement's apathy toward alt-right gangs (e.g., lack of documentation in gang databases; see chapter 2) to being sympathetic to them to directly collaborating with them (Brosseau 2016; Colson 2018; Fortin 2019; Gupta 2017; Hall 2018; Weill 2019). These observations reinforce Mills's (2003: 43) assertion that "[for] most of U.S. history, the state has functioned as a racial state protecting White supremacy." Additionally, concerns remain that law enforcement agencies are still being infiltrated by individuals supportive of white power beliefs (see Cunningham 2013; Cooter 2006; Downs 2016; FBI 2006; Jones 2015; Landers 2018; Speri 2017; Tobar 1991; Ward 2018). As described by the FBI (2006: 5), these are "ghost skins" or "those who avoid overt displays of their [white power] beliefs to blend into society and covertly advance white supremacist causes." Today the alt-right is employing the same strategy (Beckford 2019). As such, an updating from ghost skin to "*alt-right wraith*" may be more apropos to the current state of the white power movement.

The mainstreaming of the WPM is a recurrent strategy among supporters (see Cooter 2006; Dobratz & Shanks-Meile 2006; Johansson, Andreasson & Mattsson 2017; Miller-Idriss 2018, 2019; Simi & Futrell 2015) and is currently being deployed by alt-right gangs to provide a softer image to facilitate the recruitment of members and gain larger support from society (see Hawley 2018, 2019; Stern 2019). Examples of this mainstreaming to better appeal to broader society include the wearing of khaki pants and white polos by alt-righters at the 2017 Unite the Right

Rally in Charlottesville (Hermansson et al. 2020; PBS 2018a; VICE 2017) or Proud Boys' uniform of black Fred Perry polo shirts with yellow piping (Beery 2017; Cauterucci 2017; SPLC 2019; Swenson 2017).

Perry and Scrivens (2018: 170) contend that failing to respond to alt-right gangs can be read as enabling, yet "punitive responses can further marginalize and thus embitter adherents, resulting in more rather than less targeted violence." That said, if law enforcement were to take the threat of alt-right gangs being a menace to society seriously, they could have the tools to actually do something to counter the violence. For instance, over 35 years ago, much like Proud Boys, the Black Panthers established a collective identity and chapters (cliques) across the country, endorsed nationalism and street toughness, advocated a political message, and wore a recognizable uniform. But, unlike today's alt-right groups, as Bloom and Martin (2013) chronicle, the Black Panther Party was singled out by the FBI and with the help of local law enforcement was relentlessly attacked until it was eradicated (see also Cunningham 2003). Ironically, or sadly, today we see a similar concern by the FBI (2017) on "Black identity extremists," again ignoring the more pressing threat of alt-right gangs and the broader WPM (see Miah 2018; Updegrove, Cooper, Orrick & Piquero 2018). History clearly shows that when law enforcement, at the local and/or federal level, is seriously concerned about a group, they will engage in overtly oppressive actions to disrupt and disband the group, as observed with the Black Panther Party. In the end, the most obvious factor that has allowed alt-right gangs to emerge and sustain themselves is the weak response by law enforcement (Perry & Scrivens 2018, 2019; Reitman 2018).

FUTURE DIRECTIONS FOR POLICY

The United States, like Canada, has "little contemporary social science research" on alt-right gangs or groups in the broader WPM, with even "fewer efforts to methodically and systematically analyze their ideologies and activities on a national level" (Perry & Scrivens 2018: 170). For policy makers and practitioners, including law enforcement, there are several noteworthy practical implications derived from this book. As highlighted in chapter 2, law enforcement, elected officials, and the media cultivate myths about alt-right gangs, portraying these groups as fringe organizations ideologically fixated on perpetrating hate/bias-related crimes or as part of some large international conglomerate reminiscent of an organized crime group (e.g., Cosa Nostra, Sinaloa Cartel). Yet neither portrait is accurate. These imprecise depictions are due to the lack of systematic research that could provide more nuance and understanding to the structure, dynamics, and organization of alt-right gangs.

If criminal justice approaches are going to be utilized to combat alt-right gangs, it is crucial to have a firmer grasp on the reality of these white power groups.

The initial stage of this process would include the systematic collecting and cataloging of information already retrieved from field interviews, arrests, and other contacts with law enforcement about alt-right gang members into either existing gang databases or into an analogous system (see Decker & Pyrooz 2010; Katz, Webb & Schaefer 2000; Valasik et al. 2016). This would include applying and enforcing a jurisdiction's definition of a gang and gang-related crimes to include alt-right gangs (see chapter 1). Currently, it is unclear how departments are currently capturing these youth in their gang databases, if at all. Only at the correctional level (i.e., prisons), it seems, is membership in white power gangs systematically kept for inmates (see Pyrooz & Decker 2019). While gang databases are still a contentious tool utilized by law enforcement (e.g., (non)removal of desisting members, casting too wide a net, misidentifying associates, etc.), the infrastructure for such databases readily exists in many policing jurisdictions to make them a cost-effective apparatus that could easily be appropriated as a repository of information on alt-right gang members (see Barrows & Huff 2009; Huff & Barrows 2015; Densley & Pyrooz 2019b; Wright 2005). It is not uncommon for alt-right gang members to have lengthy criminal histories (e.g., drug arrests, violence, etc.), and they are likely already in a law enforcement database. For instance, alt-right gang members selling drugs are not drug-selling youth who are part of some racist subculture; rather, they are alt-right gang members who participate in the drug market, and law enforcement should monitor them for that reason. Providing police officers with this pertinent information in a straightforward manner would allow them to be able to weaken these gangs and intervene if they arrest and prosecute alt-right gang members for crimes that are not hate/bias based (see Perry & Scrivens 2018, 2019). The focus remains solely on the reactive process of charging alt-right gang members for serious acts of violence, such as Timothy McVeigh in the Oklahoma City bombing (see Crothers 2019), because domestic terrorism has not been designated a federal crime. Instead, law enforcement needs to be proactively charging and prosecuting alt-right gang members for legitimate and less serious criminal acts (see Myre 2018; Sonmez 2018).

Furthermore, coordinated efforts to systematically track alt-right gang members between corrections facilities (see Goodman 2008) and local law enforcement agencies need to be implemented. Given that the vast majority of incarcerated individuals return to society, it would be invaluable for corrections departments to pass along intelligence on an individual's white power connections to the law enforcement agency in the jurisdiction where that person is going to live. Intelligence sharing would allow for more accurate monitoring and ultimately shift behavior patterns to reduce recidivism. For instance, Perry and Scrivens (2018: 183) find that "just knowing that there is a 'specialized team' mandated to deal with hate crime and extremism, it was argued, made adherents, 'think twice about crossing the line.'"

As gang scholars can attest, effective strategies aimed at preventing or reducing the criminality of alt-right gangs need to extend beyond suppression-based efforts (e.g., aggressive policing, enhanced prosecution, tougher sentencing) if they are going to be successful in disrupting these groups (see Chaskin 2010; Decker 2003; Klein & Maxson 2006). For instance, Operation Ceasefire utilized a diverse working group that included researchers, outreach workers, and criminal justice actors (Kennedy, Piehl & Braga 1996). This working group used extensive and coordinated information to build an intervention and suppression program. This process included analyzing three main groups: the victims and offenders of Boston's youth (under 21 years old) homicides; the size, number, and location of Boston's street gangs, along with their turfs, alliances, and rivalries; and the intersection between gangs and homicides. The analysis of this triangulated dataset allowed the working group a comprehensive understanding of youth gang violence in Boston. This lesson of needing a comprehensive understanding of the alt-right gang problem is paramount if practical policy is going be used to effectively deal with alt-right gangs. In line with such a process, law enforcement needs to develop community partners that are able to gather and share intelligence and organize activities to counter extremism (see Perry & Scrivens 2018). For example, Crothers (2019: 179) points out that "a group called Unicorn Riot has also undertaken cyber operations against alt-right activists. The group has obtained the logs of servers used to organize rallies like the one in Charlottesville. It has provided those logs to the media and to lawyers leading the lawsuit against the alt-right leaders of the Charlottesville protests" (see also Hawley 2019; Hermansson et al. 2020; PBS 2018b).

Alt-right gangs, like conventional street gangs, are comprised of marginalized youth from distressed communities. Since alt-right gangs are group based and have similar proclivities to violence as conventional street gangs (see chapter 7), successful intervention programs could be used or adapted for youth vulnerable to alt-right gang membership. In designing interventions that facilitate desistance from alt-right groups, the literature on street gang desistance (e.g. Carson, Peterson & Esbensen 2013; Densley & Pyrooz 2019a; Gormally 2015; Pyrooz & Decker 2011; Pyrooz, Decker & Webb 2014; Sweeten, Pyrooz & Piquero 2013) would be a suitable starting point. One possible option is the implementation of gang alternative programs designed to supply opportunities (e.g., job training, educational assistance) to individuals outside of the gang in order to decrease group attachment and encourage desistance (Gravel, Bouchard, Descormiers, Wong & Morselli 2013). For example, outreach workers could be utilized to improve the relationships between youth sympathetic to white power ideations and better integrate communities so youth can develop a social identity that is healthier. Given the socialization and persistent intergenerational exposure to white power ideals, concerted intervention efforts will need to be coordinated not only with at-risk individuals but also with their families. Analogous efforts have been utilized throughout Europe (Hemmingsen 2015; VICE 2017) and America (Boghani 2016) to deradicalize youth sympathetic with jihadist terrorist groups (see LaFree & Freilich 2018). While empirical assessment of deradicalization efforts' effectiveness remains difficult to ascertain (Horgan & Braddock 2010), the desistance literature on conventional street gangs, informed by large longitudinal datasets, is the best starting point in the meantime to craft interventions to treat alt-right gang members.

Lastly, intervention efforts must not forget the role of digital media to communicate, recruit, and legitimate alt-right groups (see chapter 6). Digital technology provides alt-right gangs a reach beyond local communities and an ability to disseminate their message more broadly through social media (see Fielitz & Thurston 2019; Hermansson et al. 2020; Lu 2019; Stern 2019). Without working with social media platforms to limit youths' exposure to hate/bias-based social media and aggressively remove content related to the alt-right, it will be difficult to counter the influence of these groups. Such an intervention however, requires the assistance of these social media platforms at limiting user actions and restricting content, a somewhat challenging, yet not impossible, endeavor (Lima 2019; Newton 2019; Owen 2018). As Perry and colleagues (2018: 16) attest, what is needed is the "engagement of educators, social service providers, even the media. Collaborative action is key to building resilient communities."

OPERATIONALIZING THE
ALT-RIGHT GANG DEFINITION

The definition of an alt-right gang was outlined in chapter 1. With each element of the definition, we broke down the rationale and logic behind its inclusion to provide a greater awareness of what constitutes an alt-right gang. Yet, in addition to the conceptual approach presented in chapter 1, we believe the alt-right gang definition needs to be consistently operationalized. Consistency and clear guidelines are needed in order to gather empirical data in a systematic manner so that data can be examined and compared across samples. Modeled after the Eurogang approach (see Weerman et al. 2009), the alt-right gang survey instrument presented here uses a funneling technique to determine if an individual is a member of an alt-right gang without relying upon that individual's self-perception of being a gang member or associating with a gang. A series of questions are administered, with each question including an element of the alt-right gang definition. Individuals' responses to the ten questions (i.e., questions 2–11) determine whether criteria for belonging to an alt-right gang are met. Respondents' answers limit those who meet the alt-right gang definition, thereby funneling them into identification as an alt-right gang member. The first eight questions are pulled directly from The Youth Survey of the *Eurogang Program Manual* (Weerman et al. 2009), providing a consistent and proven metric to capture gang membership.

Setting the stage for the core questions is a preliminary question (question 1) that should be asked about membership in organized or formal groups. This initial question is designed to get respondents to reflect on those formal groups they belong to as a mechanism to preempt their considering these groups in the subsequent questions that follow. Next are the ten defining questions used to ascertain if an individual is a member of an alt-right gang.

Of these ten, the question asked first (question 2) is to determine whether an individual belongs to an informal group of peers. Question 3 ascertains if the group has a public-orientation, with members loitering together in public spaces. Question 4 determines if the group is durable, existing for more than three months. Questions 5 and 6 are used to ascertain if illegal behavior is part of the group's identity, being both accepted and practiced. Question 7 determines whether a respondent's group has a presence on the internet or social media. Questions 8, 9, and 10 are used to establish if a respondent's group has any leanings toward the WPM. Question 11, while not necessary to determine if the respondent is an alt-right gang member, allows individuals to consider whether they perceive their group as a gang. Question 12 is a follow-up allowing the respondent to clarify the term that is used to describe their group.

With this base set of questions, the Alt-Right Gang Survey Instrument operationalizes the definition of an alt-right gang and identifies members; it should be used in conjunction with additional questions from other surveys to better flesh out the structure, culture, and context of alt-right gangs (see Weerman et al. 2009).

ALT-RIGHT GANG SURVEY INSTRUMENT

The following questions are about your friends or the people you spend time with.

1. During the past 12 months, have you participated in any teams, scouts, sports clubs, or other formal groups in your school, neighborhood, or city?
   a. No
   b. Yes
1a. If yes, please specify _____.
2. In addition to any such formal groups, some people have a certain group of friends that they spend time with, doing things together or just hanging out. Do you have a group of friends like that? (If more than one such group exists, answer for the one most important to you.)
   a. No
   b. Yes
3. Does this group spend a lot of time together in public places like a park, the street, shopping areas, drinking or eating establishments, or in a neighborhood?
   a. No
   b. Yes
4. How long has this group existed?
   a. Less than 3 months
   b. 3 months to less than 1 year

    c. 1 to 4 years

    d. 5 to 10 years

    e. 11 to 20 years

    f. More than 20 years

5. Is doing illegal things accepted by or okay for your group?

    a. No

    b. Yes

6. Do people in your group actually do illegal things together?

    a. No

    b. Yes

7. Does your group have an online presence, either a website, social media site, imageboard, or forum that is used?

    a. No

    b. Yes

8. Does the racial or ethnic composition of your group matter?

    a. No

    b. Yes

9. Which of the following categories describe the people in your group? (Circle or check all that apply.)

9a. White

    a. All of them

    b. Most of them

    c. About half of them

    d. Less than half of them

    e. None of them

9b. Black

    a. All of them

    b. Most of them

    c. About half of them

    d. Less than half of them

    e. None of them

9c. Latino/Hispanic

    a. All of them

    b. Most of them

    c. About half of them

    d. Less than half of them

    e. None of them

9d. Asian

    a. All of them

    b. Most of them

    c. About half of them

       d. Less than half of them

       e. None of them

9e. Other

       a. All of them

       b. Most of them

       c. About half of them

       d. Less than half of them

       e. None of them

10. Does your group adopt signs, numbers, letters, or symbols to distinguish your group's identity?

       a. No

       b. Yes

10a. If yes, please specify _____.

11. Do you consider your group of friends to be a gang?

       a. No

       b. Yes

12. If you do not use the word "gang" for your group, is there some other term you would use? For example, some groups call themselves clubs, bands, crews, posses, taggers, bikers, party crews, and so on.

       If your group uses a term other than "gang," what is that term?

REFERENCES

Aba-Onu, U. F., Levy-Pounds, N., Salmen, J., & Tyner, A. (2010). Evaluation of gang databases in Minnesota and recommendations for change. *Information & Communications Technology Law, 19*(3), 223–254.

ABC News. (2018, December 12*). Proud Boys founder on whether he feels responsible for its controversial behavior.* Retrieved October 27, 2019. ABC News. https://abcnews.go .com/Nightline/video/proud-boys-founder-feels-responsible-controversial-behavior -59766444

Adams, J., & Roscigno, V. J. (2005). White supremacists, oppositional culture and the World Wide Web. *Social Forces, 84*(2), 759–778.

Adamson, C. (2000). Defensive localism in white and black: A comparative history of European-American and African-American youth gangs. *Ethnic and Racial Studies, 23*(2), 272–298.

ADL. (1988). *Young and violent: The growing menace of America's neo-Nazi skinheads.* New York: Anti-Defamation League.

ADL. (1995). *The skinhead international: A worldwide survey of neo-Nazi skinheads.* New York: Anti-Defamation League.

ADL. (2006). *Army of hate.* Retrieved from Anti-Defamation League. https://store.adl.org /army-of-hate-p316.aspx

ADL. (2017). *New hate and old: The changing face of American white supremacy.* Retrieved October 20, 2019, from Anti-Defamation League. https://www.adl.org/new-hate-and-old

ADL. (2019). *The Hammerskin Nation.* Retrieved April 29, 2019, from Anti-Defamation League. https://www.adl.org/education/resources/profiles/hammerskin-nation

ADL. (2020). *ADL H.E.A.T. Map.* Retrieved March 15, 2020, from Anti-Defamation League. https://www.adl.org/education-and-resources/resource-knowledge-base/adl-heat-map

Ahmned, N. (2020, February 26). *The alt-right has taken the political centre. It's not too late to win it back.* Retrieved March 21, 2020, from The Correspondent. https://

thecorrespondent.com/314/the-alt-right-has-taken-the-political-centre-its-not-too-late-to-win-it-back/360675125030-368a0a4b

Aho, J. A. (1990). *The politics of righteousness: Idaho Christian patriotism.* University of Washington Press.

Alleyne, E., & Pritchard, E. (2016). Psychological and behavioral characteristics differentiating gang and non-gang girls in the UK. *Journal of Criminological Research, Policy and Practice, 2*(2), 122–133.

Allyn, B. (2019, September 26). *The "OK" hand gesture is now listed as a symbol of hate.* Retrieved October 20, 2019, from NPR. https://www.npr.org/2019/09/26/764728163/the-ok-hand-gesture-is-now-listed-as-a-symbol-of-hate

Alonso, A. A. (2004). Racialized identitities and the formation of black gangs in Los Angeles. *Urban Geography, 25*(7), 658–674.

Amster, S. E. (2009). From birth of a nation to stormfront: A century of communicating hate. In B. Perry (Ed.), *Hate Crimes.* Greenwood.

Anahita, S. (2006). Blogging the borders: Virtual skinheads, hypermasculinity, and heteronormativity. *Journal of Political & Military Sociology,* 143–164.

Anderson, C. (2016). *White rage: The unspoken truth of our racial divide.* Bloomsbury Publishing.

Anderson, E. (1999). *Code of the street: Decency, violence, and the moral life of the inner city.* W.W. Norton & Company.

Antoine, L. (2018, November 8). Review of Connie O's Pub in Brooklyn, NY. Retrieved October 20, 2019, from Yelp. https://www.yelp.com/biz/connie-os-pub-brooklyn

Arnold, R. (2010). Visions of hate: Explaining neo-Nazi violence in the Russian Federation. *Problems of Post-Communism, 57*(2), 37–49.

Atkinson, D. C. (2018). Charlottesville and the alt-right: A turning point? *Politics, Groups, and Identities, 6*(2), 309–315.

Atran, S. (2017, November 6). Radical Islam and the alt-right are not so different. Retrieved October 20, 2019, from Aeon. https://aeon.co/essays/radical-islam-and-the-alt-right-are-not-so-different

Ayling, J. (2011). Criminalizing organizations: Towards deliberative lawmaking. *Law & Policy, 33*(2), 149–178.

Back, L. (2002). Aryans reading Adorno: Cyber-culture and twenty-first-century racism. *Ethnic and Racial Studies, 25*(4), 628–651.

Bacon, J., & Warren, B. (2017, August 15). Confederate monuments prompt protests across USA. Retrieved December 11, 2018, from *USA Today.* https://www.usatoday.com/story/news/nation/2017/08/15/battle-over-civil-war-monuments-prompts-rallies-across-usa/567798001/

Baele, S. J., Brace, L., & Coan, T. G. (2019). From "incel" to "saint": Analyzing the violent worldview behind the 2018 Toronto attack. *Terrorism and Political Violence.* doi: 10.1080/09546553.2019.1638256

Balch. (2006). The rise and fall of Aryan nations: A resource mobilization perspective. *Journal of Political and Military Sociology, 34.*

Bamiro, Y. [Director]. (2018). Black Rebel [Television series episode]. *Hate Thy Neighbor.* Viceland.

Barker, T. (2019). *North American criminal gangs: Street, prison, outlaw motorcycle, and drug trafficking organizations* (3rd ed.). Carolina Academic Press.

Barnes, L. (2017, August 24). *Proud Boys founder disavows violence at Charlottesville but one of its members organized the event*. Retrieved October 27, 2019, from Think Progress. https://thinkprogress.org/proud-boys-founder-tries-and-fails-to-distance-itself-from-charlottesville-6862fb8b3ae9/

Baron, S. W. (1997). Canadian male street skinheads: Street gang or street terrorists? *Canadian Review of Sociology/Revue Canadienne de Sociologie, 34*(2), 125–154.

Barrios, L. (2003). The Almighty Latin King and Queen Nation and the spirituality of resistance: Agency, social cohesion, and liberating rituals in the making of a street organization. In L. Barrios, L. Kontos & D. Brotherton (Eds.), *Gangs and society: Alternative perspectives* (pp. 119–135). Columbia University Press.

Barrouquere, B. (2019, January 30). *Feds file hate crime charges in Tree of Life Shooting, cite antisemitic posts on Gab*. Retrieved October 27, 2019, from Southern Poverty Law Center. https://www.splcenter.org/hatewatch/2019/01/30/feds-file-hate-crime-charges-tree-life-shooting-cite-antisemitic-posts-gab

Barrows, J., & Huff, C. R. (2009). Gangs and public policy. *Criminology & Public Policy, 8*(4), 675–703.

Battin, S. R., Hill, K. G., Abbott, R. D., Catalano, R. F., & Hawkins, J. D. (1998). The contribution of gang membership to delinquency beyond delinquent friends. *Criminology, 36*(1), 93–115.

Beam, L. ([1983] 1992). *Leaderless resistance. The Seditionist* (12), 12–13.

Beauchamp, Z. (2018, August 10). *Study: 11 million white Americans think like the alt-right*. Retrieved April 24, 2019, from Vox. https://www.vox.com/2018/8/10/17670992/study-white-americans-alt-right-racism-white-nationalists

Beauchamp, Z. (2019, November 18). *Accelerationism: The obsucure idea inspiring white supremacist killers around the world*. Retrieved December 11, 2019, from Vox. https://www.vox.com/the-highlight/2019/11/11/20882005/accelerationism-white-supremacy-christchurch

Beckett, K., & Herbert, S. (2010). Penal boundaries: Banishment and the expansion of punishment. *Law & Social Inquiry, 35*(1), 1–38.

Beckford, G. (2019). The new alt-right [audio podcast] *RNZ: Insight*. https://www.rnz.co.nz/national/programmes/insight/audio/2018692368/new-alt-right-political-groups-hiding-in-plain-sight-investigation

Beery, Z. (2017, June 20). *How Fred Perry polos came to symbolize hate*. Retrieved October 20, 2019, from The Outline. https://theoutline.com/post/1760/fred-perry-polo-skinheads

Belew, K. (2018). *Bring the war home: The white power movement and paramilitary America*. Harvard University Press.

Bell, K. E. (2009). Gender and gangs: A quantitative comparison. *Crime & Delinquency, 55*(3), 363–387.

Berger, J. M. (2018). *The alt-right Twitter census*. Vox-Pol. www.voxpol.eu

Berlet, C. (2008). Leaderless counterterrorism strategy: The "war on terror," civil liberties, and flawed scholarship. Retrieved May 18, 2019, from *The Public Eye Magazine*: publiceye.org/magazine/v23n3/leaderless_counterterrorism_strategy.html.

Berlet, C., & Mason, C. (2015). Swastikas in cyberspace: How hate went online. In P. A Simpson & H. Druxes (Eds.), *Digital media strategies of the far right in Europe and the United States* (pp. 21–36). Lexington Books.

Berlet, C., & Vysotsky, S. (2006). Overview of US white supremacist groups. *Journal of Political and Military Sociology, 34*(1), 11.

Bernstein, J. (2018, July 18). *Alt-Right troll to father killer: The unraveling of Lane Davis.* Retrieved October 21, 2019, from BuzzFeed News. https://www.buzzfeednews.com/article /josephbernstein/lane-davis-ralph-retort-seattle4truth-alt-right

Bernstein, M. (2017, September 8). *Portland police to halt, purge all gang designations.* Retrieved April 29, 2019, from Oregonlive. https://www.oregonlive.com/portland/2017/09 /portland_police_to_halt_purge.html

Bernstein, M. (2019a, February 15). *Lieutenant removed from Rapid Response Team as Portland police investigate his texts with Patriot Prayer's Joey Gibson.* Retrieved April 29, 2019, from Oregonlive. https://www.oregonlive.com/crime/2019/02/portland-police -lieutenant-removed-from-rapid-response-team-as-bureau-investigates-his-texts-with -patriot-prayers-joey-gibson.html

Bernstein, M. (2019b, February 21). *Mayor's staff got protest intel on Patriot Prayer from Portland cop under fire for texts with right-wing leader.* Retrieved April 29, 2019, from Oregonlive. https://www.oregonlive.com/crime/2019/02/mayors-staff-got-protest -intel-on-patriot-prayer-from-portland-cop-under-fire-for-texts-with-right-wing -leader.html

Berntzen, L. E., & Sandberg, S. (2014). The collective nature of lone wolf terrorism: Anders Behring Breivik and the anti-Islamic social movement. *Terrorism and Political Violence, 26*(5), 759–779.

Berry, D. T. (2017). *Blood and faith: Christianity in American white nationalism.* Syracuse University Press.

Bessant, J. (2018). Right-wing populism and young "Stormers": Conflict in democratic politics. In S. Pickard & J. Bessant (Eds.), *Young people re-generating politics in times of crises* (pp. 139–159). Palgrave Macmillan.

Bharath, D. (2018, February 21). Southern Poverty Law Center's new Hate Map shows 38 extremist groups in Southern California. Retrieved April 23, 2019, from *Orange County Register.* https://www.ocregister.com/2018/02/21/southern-poverty-law-centers-new -hate-map-shows-38-extremist-groups-in-southern-california/

Bhopal, K. (2018). *White privilege: The myth of a post-racial society.* Bristol Policy Press.

Bichler, G., Norris, A., Dmello, J., & Randle, J. (2019). The impact of civil gang injunctions on networked violence between the Bloods and the Crips. *Crime & Delinquency, 65*(7), 875–915.

Binelli, M. (2007, August 23). Punk rock fight club. Retrieved April 29, 2019, from *Rolling Stone.* https://www.rollingstone.com/culture/culture-news/punk-rock-fight-club -190267/

Bjerregaard, B. (2015). Legislative approaches to addressing gangs and gang-related crime. In S. H. Decker & D. C. Pyrooz (Eds.), *The handbook of gangs* (pp. 345–368). Wiley.

Bjerregaard, B., & Lizotte, A. J. (1995). Gun ownership and gang membership. *Journal of Criminal Law and Criminology, 86,* 37.

Bjerregaard, B., & Smith, C. (1993). Gender differences in gang participation, delinquency, and substance use. *Journal of Quantitative Criminology, 9*(4), 329–355.

Bjørgo, T. (2002). *Exit neo-Nazism: Reducing recruitment and promoting disengagement from racist groups* [Working paper]. Retrieved from NUPI. https://nupi.brage.unit.no /nupi-xmlui/handle/11250/2394077

Bjørgo, T. (2016). *Preventing crime: A holistic approach.* Palgrave Macmillan.

Bjørgo, T., Carlsson, Y., & Haaland, T. (2004). Hate crime or gang conflict? Violence between youth groups in a Norwegian city. In G. Mesko, M. Pagon & B. Dobovsek (Eds.), *Policing in Central and Eastern Europe: Dilemmas of contemporary criminal justice* (pp. 565–583). Faculty of Criminal Justice, University of Maribor.

Blasko, B. L., Roman, C. G., & Taylor, R. B. (2015). Local gangs and residents' perceptions of unsupervised teen groups: Implications for the incivilities thesis and neighborhood effects. *Journal of Criminal Justice, 43*(1), 20–28.

Blazak, R. (1998). Hate in the suburbs: The rise of the skinhead counterculture. In L. J. McIntyre (Ed.), *The practical skeptic: Readings in sociology.* McGraw Hill.

Blazak, R. (2001). White boys to terrorist men: Target recruitment of Nazi skinheads. *American Behavioral Scientist, 44*(6), 982–1000.

Blazak, R. (2009). The prison hate machine. *Criminology & Public Policy, 8*(3), 633–640.

Blazak, R. (2018, January 8). *2017 in review: Hate activity returns to Oregon.* Retrieved April 25, 2019, from Oregon Coalition Against Hate Crime. https://oregoncahc.org /2018/01/08/2017-in-review-hate-activity-returns-to-oregon/

Blee, K. M. (1991). Women in the 1920s' Ku Klux Klan movement. *Feminist Studies, 17*(1), 57–77.

Blee, K. M. (1996). Becoming a racist: Women in contemporary Ku Klux Klan and neo-Nazi groups. *Gender & Society, 10*(6), 680–702.

Blee, K. M. (2002). *Inside organized racism: Women in the hate movement.* University of California Press.

Blee, K. M. (2005). There's something happening here: The new left, the Klan, and FBI counterintelligence. *Contemporary Sociology, 34*(5), 548–549.

Blee, K. M. (2012). Does gender matter in the United States far-right? *Politics, Religion & Ideology, 13*(2), 253–265.

Blee, K. M. (2013). How options disappear: Causality and emergence in grassroots activist groups. *American Journal of Sociology, 119*(3), 655–681.

Blee, K. M. (2017). How the study of white supremacism is helped and hindered by social movement research. *Mobilization: An International Quarterly, 22*(1), 1–15.

Blee, K. M. (2018). *Understanding racist activism: Theory, methods, and research.* Routledge.

Blee, K., & Burke, K. (2014). Teaching about organized racism. In K. Haltinner (Ed.), *Teaching race and anti-racism in contemporary America: Adding context to colorblindness* (pp. 65–71). Springer.

Blee, K. M., & Creasap, K. A. (2010). Conservative and right-wing movements. *Annual Review of Sociology, 36*(1), 269–286.

Blee, K. M., & Linden, A. (2012). Women in extreme right parties and movements: A comparison of the Netherlands and the United States. In K. M. Blee & S. M. Deutsch (Eds.),

Women of the right: Comparisons and interplay across borders (pp. 98–114). Penn State University Press.

Blee, K., & McDowell, A. (2013). The duality of spectacle and secrecy: A case study of fraternalism in the 1920s US Ku Klux Klan. *Ethnic and Racial Studies, 36*(2), 249–265.

Blee, K. M., & Yates, E. A. (2015). The place of race in conservative and far-right movements. *Sociology of Race and Ethnicity, 1*(1), 127–136.

Bliuc, A. M., Faulkner, N., Jakubowicz, A., & McGarty, C. (2018). Online networks of racial hate: A systematic review of 10 years of research on cyber-racism. *Computers in Human Behavior, 87*, 75–86.

Bloch, S. (2019a). Broken windows ideology and the (mis)reading of graffiti. *Critical Criminology.* doi: 10.1007/s10612-019-09444-w

Bloch, S. (2019b). *Going all city.* University of Chicago Press.

Bloom, J., & Martin, W. E. (2016). *Black against empire: The history and politics of the Black Panther Party.* University of California Press.

Bogerts, L., & Fielitz, M. (2019). Do you want meme war? In M. Fielitz & N. Thurston (Eds.), *Post-digital cultures of the far right: Online actions and offline consequences in Europe and the US.* Transcript Verlag.

Boggess, L. N. (2012). It is not always black and white: An examination of black and Latino intergroup violence. *Criminal Justice Review, 37*(3), 319–336.

Boghani, P. (2016, March 18). *"Deradicalization" is coming to America. Does it work?* Retrieved October 28, 2019, from PBS *Frontline.* https://www.pbs.org/wgbh/frontline/article/deradicalization-is-coming-to-america-does-it-work/

Bogost, I. (2019, February 11). Emoji don't mean what they used to. Retrieved October 27, 2019, from *The Atlantic.* https://www.theatlantic.com/technology/archive/2019/02/how-new-emoji-are-changing-pictorial-language/582400/

Bokhari, A., & Yiannopoulos, M. (2016). An establishment conservative's guide to the alt-right. *Breitbart.* Accessed May 28, 2019. http://www.breitbart.com/tech/2016/03/29/an-establishment-conservatives-guide-to-the-alt-right/

Bolden, C. L. (2012). Liquid soldiers: Fluidity and gang membership. *Deviant Behavior, 33*(3), 207–222.

Bolden, C. L. (2014). Friendly foes: Hybrid gangs or social networking. *Group Processes & Intergroup Relations, 17*(6), 730–749.

Boman, J. H. (2016). Do birds of a feather really flock together? Friendships, self-control similarity and deviant behaviour. *British Journal of Criminology, 57*(5), 1208–1229.

Bonilla-Silva, E. (2015). The structure of racism in color-blind, "post-racial" America. *American Behavioral Scientist, 59*(11), 1358–1376.

Borgeson, K. (2003). Culture and identity among skinhead women. *Michigan Sociological Review, 17*, 99–118.

Borgeson, K., & Valeri, R. (2005). Examining differences in skinhead ideology and culture through an analysis of skinhead websites. *Michigan Sociological Review, 19*, 45–62.

Borgeson, K., & Valeri, R. (2018). *Skinhead history, identity, and culture.* Routledge.

Bowman, E., & Stewart, I. (2017, August 20). *The women behind the "alt-right."* Retrieved April 29, 2019, from NPR. https://www.npr.org/2017/08/20/544134546/the-women-behind-the-alt-right

Bowman-Grieve, L. (2009). Exploring "Stormfront": A virtual community of the radical right. *Studies in Conflict & Terrorism*, *32*(11), 989–1007.

Braga, A. A., Papachristos, A. V., & Hureau, D. M. (2014). The effects of hot spots policing on crime: An updated systematic review and meta-analysis. *Justice Quarterly*, *31*(4), 633–663.

Braga, A. A., Weisburd, D., & Turchan, B. (2019). Focused deterrence strategies effects on crime: A systematic review. *Campbell Systematic Reviews*, *15*(3), 1–65.

Braga, A. A., Zimmerman, G., Barao, L., Farrell, C., Brunson, R. K., & Papachristos, A. V. (2019). Street gangs, gun violence, and focused deterrence: Comparing place-based and group-based evaluation methods to estimate direct and spillover deterrent effects. *Journal of Research in Crime and Delinquency*. doi: 0022427818821716.

Brake, M. (1974). The skinheads: An English working class subculture. *Youth & Society*, *6*(2), 179–200.

Branas, C. C., South, E., Kondo, M. C., Hohl, B. C., Bourgois, P., Wiebe, D. J., & MacDonald, J. M. (2018). Citywide cluster randomized trial to restore blighted vacant land and its effects on violence, crime, and fear. *Proceedings of the National Academy of Sciences*, *115*(12), 2946–2951.

Brantingham, P. J., Tita, G. E., Short, M. B., & Reid, S. E. (2012). The ecology of gang territorial boundaries. *Criminology*, *50*(3), 851–885.

Brantingham, P. J., Valasik, M., & Tita, G. E. (2019). Competitive dominance, gang size and the directionality of gang violence. *Crime Science*, *8*(1), 1–20.

Bromwich, J. E. (2018, June 8). What is Atomwaffen? A neo-Nazi group, linked to multiple murders. Retrieved May 28, 2019, from *The New York Times*. https://www.nytimes.com /2018/02/12/us/what-is-atomwaffen.html

Brosseau, C. (2016, November 4). *Who's on Portland's gang list?* Retrieved May 28, 2019, from Oregon Live. https://www.oregonlive.com/portland/2016/11/at_least_i_was_on _some_kind_of.html

Brotherton, D. C., & Barrios, L. (2004). *The Almighty Latin King and Queen Nation: Street politics and the transformation of a New York City Gang*. Columbia University Press.

Brown, D. L. (2017, June 7). When Portland banned blacks: Oregon's shameful history as an "all-white" state. Retrieved May 28, 2019, from *Washington Post*: https://www .washingtonpost.com/news/retropolis/wp/2017/06/07/when-portland-banned-blacks -oregons-shameful-history-as-an-all-white-state/

Brown, G. C., Vigil, J. D., & Taylor, E. R. (2012). The ghettoization of blacks in Los Angeles: The emergence of street gangs. *Journal of African American Studies*, *16*(2), 209–225.

Brown, T. S. (2004). Subcultures, pop music and politics: Skinheads and "Nazi rock" in England and Germany. *Journal of Social History*, *38*(1), 157–178.

Brown, W. K. (1977). Black female gangs in Philadelphia. *International Journal of Offender Therapy and Comparative Criminology*, *21*(3), 221–228.

Bruneau, T., Dammert, L., & Skinner, E. (2011). *Maras: Gang violence and security in Central America*. University of Texas Press.

Bubolz, B. F., & Simi, P. (2015). Leaving the world of hate: Life-course transitions and self-change. *American Behavioral Scientist*, *59*(12), 1588–1608.

Burke, M. (2018, October 22). *Three more Proud Boys members arrested for violent Manhattan fight*. Retrieved December 11, 2018, from NBC News: https://www.nbcnews.com /news/us-news/three-more-proud-boys-members-arrested-violent-manhattan-fight -n922946.

Bullock, P., & Kerry, E. (2017). Trumpwave and fashwave are just the latest disturbing examples of the far-right appropriating electronic music. Retrieved May 28, 2019, from VICE: https://www.vice.com/en_us/article/mgwk7b/trumpwave-fashwave-far-right -appropriation-vaporwave-synthwave.

Burlein, A. (2002). *Lift high the cross: Where white supremacy and the Christian right converge*. Duke University Press

Burley, S. [@Shane_Burley] (2018, June 30). *Proud Boys were openly saying they were going to attack protesters. They just rushed the protesters when they got a chance. Brutal attack, 50 Proud Boys at least right at the front. Police lines let them through and watched.* [Tweet]. Twitter. https://twitter.com/shane_burley1/status/1013247053797867521

Burris, V., Smith, E., & Strahm, A. (2000). White supremacist networks on the internet. *Sociological Focus, 33*(2), 215–235.

Came, B. (1989, January 23). A growing menace: Violent skinheads are raising urban fears. *Maclean's*, 43–44.

Campbell, Andy. (2018, November 26). *The Proud Boys are imploding*. Retrieved April 23, 2019, from HuffPost. https://www.huffpost.com/entry/the-proud-boys-are-imploding _n_5bfc16dde4boeb6d9311e26d

Campbell, Andy. (2019, August 20). *The right, desperate to deflect its own extremism, cries "Antifa."* Retrieved October 20, 2019, from HuffPost. https://www.huffpost.com/entry/stuck -with-extremism-the-right-overreaches-to-blame-antifa_n_5d5bf7f4e4bof667ed68bbe9

Campbell, Anne. (1984). The girls in the gang. *New Society, 69*(1135), 308–311.

Campuzano, E. (2018, August 8). *I'm the reporter you saw bleeding at the Portland protests; here's my story*. Retrieved May 18, 2019, from Oregonlive. https://www.oregonlive.com /opinion/2018/08/im_the_reporter_you_saw_bleeding_at_portland_protests.html

Capatides, C. (2017, October 29). *Portland's racist past smolders beneath the surface*. Retrieved April 24, 2019, from CBS News. https://www.cbsnews.com/news/portland-race -against-the-past-white-supremacy/

Caren, N., Jowers, K., & Gaby, S. (2012, May 22). A social movement online community: Stormfront and the white nationalist movement. In *Media, Movements, and Political Change* (pp. 163–193). Emerald Group Publishing Limited.

Carmody, J. (1988, November 4). Geraldo Rivera injured in melee during taping. Retrieved May 28, 2019, from *Washington Post*. https://www.washingtonpost.com/archive /lifestyle/1988/11/04/geraldo-rivera-injured-in-melee-during-taping/14166cd2-bc3d -4871-9a97-2dc3a23bc2f3/

Carr, R., Slothower, M., & Parkinson, J. (2017). Do gang injunctions reduce violent crime? Four tests in Merseyside, UK. *Cambridge Journal of Evidence-Based Policing, 1*(4), 195–210.

Carson, D. C., Peterson, D., & Esbensen, F. A. (2013). Youth gang desistance: An examination of the effect of different operational definitions of desistance on the motivations, methods, and consequences associated with leaving the gang. *Criminal Justice Review*, *38*(4), 510–534.

Cartwright, D. S., & Howard, K. I. (1966). Multivariate analysis of gang delinquency: I. Ecologic influences. *Multivariate Behavioral Research*, *1*(3), 321–371.

Caspi, D. J., Freilich, J. D., & Chermak, S. M. (2012). Worst of the bad: Violent white supremacist groups and lethality. *Dynamics of Asymmetric Conflict*, *5*(1), 1–17.

Castle, T. (2012). Morrigan rising: Exploring female-targeted propaganda on hate group websites. *European Journal of Cultural Studies*, *15*(6), 679–694.

Castle, T., & Parsons, T. (2019). Vigilante or Viking? Contesting the mediated constructions of Soldiers of Odin Norge. *Crime, Media, Culture*, *15*(1), 47–66.

Cauterucci, C. (2017, July 10). Menswear company Fred Perry forced to denounce skinheads and alt-right bigots who love golf shirts. Retrieved April 23, 2019, from *Slate*. https://slate.com/human-interest/2017/07/fred-perry-forced-to-denounce-skinheads -and-alt-right-bigots-who-love-golf-shirts.html

Chalmers, D. M. (1987). *Hooded Americanism: The history of the Ku Klux Klan* (3rd ed.). Duke University Press.

Chaskin, R. J. (2010). *Youth gangs and community intervention: Research, practice, and evidence*. Columbia University Press.

Chermak, S. M., Freilich, J. D., & Simone, J. (2010). Surveying American state police agencies about lone wolves, far-right criminality, and far-right and Islamic jihadist criminal collaboration. *Studies in Conflict & Terrorism*, *33*(11), 1019–1041.

Chermak, S. M., Freilich, J. D., & Shemtob, Z. (2009). Law enforcement training and the domestic far right. *Criminal Justice and Behavior*, *36*(12), 1305–1322.

Chesney-Lind, M., & Hagedorn, J. M. (1999). Female gangs in America: Essays on girls, gangs and gender. Lake View Press.

Chin, K. (1996). *Chinatown gangs: Extortion, enterprise, and ethnicity*. Oxford University Press.

Christensen, L. W. (1994). *Skinhead street gangs*. Paladin Press.

Chroust, P. (2000). Neo-Nazis and Taliban on-line: Anti-modern political movements and modern media. *Democratization*, *7*(1), 102–118.

Clarke, J. (1976). The skinheads and the magical recovery of community. In S. Hall & T. Jefferson (Eds.), *Resistance through rituals: Youth subcultures in post-war Britain* (pp. 99– 102). Routledge.

CNN. (2016). *Gingrich, Camerota debate crime stats* [Video]. Retrieved from https://www .cnn.com/videos/tv/2016/12/01/gingrich-camerota-crime-stats-newday.cnn

CNN. (2019). *Fox's Tucker Carlson calls white supremacy problem a hoax* [Video]. Retrieved from YouTube. https://www.youtube.com/watch?v=GfAqQeXYPOM

Coaston, J. (2018a, August 1). #QAnon, the scarily popular pro-Trump conspiracy theory, explained. Retrieved December 11, 2018, from Vox. https://www.vox.com/policy-and -politics/2018/8/1/17253444/qanon-trump-conspiracy-theory-reddit

Coaston, J. (2018b, October 2). *4 members of an alt-right "fight club" charged with inciting a riot in Charlottesville*. Retrieved December 11, 2018, from Vox: https://www.vox .com/2018/10/2/17928174/charlottesville-unite-the-right-alt-right-violence-federal -charges

Coaston, J. (2019, April 26). *Trump's new defense of his Charlottesville comments is incredibly false*. Retrieved May 28, 2019, from Vox. https://www.vox.com/2019/4/26/18517980/trump-unite-the-right-racism-defense-charlottesville

Cohan, W. D. (2017, May 30). How Stephen Miller rode white rage from Duke's campus to Trump's West Wing. Retrieved April 25, 2019, from *Vanity Fair*. https://www.vanityfair.com/news/2017/05/stephen-miller-duke-donald-trump

Cohen, B. (2019). (((Multiple parentheses))) and burning flags: Antisemitism and media coverage of the 2016 American presidential election. *European Journal of Current Legal Issues*, 25(1).

Cohen-Almagor, R. (2013). Internet history. In R. Luppicini (Ed.), *Moral, ethical, and social dilemmas in the age of technology: Theories and practice*, 19–39. IGI Global.

Collins, K., & Roose, K. (2018, November 4). Tracing a meme from the internet's fringe to a Republican slogan. Retrieved December 11, 2018, from *The New York Times*. https://www.nytimes.com/interactive/2018/11/04/technology/jobs-not-mobs.html

Colson, N. (2018, April 17). *A new far-right threat crystallizes*. Retrieved May 28, 2019, from SocialistWorker.org. http://socialistworker.org/2018/04/17/a-new-far-right-threat-crystallizes

Conti, A., & Cooper, W. (2018, February 12). *Learn to spot the secret signals of far-right fashion*. Retrieved May 28, 2019, from VICE. https://www.vice.com/en_us/article/59wjq8/learn-to-spot-the-secret-signals-of-far-right-fashion

Cooter, A. (2011). Neo-Nazi nationalism. *Studies in Ethnicity and Nationalism*, 11(3), 365–383.

Cooter, A. B. (2006). Neo-Nazi normalization: The skinhead movement and integration into normative structures. *Sociological Inquiry*, 76(2), 145–165.

Coplon, J. (1988, December 1). Skinhead nation. *Rolling Stone*, 54.

Coppins, M. (2018, May 28). Trump's right-hand troll. Retrieved December 11, 2018, from *The Atlantic*. https://www.theatlantic.com/politics/archive/2018/05/stephen-miller-trump-adviser/561317/

Corb, A. (2011). *Into the minds of mayhem: White supremacy, recruitment and the internet*. Report commissioned by Google Ideas.

Corb, A., & Grozelle, R. (2014). A new kind of terror: Radicalizing youth in Canada. *Journal Exit-Deutschland*, 1(0), 32–58.

Corte, U., & Edwards, B. (2008). White power music and the mobilization of racist social movements. *Music and Arts in Action*, 1(1), 4–20.

Cosgrove, J. (2018, July 17). Must reads: The Proud Boys walk into a bar. A fight breaks out. Now a Los Angeles bar deals with the consequences. Retrieved May 18, 2019, from *Los Angeles Times*. https://www.latimes.com/local/lanow/la-me-ln-proud-boys-bar-20180717-story.html

Costello, M., Barrett-Fox, R., Bernatzky, C., Hawdon, J., & Mendes, K. (2018). Predictors of viewing online extremism among America's youth. *Youth & Society*. doi: 0044118X18768115.

Costello, M., & Hawdon, J. (2018). Who are the online extremists among us? Sociodemographic characteristics, social networking, and online experiences of those who produce online hate materials. *Violence and Gender*, 5(1), 55–60.

Cotter, J. M. (1999). Sounds of hate: White power rock and roll and the neo-Nazi skinhead subculture. *Terrorism and Political Violence*, 11(2), 111–140.

Coutts, S. (2017, August 28). *How hate goes "mainstream": Gavin McInnes and the Proud Boys*. Retrieved May 28, 2019, from Rewire.News. https://rewire.news/article/2017/08/28/hate-goes-mainstream-gavin-mcinnes-proud-boys/

Craig, W. M., Vitaro, F., Gagnon, L., & Tremblay, R. E. (2002). The road to gang membership: characteristics of male gang and nongang members from ages 10 to 14. *Social Development, 11*(1), 53–68.

Crew, D. O. (2003). *Ku Klux Klan sheet music: An illustrated catalogue of published music, 1867–2002*. McFarland.

Cristofaro, E. D. (2018, December 12). *Memes are taking the alt-right's message of hate mainstream*. Retrieved May 28, 2019, from The Conversation. http://theconversation.com/memes-are-taking-the-alt-rights-message-of-hate-mainstream-108196

Crofts, T. (2011). The law and (anti-social behaviour) order campaign in Western Australia. *Current Issues in Criminal Justice, 22*(3), 399–414.

Crosbie, J. (2018, November 28). *The Proud Boys just accidentally doxxed their new "elders."* Retrieved April 23, 2019, from Splinter. https://splinternews.com/proud-boys-failed-to-redact-their-new-dumb-bylaws-and-a-1830700905

Crothers, L. (2019). *Rage on the right: The American militia movement from Ruby Ridge to the Trump presidency*. Rowman & Littlefield.

Cruz, J. M. (2010). Central American Maras: From youth street gangs to transnational protection rackets. *Global Crime, 11*(4), 379–398.

Cunningham, D. (2013). *Klansville, U.S.A.: The rise and fall of the civil rights-era Ku Klux Klan*. Oxford University Press.

Cunningham, K. J. (2003). Cross-regional trends in female terrorism. *Studies in Conflict & Terrorism, 26*(3), 171–195.

Cureton, S. R. (2009). Something wicked this way comes: A historical account of black gangsterism offers wisdom and warning for African American leadership. *Journal of Black Studies, 40*(2), 347–361.

Cureton, S. R. (2011). *Black vanguards and black gangsters: From seeds of discontent to a declaration of war*. University Press of America.

Curry, G. D. (2000). Self-reported gang involvement and officially recorded delinquency. *Criminology, 38*(4), 1253–1274.

Curry, G. D. (2011). Gangs, crime, and terrorism. In B. Forst, J. R. Greene & J. P. Lynch (Eds.), *Criminologists on Terrorism and Homeland Security* (pp. 97–112). Cambridge University Press.

Curry, G. D. (2015). The logic of defining gangs revisited. In S. H. Decker & D. Pyrooz (Eds.). *The handbook of gangs* (pp. 7–27). Wiley.

Curry, G. D., & Decker, S. H. (1998). *Confronting gangs: Crime and community*. Roxbury.

Curry, G. D., Decker, S. H., & Pyrooz, D. (2014). *Confronting gangs: Crime and community* (3rd ed.). Oxford University Press.

Dandurand, Y. (2015). Social inclusion programmes for youth and the prevention of violent extremism. In M. Lombardi et al. (Eds.), *Countering radicalisation and violent extremism among youth to prevent terrorism* (pp. 23–36). IOS Press.

Daniels, J. (2009a). Cloaked websites: Propaganda, cyber-racism and epistemology in the digital era. *New Media & Society, 11*(5), 659–683.

Daniels, J. (2009b). *Cyber racism: White supremacy online and the new attack on civil rights.* Rowman & Littlefield.

Daniels, J. (2013). Race and racism in internet studies: A review and critique. *New Media & Society, 15*(5), 695–719.

Daniels, J. (2018). The algorithmic rise of the "alt-right." *Contexts, 17*(1), 60–65.

Daniels, J., & LaLone, N. (2012). Racism in video gaming: Connecting extremist and mainstream expressions of white supremacy. In D. G. Embrick, T. J. Wright & A. Lucacs (Eds.), *Social exclusion, power, and video game play: New research in digital media and technology* (pp. 85–100). Lexington Books.

Darby, S. (2017, September). The rise of the Valkyries. *Harper's Magazine.* Retrieved December 11, 2018, from Harpers: https://harpers.org/archive/2017/09/the-rise-of-the-valkyries/

Darmstadt, A., Prinz, M., & Saal, O. (2019). *The murder of Keira: Misinformation and hate speech as far-right online strategies.* In M. Fielitz & N. Thurston (Eds.), *Post-digital cultures of the far right: Online actions and offline consequences in Europe and the US* (pp. 155–168). Transcript Verlag.

Dawkins, R. (1976). *The selfish gene* (4th ed.). Oxford University Press.

De Waele, M., & Pauwels, L. (2016). Why do Flemish youth participate in right-wing disruptive groups? In *Gang transitions and transformations in an international context* (pp. 173–200). Springer International Publishing.

Décary-Hétu, D., & Morselli, C. (2011). Gang presence in social network sites. *International Journal of Cyber Criminology, 5*(2).

Decker, S. H. (1996). Collective and normative features of gang violence. *Justice Quarterly, 13*(2), 243–264.

Decker, S. H. (2003). *Policing gangs and youth violence: Where do we stand. Where Do we go from here.* Wadsworth.

Decker, S. H., & Curry, G. D. (2002). Gangs, gang homicides, and gang loyalty: Organized crimes or disorganized criminals. *Journal of Criminal Justice, 30*(4), 343–352.

Decker, S. H., & Pyrooz, D. (2010). Gang violence worldwide: Context, culture, and country. In *Small arms survey 2010* (pp. 129–155). Cambridge University Press.

Decker, S. H., & Pyrooz, D. (2011). Gangs, terrorism, and radicalization. *Journal of Strategic Security, 4*(4), 151–166.

Decker, S. H., & Pyrooz, D. C. (2015a). "I'm down for a jihad": How 100 years of gang research can inform the study of terrorism, radicalization and extremism. *Perspectives on Terrorism, 9*(1), 104–112.

Decker, S. H., & Pyrooz, D. C. (2015b). *The handbook of gangs.* John Wiley & Sons.

Decker, S. H., Pyrooz, D. C., Sweeten, G., & Moule, R. K. (2014). Validating self-nomination in gang research: Assessing differences in gang embeddedness across non-, current, and former gang members. *Journal of Quantitative Criminology, 30*(4), 577–598.

Decker, S. H., & Van Winkle, B. (1994). "Slinging dope": The role of gangs and gang members in drug sales. *Justice Quarterly, 11*(4), 583–604.

Decker, S. H., & Van Winkle, B. (1996). *Life in the gang: Family, friends and violence.* Cambridge University Press.

Decker, S. H., & Weerman, F. (2005). *European street gangs and troublesome youth groups.* AltaMira Press.

DeCook, J. R. (2018). Memes and symbolic violence: #Proudboys and the use of memes for propaganda and the construction of collective identity. *Learning, Media and Technology, 43*(4), 485–504.

Dekleva, B. (2001). Gang-like groups in Slovenia. In Malcolm W. Klein, H. J. Kerner, C. L. Maxson & E. G. M. Weitekamp (Eds.), *The Eurogang Paradox: Street Gangs and Youth Groups in the U.S. and Europe* (pp. 273–281). Springer.

Delaney, T. (2014). *American street gangs* (2nd ed.). Pearson.

Densley, J. (2013). *How gangs work: An ethnography of youth violence.* Palgrave.

Densley, J., McLean, R., Deuchar, R., & Harding, S. (2018). An altered state? Emergent changes to illicit drug markets and distribution networks in Scotland. *International Journal of Drug Policy, 58*, 113–120.

Densley, J. A., & Pyrooz, D. C. (2019a). A signaling perspective on disengagement from gangs. *Justice Quarterly, 36*(1), 268–283.

Densley, J., & Pyrooz, D. (2019b). The Matrix in context: Taking stock of police gang databases in London and beyond. *Youth Justice.* doi: 10.1177/1473225419883706

Department of Justice. (2019, February 12). Multiple white supremacist gang members among 54 defendants charged in RICO indictment. Retrieved May 18, 2019, from https://www.justice.gov/opa/pr/multiple-white-supremacist-gang-members-among -54-defendants-charged-rico-indictment

Deuchar, R., Harding, S., McLean, R., & Densley, J. A. (2018). Deficit or credit? A comparative, qualitative study of gender agency and female gang membership in Los Angeles and Glasgow. *Crime & Delinquency.* doi: 0011128718794192.

Dickson, E. J. (2019, August 15). Are the Proud Boys done or are they just getting started? Retrieved October 31, 2019, from *Rolling Stone.* https://www.rollingstone.com/culture /culture-features/proud-boys-antifa-attack-trump-rally-2020-election-862538/

Dignam, P. A., & Rohlinger, D. A. (2019). Misogynistic men online: How the red pill helped elect Trump. *Signs: Journal of Women in Culture and Society, 44*(3), 589–612.

Disser, N. (2016, July 28). *Gavin McInnes and his 'Proud Boys' want to make men great again.* Retrieved December 11, 2018, from Bedford + Bowery. https://web.archive.org /web/20190309220550/https://bedfordandbowery.com/2016/07/gavin-mcinnes-and -his-proud-boys-want-to-make-white-men-great-again/

Dobratz, B. A., & Shanks-Meile, S. L. (2000). *The white separatist movement in the United States.* Johns Hopkins University Press

Dobratz, B. A., & Shanks-Meile, S. L. (2006). The strategy of white separatism. *Journal of Political and Military Sociology, 34*(1), 49–80.

Dobratz, B. A., & Waldner, L. K. (2006). In search of understanding the white power movement: An introduction. *Journal of Political and Military Sociology; DeKalb, 34*(1), 1–9.

Dobratz, B., & Waldner, L. (2012). Repertoires of contention: White separatist views on the use of violence and leaderless resistance. *Mobilization: An International Quarterly, 17*(1), 49–66.

Donovan, J., Lewis, B., Friedberg, B., Fielitz, M., & Thurston, N. (2019). Parallel ports: Sociotechnical change from the alt-right to alt-tech. In M. Fielitz & N. Thurston (Eds.), *Post-digital cultures of the far right: Online actions and offline consequences in Europe and the US* (pp. 49–66). Transcript Verlag.

Dorais, M., & Corriveau, P. (2009). *Gangs and girls: Understanding juvenile prostitution.* McGill-Queen's University Press.

Downs, C. (2016, November 16). For white nationalists, Trump win a dream come true, says alt-right leader from Dallas. Retrieved December 11, 2018, from *Dallas News.* https://www.dallasnews.com/news/politics/2016/11/16/for-white-nationalists-trump-win-a-dream-come-true-says-alt-right-leader-from-dallas/

Drabble, J. (2007). From white supremacy to white power: The FBI, Cointelpro-white hate, and the Nazification of the Ku Klux Klan in the 1970s. *American Studies, 48*(3), 49.

Druxes, H. (2015). Manipulating the media: The German new right's virtual and violent identities. In: P. A. Simpson and H. Druxes (Eds.), *Digital media strategies of the far right in Europe and the United States* (pp. 123–139). Lexington Books.

Du Bois, W. E. B. (1935). *Black reconstruction: An essay toward a history of the part which black folk played in the attempt to reconstruct democracy in America, 1860–1880.* Harcourt, Brace.

Duane, D. (2019, September 28). The long, strange tale of California's surf Nazis. Retrieved October 31, 2019, from *The New York Times.* https://www.nytimes.com/2019/09/28/opinion/sunday/surf-racism.html

Duckitt, J., & Sibley, C. G. (2010). Right-wing authoritarianism and social dominance orientation differentially moderate intergroup effects on prejudice. *European Journal of Personality, 24*(7), 583–601.

Duggan, P. (2018, October 2). Four alleged members of hate group charged in 2017 "Unite the Right" rally in Charlottesville. Retrieved December 11, 2018, from *Washington Post.* https://www.washingtonpost.com/local/public-safety/federal-officials-to-announce-additional-charges-in-2017-unite-the-right-rally-in-charlottesville/2018/10/02/60881262-c651-11e8-9b1c-a90f1daae309_story.html

Dumke, M. (2018a, April 20). *Chicago's gang database isn't just about gangs.* Retrieved May 18, 2019, from ProPublica. https://www.propublica.org/article/chicago-gang-database-is-not-just-about-gangs

Dumke, M. (2018b, July 19). *Like Chicago police, Cook County and Illinois officials track thousands of people in gang databases.* Retrieved May 18, 2019, from ProPublica. https://www.propublica.org/article/politic-il-insider-additional-gang-databases-illinois-cook-county

Dunbar, A., & Kubrin, C. E. (2018). Imagining violent criminals: An experimental investigation of music stereotypes and character judgments. *Journal of Experimental Criminology, 14*(4), 507–528.

Dunbar, A., Kubrin, C. E., & Scurich, N. (2016). The threatening nature of "rap" music. *Psychology, Public Policy, and Law, 22*(3), 280–292.

Durán, R. J. (2009). The core ideals of the Mexican American gang living the presentation of defiance. *Aztlan: A Journal of Chicano Studies, 34*(2), 99–134.

Durán, R. J. (2013). *Gang life in two cities: An insiders journey.* Columbia University Press.

Dyck, K. (2017). *Reichsrock: The international web of white-power and neo-Nazi hate music.* Rutgers University Press.

Dyson-Hudson, R., & Smith, E. A. (1978). Human territoriality: An ecological reassessment. *American Anthropologist, 80*(1), 21–41.

Eatwell, R. (2018). Charisma and the radical right. In J. Rydgren (Ed.), *The Oxford handbook of the radical right* (pp. 251–268). Oxford University Press.

Ehrenreich, E. (2007). *The Nazi ancestral proof.* Indiana University Press.

Ellinas, A. (2018). Media and the radical right. In J. Rydgren (Ed.), *The Oxford handbook of the radical right.* Oxford University Press.

Ellis, E. G. (2018). The alt-right are savvy internet users. Stop letting them surprise you. Retrieved May 28, 2019, from *Wired.* https://www.wired.com/story/alt-right-youtube -savvy-data-and-society/

Enloe, C., Graff, A., Kapur, R., & Walters, S. D. (2019). Ask a feminist: Gender and the rise of the global right. *Signs: Journal of Women in Culture and Society, 44*(3), 823–844.

Enstad, J. D. (2017). "Glory to Breivik!" The Russian far right and the 2011 Norway attacks. *Terrorism and Political Violence, 29*(5), 773–792.

Esbensen, F.-A., & Carson, D. C. (2012). Who are the gangsters? An examination of the age, race/ethnicity, sex, and immigration status of self-reported gang members in a seven-city study of American youth. *Journal of Contemporary Criminal Justice, 28*(4), 465–481.

Esbensen, F.-A., & Maxson, C. L. (2011). *Youth gangs in international perspective: Results from the Eurogang program of research.* Springer Science & Business Media.

Esbensen, F.-A., & Maxson, C. L. (2018). The Eurogang program of research. In *Oxford research encyclopedia of criminology and criminal justice.* https://doi.org/10.1093/acrefore /9780190264079.013.421

Esbensen, F.-A., & Osgood, D. W. (1999). Gang resistance education and training (GREAT): results from the national evaluation. *Journal of Research in Crime and Delinquency, 36*(2), 194–225.

Esbensen, F.-A., Osgood, D. W., Peterson, D., Taylor, T. J., & Carson, D. C. (2013). Short- and long-term outcome results from a multisite evaluation of the G.R.E.A.T. program. *Criminology & Public Policy, 12*(3), 375–411.

Esbensen, F.-A., Osgood, D. W., Taylor, T. J., Peterson, D., & Freng, A. (2001). How great is G.R.E.A.T.? Results from a longitudinal quasi-experimental design. *Criminology & Public Policy, 1*(1), 87–118.

Esbensen, F.-A., Peterson, D., Taylor, T. J., & Freng, A. (2010). *Youth violence: Understanding the role of sex, race/ethnicity, and gang membership.* Temple University Press.

Esbensen, F.-A., Peterson, D., Taylor, T. J., Freng, A., Osgood, D. W., Carson, D. C., & Matsuda, K. N. (2011). Evaluation and evolution of the gang resistance education and training (G.R.E.A.T.) program. *Journal of School Violence, 10*(1), 53–70.

Esbensen, F.-A., Peterson, D., Taylor, T. J., & Osgood, D. W. (2012). Results from a multi-site evaluation of the G.R.E.A.T. program. *Justice Quarterly, 29*(1), 125–151.

Esbensen, F.-A., Tibbetts, S. G., & Gaines, L. K. (2004). *American youth gangs at the millennium.* Waveland Press.

Esbensen, F.-A., & Tusinski, K. (2007). Youth gangs in the print media. *Journal of Criminal Justice and Popular Culture, 14*(1), 21–38.

Esbensen, F.-A., & Winfree, L. T. (1998). Race and gender differences between gang and nongang youths: Results from a multisite survey. *Justice Quarterly, 15*(3), 505–526.

Esbensen, F.-A., Winfree, L. T., He, N., & Taylor, T. J. (2001). Youth gangs and definitional issues: When is a gang a gang, and why does it matter? *Crime & Delinquency, 47*(1), 105–130.

Esposito, L. (2019). *The alt-right as a revolt against neoliberalism and political correctness: The role of collective action frames. Perspectives on Global Development and Technology, 18*(1–2), 93–11. https://doi.org/10.1163/15691497-12341507

Etter, G. W. (1999). Skinheads: Manifestations of the warrior culture of the new urban tribes. *Journal of Gang Research, 6*(3), 9–21.

Ezekiel, R. S. (1996). *Racist mind: Portraits of American neo-Nazis and Klansmen.* Penguin.

Ezekiel, R. S. (2002). An ethnographer looks at neo-Nazi and Klan groups: The racist mind revisited. *American Behavioral Scientist, 46*(1), 51–71.

Fangen, K. (1997). Separate or equal? The emergence of an all-female group in Norway's rightist underground. *Terrorism and Political Violence, 9*(3), 122–164.

Fangen, K. (1998). Right-wing skinheads: Nostalgia and binary oppositions. *Young, 6*(3), 33–49.

Farrington, D. P., Ttofi, M. M., & Coid, J. W. (2009). Development of adolescence-limited, late-onset, and persistent offenders from age 8 to age 48. *Aggressive Behavior, 35*(2), 150–163.

FBI. (2006). *White supremacist infiltration of law enforcement.* Retrieved December 11, 2018, from Federal Bureau of Investigation. http://s3.documentcloud.org/documents/402521/doc-26-white-supremacist-infiltration.pdf

FBI. (2017). *Black identity extremists likely motivated to target law enforcement officers* (p. 12). Retrieved December 11, 2018, from Federal Bureau of Investigation. https://www.documentcloud.org/documents/4067711-BIE-Redacted.html

Feagin, J. R., Vera, H., & Batur, P. (2001). *White racism: The basics.* Routledge.

Feischmidt, M., & Pulay, G. (2017). "Rocking the nation": The popular culture of neo-nationalism. *Nations and Nationalism, 23*(2), 309–326.

Felson, M. (2006). *Crime and Nature.* Sage.

Ferber, A. L. (1998). *White man falling: Race, gender, and white supremacy.* Rowman & Littlefield.

Feuer, A. (2018, October 16). Proud Boys founder: How he went from Brooklyn hipster to far-right provocateur. Retrieved December 11, 2018, from *The New York Times.* https://www.nytimes.com/2018/10/16/nyregion/proud-boys-gavin-mcinnes.html

Fielitz, M., & Thurston, N. (2019). *Post-digital cultures of the far right: Online actions and offline consequences in Europe and the US.* Transcript Verlag.

Finklestein, J., Zannettou, S., Bradlyn, B., & Blackburn, J. (2018). *A Quantitative approach to understanding online antisemitism.* Retrieved from Arxiv. http://arxiv.org/abs/1809.01644

Finn, J. E. (2019). *Fracturing the founding: How the alt-right corrupts the Constitution.* Rowman & Littlefield.

Finnegan, W. (1997, November 24). The unwanted. Retrieved May 18, 2018, from *The New Yorker:* https://www.newyorker.com/magazine/1997/12/01/the-unwanted

First Vigil. (2019). *Cases by right-wing group.* Retrieved May 18, 2019, from First Vigil. https://first-vigil.com/pages/by_group/

Fleisher, M. S. (1998). *Dead end kids: Gang girls and the boys they know.* University of Wisconsin Press.

Fleisher, M. S. (2005). Fieldwork research and social network analysis: Different methods creating complementary perspectives. *Journal of Contemporary Criminal Justice, 21*(2), 120–134.

Fleisher, M. S., & Decker, S. H. (2001). Overview of the challenge of prison gangs. *Corrections Management Quarterly, 5*(1), 1–9.

Flores, G. (2017, December 3). Massive Chicago gang database under fire: Database is racially skewed, data shows; and violates spirit of sanctuary city, advocates say. Retrieved May 28, 2019, from *Social Justice News Nexus*. http://sjnnchicago.medill.northwestern .edu/blog/2017/12/03/massive-chicago-gang-database-fire-database-racially-skewed -data-shows-violates-spirit-sanctuary-city-advocates-say/

Flynn, K., & Gerhardt, G. (1989). *The silent brotherhood: Inside America's racist underground*. Free Press.

Fong, R. S. (1990). Organizational structure of prison gangs: A Texas case study. *Federal Probation, 54*(1), 36–43.

Forbes, R., & Stampton, E. (2015). *The white nationalist skinhead movement: UK & USA 1979–1993*. Feral House.

Forscher, P. S., & Kteily, N. (2019). A psychological profile of the alt-right. *Perspectives on Psychological Science*. https://doi.org/10.1177/1745691619868208

Fortin, J. (2019, February 17). *Probe opened into police texts with right-wing activist*. Retrieved May 28, 2019, from SFGate: https://www.sfgate.com/nation/article/Probe -opened-into-police-texts-with-right-wing-13623869.php

Fox, K. A. (2017). Gangs, gender, and violent victimization. *Victims & Offenders, 12*(1), 43–70.

Francisco, J., & Martinez, E. (2003). Urban street activists: Gang and community efforts to bring peace and justice to Los Angeles neighborhoods. In *Gangs and society: Alternative perspectives* (pp. 95–115). Columbia University Press.

Fraser, A. (2013). Street habitus: Gangs, territorialism and social change in Glasgow. *Journal of Youth Studies, 16*(8), 970–985.

Fraser, A. (2017). *Gangs 7 crime: Critical alternatives*. Sage.

Freeman, A. (2017, August 30). *Milk, a symbol of neo-Nazi hate*. Retrieved April 29, 2019, from The Conversation. http://theconversation.com/milk-a-symbol-of-neo-nazi-hate -83292

Freilich, J. D., Chermak, S. M., & Caspi, D. (2009). Critical events in the life trajectories of domestic extremist white supremacist groups: A case study analysis of four violent organizations. *CAPP Criminology & Public Policy, 8*(3), 497–530.

Fremon, C. (2008). *G-dog and the homeboys: Father Greg Boyle and the gangs of East Los Angeles*. University of New Mexico Press.

Freng, A., Davis, T., McCord, K., & Roussell, A. (2012). The new American gang? Gangs in Indian country. *Journal of Contemporary Criminal Justice, 28*(4), 446–464.

Freng, A., & Winfree, L. T. Jr. (2004). Exploring race and ethnic differences in a sample of middle school gang members. In F. A. Esbensen, S. G. Tibbetts & L. K. Gaines (Eds.), *American Youth Gangs at the Millennium* (pp. 142–162). Waveland Press.

Froio, C., & Ganesh, B. (2019). The transnationalisation of far right discourse on Twitter. *European Societies, 21*(4), 513–539.

Futrell, R., & Simi, P. (2004). Free spaces, collective identity, and the persistence of U.S. white power activism. *Social Problems, 51*(1), 16–42.

Futrell, R., & Simi, P. (2017). The [un]surprising alt-right. *Contexts, 16*(2), 76.

Futrell, R., Simi, P., & Gottschalk, S. (2006). Understanding music in movements: The white power music scene. *The Sociological Quarterly, 47*(2), 275–304.

Gab. (2019a). Gab social. Retrieved October 27, 2019, from Gab Social hosted on gab.com https://gab.com/about.

Gab. (2019b). Gab social. Retrieved October 31, 2019, from Gab Social hosted on gab.com. https://gab.com/

Gambert, I., & Linné, T. (2018, April 26). *How the alt-right uses milk to promote white supremacy*. Retrieved April 29, 2019, from The Conversation. http://theconversation.com /how-the-alt-right-uses-milk-to-promote-white-supremacy-94854

Gambetta, D. (2009). *Codes of the underworld: How criminals communicate*. Princeton University Press.

Gardell, M. (2003). *Gods of the blood: The pagan revival and white separatism*. Duke University Press.

Gardell, M. (2018). Urban terror: The case of lone wolf Peter Mangs. *Terrorism and Political Violence, 30*(5), 793–811.

Garot, R. (2010). *Who you claim: Performing gang identity in school and on the streets*. New York University Press.

Garot, R., & Katz, J. (2003). Provocative looks: Gang appearance and dress codes in an inner-city alternative school. *Ethnography, 4*(3), 421–454.

Gaston, S., & Huebner, B. M. (2015). Gangs in correctional institutions. In H. Decker & D. Pyrooz (Eds.), *The handbook of gangs* (pp. 328–344). Wiley.

Gatz, M., & Klein, M. W. (1993). Europe's new gangs break American pattern by crossing ethnic lines, commuting to turf. *Psychology International, 4*(2), 1, 10–11.

Geiling, N. (2015, February 18). How Oregon's second largest city vanished in a day. *Smithsonian*. Retrieved from https://www.smithsonianmag.com/history/vanport-oregon -how-countrys-largest-housing-project-vanished-day-180954040/

Gerstenfeld, P. B., & Grant, D. R. (2004). *Crimes of hate: Selected readings*. Sage.

Gil, D. D., & Lopez, A. F. (2017). Violent urban gangs. Main perpetrators in hate crimes. In M. Elósegui & C. Hermida (Eds.), *Racial justice, policies and courts' legal reasoning in Europe* (pp. 131–153). Springer.

Gillespie, T. (2010): The politics of "platforms." *New Media & Society, 12*(3), 347–364.

Gogarty, L. A. (2017). The art right. *Art Monthly; London* (405), 6–10.

Goodman, P. (2008). "It's just black, white, or Hispanic": An observational study of racializing moves in California's segregated prison reception centers. *Law & Society Review, 42*(4), 735–770.

Goodman, P. (2014). Race in California's prison fire camps for men: Prison politics, space, and the racialization of everyday life. *American Journal of Sociology, 120*(2), 352–394.

Goodrick-Clarke, N. (1985). *The occult roots of Nazism: The Ariosophists of Austria and Germany: 1890–1935*. The Aquarian-Press.

Goodrick-Clarke, N. (2002). *Black sun: Aryan cults, esoteric Nazism, and the politics of identity*. New York University Press

Gordon, G. (2018, December 13). American women of the far right. Retrieved April 29, 2019, from *The New York Review of Books*. https://www.nybooks.com/daily/2018/12/13 /american-women-of-the-far-right/

Gordon, L. (2018). *The second coming of the KKK: The Ku Klux Klan of the 1920s and the American political tradition*. Liveright Publishing.

Gormally, S. (2015). "I've been there, done that . . .": A study of youth gang desistance. *Youth Justice, 15*(2), 148–165.

Gottfredson, M. R., & Hirschi, T. (1990). *A general theory of crime*. Stanford University Press.

Gover, A. R., Jennings, W. G., & Tewksbury, R. (2009). Adolescent male and female gang members' experiences with violent victimization, dating violence, and sexual assault. *American Journal of Criminal Justice, 34*(1), 103–115.

Grannis, R. (2009). *From the ground up: Translating geography into community through neighbor networks*. Princeton University Press.

Grasmick, H. G., Tittle, C. R., Bursik, R. J., & Arneklev, B. J. (1993). Testing the core empirical implications of Gottfredson and Hirschi's general theory of crime. *Journal of Research in Crime and Delinquency, 30*(1), 5–29.

Gravel, J., Allison, B. A., West-Fagan, J., McBride, M., & Tita, G. E. (2018). Birds of a feather fight together: Status-enhancing violence, social distance and the emergence of homogenous gangs. *Journal of Quantitative Criminology, 34*(1), 189–219.

Gravel, J., Bouchard, M., Descormiers, K., Wong, J. S., & Morselli, C. (2013). Keeping promises: A systematic review and a new classification of gang control strategies. *Journal of Criminal Justice, 41*(4), 228–242.

Gravel, J., Wong, J. S., & Simpson, R. (2018). Getting in people's faces: On the symbiotic relationship between the media and police gang units. *Deviant Behavior, 39*(2), 257–273.

Green, D. P., Glaser, J., & Rich, A. (1998). From lynching to gay bashing: The elusive connection between economic conditions and hate crime. *Journal of Personality and Social Psychology, 75*(1), 82–92.

Green, D. P., Strolovitch, D. Z., & Wong, J. S. (1998). Defended neighborhoods, integration, and racially motivated crime. *American Journal of Sociology, 104*(2), 372–403.

Grogger, J. (2002). The effects of civil gang injunctions on reported violent crime: Evidence from Los Angeles County. *The Journal of Law & Economics, 45*(1), 69–90.

Grogger, J. (2005). What we know about gang injunctions. *Criminology & Public Policy, 4*, 637.

Gunnels, J. (2009). "A Jedi like my father before me": Social identity and the New York Comic Con. *Transformative Works and Cultures, 3*.

Gupta, A. (2017, June 8). Playing cops: *Militia member aids police in arresting protester at Portland alt-right rally*. Retrieved May 28, 2019, from The Intercept. https://theintercept .com/2017/06/08/portland-alt-right-milita-police-dhs-arrest-protester/

Gushue, K., Lee, C., Gravel, J., & Wong, J. S. (2018). Familiar gangsters: Gang Violence, brotherhood, and the media's fascination with a crime family. *Crime & Delinquency, 64*(12), 1612–1635.

Hagan, J. (1993). The social embeddedness of crime and unemployment. *Criminology, 31*(4), 465–491.

Hagedorn, J. M. (1998). Frat boys, bossmen, studs, and gentlemen: A typology of gang masculinities. In *Masculinities and violence* (pp. 152–167). Bowker, L. H. (Ed.). London: Sage Publications.

Hagedorn, J. (2008). *A world of gangs: Armed young men and gangsta culture*. University of Minnesota Press.

Hale, W. C. (2012). Extremism on the World Wide Web: A research review. *Criminal Justice Studies, 25*(4), 343–356.

Hall, A. (2017, November 26). *Controversial Proud Boys embrace "Western values," reject feminism and political correctness*. Retrieved May 28, 2019, from WisconsinWatch.

https://www.wisconsinwatch.org/2017/11/controversial-proud-boys-embrace-western-values-reject-feminism-and-political-correctness/

Hall, A. (2018, October 5). *The Proud Boys: Drinking club or misogynist movement?* Retrieved April 24, 2019, from *To the Best of Our Knowledge*, Wisconsin Public Radio. https://www.ttbook.org/interview/proud-boys-drinking-club-or-misogynist-movement

Hallsworth, S., & Young, T. (2008). Gang talk and gang talkers: A critique. *Crime, Media, Culture, 4*(2), 175–195.

Hamm, B. I. (2001). A human rights approach to development. *Human Rights Quarterly, 23*, 1005–1031.

Hamm, M. S. (1993). *American skinheads: The criminology and control of hate crime.* Westport: Praeger.

Haney-Lopez, I. (2015). *Dog whistle politics: How coded racial appeals have reinvented racism and wrecked the middle class.* Oxford University Press.

Hankes, K. (2019, July 3). *SPLC: Hate groups have long adopted symbols of U.S. history to promote white supremacy.* Retrieved October 27, 2019, from Southern Poverty Law Center. https://www.splcenter.org/news/2019/07/03/splc-hate-groups-have-long-adopted-symbols-us-history-promote-white-supremacy

Hankes, K., Janik, R., & Hayden, E. (2019, April 28). *Shooting at Poway Synagogue underscores link between internet radicalization and violence.* Retrieved May 28, 2019, from Southern Poverty Law Center website. https://www.splcenter.org/hatewatch/2019/04/28/shooting-poway-synagogue-underscores-link-between-internet-radicalization-and-violence

Hann, M. (2016, December 14). "Fashwave": Synth music co-opted by the far right. *The Guardian.* Retrieved from https://www.theguardian.com/music/musicblog/2016/dec/14/fashwave-synth-music-co-opted-by-the-far-right

Hanrahan, J. (2018, June 26). *Unravelling Atomwaffen Division.* Retrieved May 28, 2019, from Jake Hanrahan. https://medium.com/@Hanrahan/atomwaffendown-c662cb4d1aa6

Harding, S. (2014). *The street casino: Survival in violent street gangs.* Policy Press.

Harkness, G. (2013). Gangs and gangsta rap in Chicago: A microscenes perspective. *Poetics, 41*(2), 151–176.

Harmon, A. (2018, October 19). Why white supremacists are chugging milk (and why geneticists are alarmed). Retrieved May 28, 2019, from *The New York Times*: https://www.nytimes.com/2018/10/17/us/white-supremacists-science-dna.html

Harris, K. (2010). *Organized Crime in California.* California Department of Justice, Division of Law Enforcement, Bureau of Investigation and Intelligence. https://oag.ca.gov/sites/all/files/agweb/pdfs/publications/org_crime2010.pdf

Hatmaker, T. (2018, August 10). *Facebook is the recruiting tool of choice for far-right group the Proud Boys.* Retrieved April 23, 2019, from TechCrunch. http://social.techcrunch.com/2018/08/10/proud-boys-facebook-mcinnes/

Hawley, G. (2017). *Making sense of the alt-right.* Columbia University Press.

Hawley, G. (2018, August 9). *The demography of the alt-right.* Institute for Family Studies. https://ifstudies.org/blog/the-demography-of-the-alt-right

Hawley, G. (2019). *The alt-right: What everyone needs to know.* Oxford University Press.

Hayden, M. E. (2017, October 28). Antifa claims victory after alt-right pulls out of second Tennessee "White Lives Matter" rally. Retrieved October 27, 2019, from *Newsweek.*

https://www.newsweek.com/antifa-claims-victory-after-alt-right-pulls-out-second
-half-white-lives-matter-695634

Hayward, R. A., & Honegger, L. (2014). Gender differences in juvenile gang members: An exploratory study. *Journal of Evidence-Based Social Work, 11*(4), 373–382.

Hebdige, D. (1979). *Subculture: The meaning of style.* Methuen.

Heim, J. (2017, August 14). How a rally of white nationalists and supremacists at the University of Virginia turned into a "tragic, tragic weekend." Retrieved April 30, 2019, from *Washington Post.* https://www.washingtonpost.com/graphics/2017/local/charlottesville-timeline/

Heim, J. (2018, June 20). "Unite the Right" organizer gets approval for rally anniversary event in D.C. *Washington Post.* https://www.washingtonpost.com/local/education/unite-the -right-organizer-gets-approval-for-rally-anniversary-event-in-dc/2018/06/20/597a1b1a -74a7-11e8-9780-b1dd6a09b549_story.html

Helmreich, W. B. (1973). Black crusaders: The rise and fall of political gangs. *Society, 11*(1), 44–50.

Hemmingby, C., & Bjørgo, T. (2018). Terrorist target selection: The case of Anders Behring Breivik. *Perspectives on Terrorism, 12*(6), 164–176.

Hemmingsen, A. (2015). *An introduction to the Danish approach to countering and preventing extremism and radicalization.* DIIS Reports No. 2015:15. Danish Institute for International Studies.

Hermansson, P., Lawrence, D., Mulhall, J. & Murdoch, S. (2020). *The international alt-right: Fascism for the 21st century?* Routledge.

Hennigan, K. M., & Sloane, D. (2013). Improving civil gang injunctions. *Criminology & Public Policy, 12*(1), 7–41.

Hennigan, K., & Spanovic, M. (2012). Gang dynamics through the lens of social identity theory. In F. A. Esbensen & C. L. Maxson (Eds.), *Youth gangs in international perspective: Results from the Eurogang program of research* (pp. 127–149). Springer.

Hicks, W. L. (2004). Skinheads: A three nation comparison. *Journal of Gang Research, 11*, 51–74.

Hill, K. G., Howell, J. C., Hawkins, J. D., & Battin-Pearson, S. R. (1999). Childhood risk factors for adolescent gang membership: Results from the Seattle social development project. *Journal of Research in Crime and Delinquency, 36*(3), 300–322.

Hipp, J. R., Tita, G. E., & Boggess, L. N. (2009). Intergroup and intragroup violence: Is violent crime an expression of group conflict or social disorganization? *Criminology, 47*(2), 521–564. https://doi.org/10.1111/j.1745-9125.2009.00150.x

Hirschi, T., & Gottfredson, M. (1983). Age and the explanation of crime. *American Journal of Sociology, 89*(3), 552–584.

Hitler, A. ([1925] 2008). *Mein Kampf.* Samaira Book Publishers.

Hobbs, A. (2017, August 21). The US government destroyed the Ku Klux Klan once. It could do so again. Retrieved May 28, 2019, from *The Guardian.* https://www.theguardian.com /commentisfree/2017/aug/21/us-government-ku-klux-klan-charlottesville

Hochschild, A. R. (2016). *Strangers in their own land: Anger and mourning on the American right.* The New Press.

Hodge, E., & Hallgrimsdottir, H. (2019, February). Networks of hate: The alt-right, "troll culture," and the cultural geography of social movement spaces online. *Journal of Borderlands Studies,* 1–18.

Hogan, M. (2017, August 17). *Is white power music finally getting booted from the internet?* Retrieved April 29, 2019, from Pitchfork. https://pitchfork.com/thepitch/is-white -power-music-finally-getting-booted-from-the-internet/

Holt, J. (2018, November 19). *We were promised Proud Boys. Philadelphia had other ideas.* Retrieved December 11, 2018, from Right Wing Watch. https://www.rightwingwatch .org/post/we-were-promised-proud-boys-philadelphia-had-other-ideas/

Holt, T. J. (2007). Subcultural evolution? Examining the influence of on- and off-line experiences on deviant subcultures. *Deviant Behavior, 28*(2), 171–198.

Honko, L. (1972). The problem of defining myth. *Scripta Instituti Donneriani Aboensis, 6*, 7–19.

Horgan, J., Altier, M. B., Shortland, N., & Taylor, M. (2016). Walking away: The disengagement and de-radicalization of a violent right-wing extremist. *Behavioral Sciences of Terrorism and Political Aggression, 9*(2), 63–77.

Horgan, J., & Braddock, K. (2010). Rehabilitating the terrorists? Challenges in assessing the effectiveness of de-radicalization programs. *Terrorism and Political Violence,* (22), 267–291.

Horowitz, D. (1999). *Inside the klavern: The secret history of a Ku Klux Klan of the 1920s.* Southern Illinois University Press.

Horowitz, R. L. (1983). *Honor and the American dream: Culture and identity in a Chicano community.* Rutgers University Press.

Howell, J. C. (2007). Menacing or mimicking? Realities of youth gangs. *Juvenile and Family Court Journal, 58*(2), 39–50.

Howell, J. C. (2010). *Gang prevention: An overview of research and programs.* United States Office of Juvenile Justice and Delinquency Prevention. https://www.ncjrs.gov/pdffiles1 /ojjdp/231116.pdf

Howell, J. C., & Egley, A. (2005). Moving risk factors into developmental theories of gang membership. *Youth Violence and Juvenile Justice, 3*(4), 334–354.

Howell, J. C., & Griffiths, E. (2018). *Gangs in America's communities* (3rd ed.). Sage.

Howell, J. C., Starbuck, D., & Lindquist, D. J. (2001). *Hybrid and other modern gangs.* United States Office of Juvenile Justice and Delinquency Prevention.

Howell, K. B. (2011). Fear itself: The impact of allegations of gang affiliation on pre-trial detention criminal law issue. *St. Thomas Law Review,* (4), 620–660.

Howell, K. B. (2015). Gang policing: The post stop-and-frisk justification for profile-based policing. *University of Denver Criminal Law Review,* 1–32.

Howle, E. (2016). *The CalGang criminal intelligence system.* Retrieved from California State Auditor. https://www.auditor.ca.gov/pdfs/reports/2015-130.pdf

Huff, C. R. (2002). Gangs and public policy: Prevention, intervention, and suppression. In C. R. Huff (Ed.), *Gangs in America III* (pp. 287–294). Sage.

Huff, C. R., & Barrows, J. (2015). Documenting gang activity. In S. H. Decker & D. Pyrooz (Eds.), *The handbook of gangs* (pp. 59–77). Wiley.

Hughes, E. C. ([1948] 1984). The study of ethnic relations. In E. Hughes (Ed.), *The sociological eye: Selected papers* (pp. 153–58). Transaction.

Hughes, L. A. (2013). Group cohesiveness, gang member prestige, and delinquency and violence in Chicago, 1959–1962. *Criminology, 51*(4), 795–832.

Hughes, L. A., Botchkovar, E. V., & Short, J. F. (2019). "Bargaining with patriarchy" and "bad girl femininity": Relationship and behaviors among Chicago girl gangs, 1959–62. *Social Forces*.

Hughes, L. A., & Short, J. F. (2013). Partying, cruising, and hanging in the streets: Gangs, routine activities, and delinquency and violence in Chicago, 1959–1962. *Journal of Quantitative Criminology, 30*(3), 415–451.

Humphrey, S. (2019, June 28). Insecure, attention-starved right wingers are marching in Portland Saturday; Here's how to beat 'em. Retrieved October 27, 2019, from *Portland Mercury*. https://www.portlandmercury.com/blogtown/2019/06/28/26720951/insecure -attention-starved-right-wingers-are-marching-in-portland-saturday-heres-how-to -beat-em

Irwin-Rogers, K., Densley, J., & Pinkney, C. (2018). Gang violence and social media. In J. L. Ireland, C. A. Ireland & P. Birch (Eds.), *The Routledge international handbook of human aggression*. Routledge.

It's Going Down (IGD). (2018, November 15). *Republican circles embracing Proud Boys in recount fight*. Retrieved April 23, 2019, from It's Going Down. https://itsgoingdown.org /florida-proud-boys/

Jackson, P., & Gable, G. (2011). Far-right.com: Nationalist extremism on the internet. Retrieved from *Searchlight Magazine*: http://www.searchlightmagazine.com/blogs /searchlight-blog/mapping-the-far-right

Jan, T. (2017, November 16). What happens when neo-Nazis hijack your brand. Retrieved May 18, 2019, from *Washington Post*. https://www.washingtonpost.com/business /economy/what-happens-when-nazis-hijack-your-brand/2017/11/16/8871c7ba-c98f -11e7-8321-481fd63f174d_story.html

Jansyn, L. R. (1966). Solidarity and delinquency in a street corner group. *American Sociological Review, 31*(5), 600–614.

Jeffries, L. (2018). The white meme's burden: Replication and adaptation in twenty-first century white supremacist internet cultures. *Reception: Texts, Readers, Audiences, History, 10*(1), 50–73.

Jipson, A., & Becker, P. J. (2019, March 21). *White nationalism, born in the USA, is now a global terror threat*. Retrieved May 28, 2019, from WallStreetWindow.com. https:// wallstreetwindow.com/2019/03/white-nationalism-born-in-the-usa-is-now-a-global -terror-threat-jipson-and-becker-03-21-2019/

Joe, K. A., & Chesney-Lind, M. (1995). "Just every mother's angel": An analysis of gender and ethnic variations in young gang membership. *Gender & Society, 9*(4), 408–431.

Johansson, T., Andreasson, J., & Mattsson, C. (2017). From subcultures to common culture: Bodybuilders, skinheads, and the normalization of the marginal. *SAGE Open*, doi: 10.1177/2158244017706596

Johnson, D. (2019). *Hateland: A long, hard look at America's extremist heart*. Prometheus Books.

Jones, S. V. (2015). Law enforcement and white power: An FBI report unraveled. *Thurgood Marshall Law Review, 41*, 103.

Joosse, P. (2017). Leaderless resistance and the loneliness of lone wolves: Exploring the rhetorical dynamics of lone actor violence. *Terrorism and Political Violence, 29*(1), 52–78.

Kaffine, D. T. (2009). Quality and the commons: The surf gangs of California. *The Journal of Law and Economics, 52*(4), 727–743.

Kaplan, J. (1997). *Radical religion in America: Millenarian movements from the far right to the Children of Noah.* Syracuse University Press.

Kaplan, J, Weinberg, L., & Oleson, T. (2003). Dreams and realities in cyberspace: White Aryan Resistance and the World Church of the Creator. *Patterns of Prejudice, 37,* 139–156.

Katz, C. M., Webb, V. J., & Schaefer, D. R. (2000). The validity of police gang intelligence lists: Examining differences in delinquency between documented gang members and nondocumented delinquent youth. *Police Quarterly, 3*(4), 413–437.

Kavanaugh, S. D. (2018, October 13). Bear spray, bloody brawls at Patriot Prayer "law and order" march in Portland. Retrieved December 11, 2018, from *The Oregonian.* https://www.oregonlive.com/portland/2018/10/patriot_prayer_flash_march_cal.html

Keane, D. (1993). *Skinheads USA: Soldiers of the race war.* United States: Home Box Office.

Kelley, B. J. (2017, October 17). *Fashwave, the electronic music of the alt-right, is just more hateful subterfuge.* Retrieved May 28, 2019, from Southern Poverty Law Center. https://www.splcenter.org/hatewatch/2017/10/17/fashwave-electronic-music-alt-right-just-more-hateful-subterfuge

Kelly, A. (2018, June 1). The housewives of white supremacy. Retrieved May 28, 2019, *The New York Times.* https://www.nytimes.com/2018/06/01/opinion/sunday/tradwives-women-alt-right.html

Kennedy, D. M., Piehl, A. M., & Braga, A. A. (1996). Youth violence in Boston: Gun markets, serious youth offenders, and a use-reduction strategy. *Law and Contemporary Problems, 59,* 147.

Kersten, J. (2001). Groups of violent young males in Germany. In In M. W. Klein, H. J. Kerner, C. L. Maxson & E. G. M. Weitekamp (Eds.), *The Eurogang paradox: Street gangs and youth groups in the U.S. and Europe* (pp. 247–255). Springer.

Kestenbaum, S. (2018, February 1). *What is Atomwaffen Division, the Nazi group tied to the murder of Blaze Bernstein?* Retrieved April 25, 2019, from The Forward. https://forward.com/news/393099/what-is-atomwaffen-division-the-nazi-group-tied-to-the-murder-of-blaze-bern/

Kimmel, M. S. (1996). *Manhood in America: A cultural history.* Free Press.

Kimmel, M. S. (2008). *Guyland: The perilous world where boys become men.* HarperCollins.

Kimmel, M. S. (2013). *Angry white men: American masculinity at the end of an era.* Nation Books.

Kimmel, M. S. (2018). *Healing from hate.* University of California Press.

King, D. (1988, April 9). Skinheads: Aimless violence sparks a police crackdown. *The Globe and Mail,* pp. A1–A4.

Kinnes, I. (2012). Contesting police governance: Respect, authority and belonging in organised violent gangs in Cape Town. *Acta Criminologica: Southern African Journal of Criminology, 2012*(2), 31–46.

Kinsella, W. (1994). *Web of hate: Inside Canada's far right network.* Harper & Collins.

Klapsis, A. (2019). The alt-right ideology in Russia. In A. Waring (Ed.), *The new authoritarianism. Vol. 2. A risk analysis of the European alt-right phenomenon.* Ibidem-Verlag.

Klein, A. (2019). From Twitter to Charlottesville: Analyzing the fighting words between the alt-right and Antifa. *International Journal of Communication, 13,* 297–318.

Klein, M. W. (1971). *Street gangs and street workers.* Prentice-Hall.

Klein, M. W. (1995). *The American street gang. Its nature, prevalence, and control.* Oxford University Press.

Klein, M. W. (1996). Gangs in the United States and Europe. *European Journal on Criminal Policy and Research, 4*(2), 63–80.

Klein, M. W. (2001). Other gang situations in Europe. In Malcolm W. Klein, H.-J. Kerner, C. L. Maxson & E. G. M. Weitekamp (Eds.), *The Eurogang paradox: Street gangs and youth groups in the U.S. and Europe* (pp. 209–213). Springer.

Klein, M. W. (2009). *The street gangs of Euroburg: A story of research.* iUniverse.

Klein, M. W., & Crawford, L. Y. (1967). Groups, gangs, and cohesiveness. *Journal of Research in Crime and Delinquency, 4*(1), 63–75.

Klein, M. W., Kerner, H.-J., Maxson, C., & Weitekamp, E. (Eds.). (2001). *The Eurogang paradox: Street gangs and youth groups in the U.S. and Europe.* Springer.

Klein, M. W., & Maxson, C. L. (1989). Street gang violence. In N. A. Wiener & M. E. Wolfgang (Eds.), *Violent crime, violent criminals* (pp. 198–234). Sage.

Klein, M. W., & Maxson, C. L. (2006). *Street gang patterns and policies.* Oxford University Press.

Knox, G. W., Martin, B., Tromanhauser, E. D., McCurrie, T. F., & Laskey, J. A. (1995). A research note: Preliminary results of the 1995 National Prosecutor's Survey. *Journal of Gang Research, 2*(4), 59–71.

Koehler, D. (2017). *Right-wing terrorism in the 21st century: The "National Socialist Underground" and the history of terror from the far-right in Germany.* Routledge.

Kontos, L., Brotherton, D. C., & Barrios, L. (Eds.). (2003). *Gangs and society: Alternative perspectives.* Columbia University Press.

Koster, W. D., & Houtman, D. (2008). "Stormfront is like a second home to me." *Information, Communication & Society, 11*(8), 1155–1176.

Koulouris, T. (2018). Online misogyny and the alternative right: Debating the undebatable. *Feminist Media Studies, 18*(4), 750–761.

KPIX. (2017, April 27). *Heavy police presence keeps Berkeley Coulter protests peaceful.* CBS. Retrieved May 18, 2019, from https://sanfrancisco.cbslocal.com/2017/04/27/political-violence-berkeley-ann-coulter-alt-right/

Kubrin, C. E. (2005). Gangstas, thugs, and hustlas: Identity and the code of the street in rap music, *Social problems, 52*(3), 360–378. https://papers.ssrn.com/abstract=2028168

Kubrin, C. E. (2006). "I see death around the corner": Nihilism in rap music. *Sociological Perspectives, 48*(4), 433–459.

Kubrin, C. E., & Nielson, E. (2014). Rap on trial. *Race and Justice, 4*(3), 185–211.

Kubrin, C. E., & Wadsworth, T. (2003). Identifying the structural correlates of African American killings: What can we learn from data disaggregation? *Homicide Studies, 7*(1), 3–35.

Kubrin, C. E., & Weitzer, R. (2003). Retaliatory homicide: Concentrated disadvantage and neighborhood culture. *Social Problems, 50*(2), 157–180.

Kun, J., & Pulido, L. (2013). *Black and brown in Los Angeles: Beyond conflict and coalition.* University of California Press.

Kundnani, A. (2012). Radicalisation: The journey of a concept. *Race & Class, 54*(2), 3–25.

Kutner, S. (2019). Proud Boys incidents 2016–2019. Retrieved October 30, 2019, from https://www.arcgis.com/home/webmap/viewer.html?webmap=46c5dd159e984d59b636 229a55561807&extent=-146.5001,22.4863,-45.4259,57.7828

LaFree, G., & Freilich, J. D. (2018). Government policies for counteracting violent extremism. *Annual Review of Criminology, 2*(1), 383–404.

Lahey, B. B., Goodman, S. H., Waldman, I. D., Bird, H., Canino, G., Jensen, P., . . . Applegate, B. (1999). Relation of age of onset to the type and severity of child and adolescent conduct problems. *Journal of Abnormal Child Psychology, 27*(4), 247–260.

Lamoureux, M., & Makuch, B. (2018a, November 20). *Neo-Nazis are organizing secretive paramilitary training across America.* Retrieved May 28, 2019, from VICE. https:// www.vice.com/en_us/article/a3mexp/neo-nazis-are-organizing-secretive-paramilitary -training-across-america

Lamoureux, M., & Makuch, B. (2018b, June 19). *Atomwaffen, an American neo-Nazi terror group, is in Canada.* Retrieved October 20, 2019, from VICE. https://www.vice.com/en _us/article/a3a8ae/atomwaffen-an-american-neo-nazi-terror-group-is-in-canada

Landers, J. (2018, March 9). *A leaked message board shows what white supremacists think of the police.* Retrieved October 28, 2019, from Rewire.News. https://rewire.news/ article/2018/03/09/leaked-message-board-shows-white-supremacists-think-police/

Landre, R., Miller, M., & Porter, D. (1997). *Gangs: A handbook for community awareness.* Checkmark Books.

Langer, E. (2003). *A hundred little Hitlers: The death of a black man, the trial of a white racist, and the rise of the neo-Nazi movement in America.* Picador.

Laqueur, W., & Wall, C. (2018). *The future of terrorism: ISIS, al-Qaeda, and the alt-right.* St. Martin's Press.

Latif, M., Blee, K., DeMichele, M., Simi, P., & Alexander, S. (2019). Why white supremacist women become disillusioned, and why they leave. *The Sociological Quarterly,* 1–22. https://doi.org/10.1080/00380253.2019.1625733

Lauger, T. R., & Densley, J. A. (2018). Broadcasting badness: Violence, identity, and performance in the online gang rap scene. *Justice Quarterly, 35*(5), 816–841.

Lavoie, D., & Kunzelman, M. (2018, October 3). 4 men arrested in connection with violent Virginia rally. *Twin Cities.* Retrieved from https://www.twincities.com/2018/10/02 /multiple-people-arrested-over-2017-white-nationalist-rally/

Leap, J. (2012). *Jumped in: What gangs taught me about violence, drugs, love, and redemption.* Beacon Press.

Lehr, P. (2013). Still blind in the right eye? A comparison of German responses to political violence from the extreme left and the extreme right. In M. Taylor, P. M. Currie & D. Holbrook (Eds.), *Extreme right-wing political violence and terrorism* (pp. 187–221). Bloomsbury Academic.

Lennings, C. J., Amon, K. L., Brummert, H., & Lennings, N. J. (2010). Grooming for terror: The internet and young people. *Psychiatry, Psychology and Law, 17*(3), 424–437.

Leovy, J. (2015). *Ghettoside: A True Story of Murder in America.* Spiegel & Grau.

Levin, B. (2002). Cyberhate: A legal and historical analysis of extremists' use of computer networks in America. *American Behavioral Scientist, 45*(6), 958–988.

Levin, B., & Grisham, K. (2016). *Special status report: Hate crime in the United States* (20 state compilation of official data). Center for the Study of Hate & Extremism at the California State University.

Levin, B., & Nakashima, L. (2019). *Report to the nation: Illustrated almanac-decade summary: hate & extremism.* Center for the Study of Hate & Extremism. https://www.csusb .edu/sites/default/files/ALMANAC%20CSHE%20Nov.%202019_11.12.19_1130amPT _final.pdf

Levin, B., & Reitzel, J. D. (2018). *Report to the nation: Hate crimes rise in U.S. cities and counties in time of division and foreign interference.* Center for the Study of Hate & Extremism. https://www.csusb.edu/sites/default/files/2018%20Hate%20Final%20Report %205-14.pdf

Levitt, S. D., & Venkatesh, S. A. (2000). An economic analysis of a drug-selling gang's finances. *The Quarterly Journal of Economics, 115*(3), 755–789.

Lewis, K., & Papachristos, A. V. (2019). Rules of the game: Exponential random graph models of a gang homicide network. *Social Forces* soz106. https://doi.org/10.1093/sf /soz106.

Lewis, M., & Serbu, J. (1999). Kommemorating the Ku Klux Klan. *The Sociological Quarterly, 40*(1), 139–158.

Lewis, R. (2018, September 18). *Alternative influence.* Retrieved October 20, 2019, from Data & Society. https://datasociety.net/output/alternative-influence/

Ley, D., & Cybriwsky, R. A. (1974). Urban graffiti as territorial markers. *Annals of the Association of American Geographers, 64*(4), 491–505.

Liebow, E. (1967). *Tally's corner: A study of Negro streetcorner men.* Little, Brown.

Lien, I. L. (2001). The concept of honor, conflict and violent behavior among youths in Oslo. In *The Eurogang paradox: Street gangs and youth groups in the U.S. and Europe* (pp. 165–174). Springer.

Lima, C. (2019, May 2). Facebook wades deeper into censorship debate as it bans "dangerous" accounts. Retrieved May 18, 2019, from Politico. https://www.politico.com/story /2019/05/02/facebook-bans-far-right-alex-jones-1299247

Lima, L., Reis, J. C. S., Melo, P., Murai, F., Araujo, L., Vikatos, P., & Benevenuto, F. (2018). Inside the right-leaning echo chambers: Characterizing Gab, an unmoderated social system. 2018 IEEE/ACM International Conference on Advances in Social Networks Analysis and Mining (ASONAM), 515–522.

Lind, D. (2017, August 12). *Unite the Right, the violent white supremacist rally in Charlottesville, explained.* Retrieved October 27, 2019, from Vox. https://www.vox.com/2017/8/12 /16138246/charlottesville-nazi-rally-right-uva

Lombardo, P. (2011). *A century of eugenics in America.* Indiana University Press.

Longerich, P. (2012). *Holocaust: The Nazi persecution and murder of the Jews.* Oxford University Press.

Lopez, G. (2017, August 18). The radicalization of white Americans. Retrieved April 30, 2019, from Vox. https://www.vox.com/identities/2017/8/18/16151924/radicalization -white-supremacists-nazis

Lopez, R. (2017). Answering the alt-right. Retrieved October 20, 2019, from *National Affairs.* https://www.nationalaffairs.com/publications/detail/answering-the-alt-right

Lough, A. (Director) (2018). *Alt-right: Age of rage* [Video]. Gravitas Ventures.

Love, N. S. (2012). Privileged intersections: The race, class, and gender politics of Prussian Blue. *Music and Politics, 6*(1), 1–21.

Love, N. S. (2016). *Trendy fascism: White power music and the future of democracy.* State University of New York Press.

Love, N. S. (2017). Back to the future: Trendy fascism, the Trump effect, and the alt-right. *New Political Science, 39*(2), 263–268.

Lu, Y. (2019, February 23). When the alt-right loves your app. Retrieved October 28, 2019, from *New York Magazine.* http://nymag.com/intelligencer/2019/02/when-the-alt-right -loves-your-app.html

Lyman, S. M., & Scott, M. B. (1967). Territoriality: A neglected sociological dimension. *Social Problems, 15*(2), 236–249.

Lyons, M. N. (2017). *Ctrl-Alt-Delete: The origins and ideology of the alternative right.* Kersplebedeb Publishing.

Lyons, M. N. (2018). *Insurgent supremacists.* Kersplebedeb Publishing.

Maclean, N. (1994). *Behind the mask of chivalry: The making of the second Ku Klux Klan.* Oxford University Press.

Magnus, A. M., & Scott, D. W. (2020). A culture of masculinity or survival? Gendered perspectives of violence among incarcerated youth. *Deviant Behavior.* doi: 10.1080/01639625.2020.1724381

Main, T. J. (2018). *The rise of the Alt-Right.* Brookings Institution Press.

Makarenko, T. (2004). The crime-terror continuum: Tracing the interplay between transnational organised crime and terrorism. *Global Crime, 6,* 129–145.

Makuch, B., & Lamoureux, M. (2019a, August 16). *International neo-Nazi extremist group claims prior knowledge of Vegas bomb plot.* Retrieved October 20, 2019, from VICE. https://www.vice.com/en_us/article/bjwxa8/international-neo-nazi-extremist-group -claims-prior-knowledge-of-vegas-bomb-plot

Makuch, B., & Lamoureux, M. (2019b, September 17). *Neo-Nazis are glorifying Osama bin Laden.* Retrieved October 20, 2019, from VICE. https://www.vice.com/en_us/article /bjwv4a/neo-nazis-are-glorifying-osama-bin-laden

Marantz, A. (2019). *Antisocial: Online extremists, techno-utopians, and the hijacking of the American conversation.* Viking.

Marcotte, A. (2018) *Troll nation.* Hot Books.

Marcotte, A. (2019, October 8). Trolls have taken over our democracy. Silicon Valley helped. Retrieved October 27, 2019, from *Salon.* https://www.salon.com/2019/10/08 /trolls-have-taken-over-our-democracy-silicon-valley-helped/

Martinez, C. (2016). *The neighborhood has its own rules: Latinos and African Americans in South Los Angeles.* New York University Press.

Martinez, C. (2017). Responding to violence, keeping the peace: Relations between black and Latino youth. *The ANNALS of the American Academy of Political and Social Science, 673*(1), 169–189.

Martinez, C. G. (2008). *The transformation of a Los Angeles ghetto: Latino immigration, and the new urban social order* [Doctoral dissertation]. University of California, Berkeley. https://scholar.google.com/citations?user=4xmsjYYAAAAJ&hl=en

Martinez, N. (2018, August 30). *How the Facebook right-wing propaganda machine works.* Retrieved April 24, 2019, from Media Matters for America. https://www.mediamatters .org/blog/2018/08/31/how-facebook-right-wing-propaganda-machine-works/221151

Massanari, A. L. (2018). Rethinking Research Ethics, Power, and the Risk of Visibility in the Era of the "Alt-Right" Gaze. *Social Media + Society.* https://doi.org/10.1177 /2056305118768302

Matsuda, K. N., Melde, C., Taylor, T. J., Freng, A., & Esbensen, F.-A. (2013). Gang membership and adherence to the "code of the street." *Justice Quarterly, 30*(3), 440–468.

Mattheis, A. (2018). Shieldmaidens of whiteness: (Alt) maternalism and women recruiting for the far/alt-right. *Journal for Deradicalization,* (17), 128–162.

Maxson, C. L. (1998). *Gang members on the move.* Juvenile Justice Bulletin. Youth Gang Series. Department of Justice.

Maxson, C. L., Bradstreet, C. E., Gascon, D., Gerlinger, J., Grebenkemper, J., Haerle, D., . . . Scott, D. (2012). *Gangs and violence in California's youth correctional facilities: A research foundation for developing effective gang policies* (pp. 1–59). University of California, Irvine, Department of Criminology, Law and Society. https://www.cdcr.ca.gov/Juvenile_Justice /docs/Gangs_Violence_in_CA_Youth_Correctional_Facilities_UCI_Research_.pdf

Maxson, C. L., Egley, A. Jr., Miller, J., & Klein, M. W. (2014). Section VIII introduction. In C. L. Maxson, A. Egley Jr., J. Miller & M. W. Klein (Eds.), *The Modern Gang Reader* (4th ed.). Oxford University Press.

Maxson, C. L., & Esbensen, F.-A. (2016). Participation in and transformation of gangs (and gang research) in an international context: Reflections on the Eurogang Research Program. In C. Maxson & F.-A. Esbensen (Eds.), *Gang transitions and transformations in an international context* (pp. 1–11). Springer.

Maxson, C. L., Gordon, M., & Klein, M. (1985). Differences between gang and nongang homicides. *Criminology, 23*(2), 209–222.

Maxson, C. L., Hennigan, K. & Sloane, D. (2005). "It's getting crazy out there": Can a civil gang injunction change a community? *Criminology & Public Policy, 4*(3), 577–605.

Maxson, C. L., & Klein, M. (1990). Street gang violence: Twice as great, or half as great. *Gangs in America, 1,* 70.

Maxson, C. L., & Klein, M. (1995). Investigating gang structures. *Journal of Gang Research, 3*(1), 33–40.

Maxson, C. L., & Klein, M. W. (1996). Defining gang homicide: An updated look at member and motive approaches. In C. R. Huff (Ed.), *Gangs in America* (2nd ed., pp. 3–20). Sage.

Maxson, C. L., & Klein, M. (2002). "Play groups" no longer: Urban street gangs in the Los Angeles region. In M. Dear (Ed.), *From Chicago to LA: Making sense of urban theory* (pp. 239–266). Sage.

May, R. (2018, October 1). Hearing hate: White power music. Retrieved April 29, 2019, from https://www.europenowjournal.org/2018/10/01/hearing-hate-white-power-music/

May, R., & Feldman, M. (2018). Understanding the alt-right. Ideologues, "lulz" and hiding in plain sight. In M. Fielitz & N. Thurston (Eds.), *Post-digital cultures of the far right: Online actions and offline consequences in Europe and the US.* Transcript Verlag.

McAuliffe, T. (2019). *Beyond Charlottesville: Taking a stand against white nationalism.* United States: St. Martin's Publishing Group.

McCleery, M., & Edwards, A. (2019). A micro-sociological analysis of homegrown violent extremist attacks in the UK in 2017. *Dynamics of Asymmetric Conflict, 12*(1), 4–19.

McCoy, T. (2018, April 20). "Imploding": Financial troubles. Lawsuits. Trailer park brawls. Has the alt-right peaked? Retrieved December 11, 2018, from *Washington Post.* https://www.washingtonpost.com/local/social-issues/imploding-lawsuits-fundraising-troubles-trailer-park-brawls-has-the-alt-right-peaked/2018/04/20/0a2fb786-39a6-11e8-9c0a-85d477d9a226_story.html

McDevitt, J., Levin, J., & Bennett, S. (2002). Hate crime offenders: An expanded typology. *Journal of Social Issues, 58*(2), 303–317.

McFarland, P. (2008). *Chicano rap.* University of Texas Press.

McInnes, G. (2016, September 15). Introducing: The Proud Boys. Retrieved December 11, 2018, from *Taki's Magazine.* https://www.takimag.com/article/introducing_the_proud_boys_gavin_mcinnes/

McInnes, G. (2017, August 21). We are not alt-right. Retrieved October 20, 2019, from *Proud Boy Magazine.* https://officialproudboys.com/proud-boys/we-are-not-alt-right/

McLean, R., Deuchar, R., Harding, S., & Densley, J. (2019). Putting the "street" in gang: Place and space in the organization of Scotland's drug-selling gangs. *The British Journal of Criminology, 59*(2), 396–415.

McVeigh, R. (2009). *The rise of the Ku Klux Klan: Right-wing movements and national politics.* University of Minnesota Press.

McVeigh, R., & Estep, K. (2019). *The politics of losing: Trump, the Klan, and the mainstreaming of resentment.* Columbia University Press.

Melde, C., & Esbensen, F.-A. (2011). Gang membership as a turning point in the life course. *Criminology, 49*(2), 513–552.

Melde, C., & Esbensen, F.-A. (2013). Gangs and violence: Disentangling the impact of gang membership on the level and nature of offending. *Journal of Quantitative Criminology, 29*(2), 143–166.

Melde, C., & Weerman, F. (2020). *Understanding gangs in the era of internet and social media.* Springer.

Messner, B., Jipson, A., Becker, P., & Byers, B. (2007). The hardest hate: A sociological analysis of country hate music. *Popular Music and Society, 30*(4), 513–531.

Mettler, K. (2016, November 15). We live in crazy times: Neo-Nazis have declared New Balance the "official shoes of white people." *Washington Post.* https://www.washingtonpost.com/news/morning-mix/wp/2016/11/15/the-crazy-reason-neo-nazis-have-declared-new-balance-the-official-shoes-of-white-people/

Miah, M. (2018). *Black nationalism, Black solidarity.* Retrieved October 28, 2019, from Solidarity. http://solidarity-us.org/atc/192/p5171/

Michael, G. (2012). *Lone wolf terror and the rise of leaderless resistance.* Vanderbilt University Press.

Miller, C. (2018, November 14). *Azov, Ukraine's most prominent ultranationalist group, sets its sights on U.S., Europe.* Retrieved October 20, 2019, from RadioFreeEurope/RadioLiberty website. https://www.rferl.org/a/azov-ukraine-s-most-prominent-ultranationalist-group-sets-its-sights-on-u-s-europe/29600564.html

Miller, J. (2001). *One of the guys: Girls, gangs, and gender.* Oxford University Press.

Miller, J., & Brunson, R. K. (2000). Gender dynamics in youth gangs: A comparison of males' and females' accounts. *Justice Quarterly, 17*(3), 419–448.

Miller, W. B. (1966). Violent crimes in city gangs. *The ANNALS of the American Academy of Political and Social Science, 364*(1), 96–112.

Miller, W. B. (1973). The molls. *Society, 11*(1), 32–35.

Miller-Idriss, C. (2018). *The extreme gone mainstream: Commercialization and far right youth culture in Germany*. Princeton University Press.

Miller-Idriss, C. (2019). What makes a symbol far right? In M. Fielitz & N. Thurston (Eds.), *Post-digital cultures of the far right: Online actions and offline consequences in Europe and the US* (p. 123). Transcript Verlag.

Miller-Idriss, C., & Pilkington, H. (2017). In search of the missing link: Gender, education and the radical right. *Gender and Education, 29*(2), 133–146.

Mills, C. E., Freilich, J. D., & Chermak, S. M. (2017). Extreme hatred: Revisiting the hate crime and terrorism relationship to determine whether they are "close cousins" or "distant relatives." *Crime & Delinquency, 63*(10), 1191–1223.

Mills, C. W. (2013). White supremacy as sociopolitical system: A philosophical perspective. In *White out* (pp. 42–55). Routledge.

Mills, E. S. (1990). Housing economics: A synthesis. In M. Chetterji & R. E. Kuenne (Eds.), *New frontiers in regional science: Essays in honor of Walter Isard* (vol. 1, pp. 257–274). New York University Press.

Mitchell, M. M., Fahmy, C., Pyrooz, D. C., & Decker, S. H. (2017). Criminal crews, codes, and contexts: Differences and similarities across the code of the street, convict code, street gangs, and prison gangs. *Deviant Behavior, 38*(10), 1197–1222.

Mittos, A., Blackburn, J., & De Cristofaro, E. (2018). "23andMe confirms: I'm super white": Analyzing twitter discourse on genetic testing. *ArXiv*:1801.09946 [Cs].

Monod, J. (1967). Juvenile gangs in Paris: Toward a structural analysis. *Journal of Research in Crime and Delinquency, 4*(1), 142–165.

Montejano, D. (2010). *Quixote's soldiers: A local history of the Chicano movement, 1966–1981*. University of Texas Press.

Moore, D. (1994). *The lads in action: Social process in an urban youth subculture*. Arena.

Moore, J. (1994). The Chola life course: Chicana heroin users and the barrio gang. *The International Journal of the Addictions, 29*(9), 1115–1126.

Moore, J. B. (1993). *Skinheads shaved for battle: A cultural history of American skinheads*. Bowling Green State University Popular Press.

Moore, J. W. (1978). *Homeboys: Gangs, drugs, and prison in the barrios of Los Angeles*. Temple University Press.

Moore, J. W. (1991). *Going down to the barrio: Homeboys and homegirls in change*. Temple University Press.

Moore, J. W., Vigil, D., & Garcia, R. (1983). Residence and territoriality in Chicano gangs. *Social Problems, 31*(2), 182–194.

Moravcová, E. (2012). Methodological aspects of gang membership: The case of the Czech Republic. *Acta Universitatis Carolinae Philosophica et Historica, XVIII*(2), 69–83.

Morris, F. (2017, January 13). White nationalists' enthusiasm for Trump cools. Retrieved October 20, 2019, from https://www.wbur.org/npr/509533142/white-nationalists-enthusiasm-for-trump-cools

Morris, T. (2017). *Dark ideas: How neo-Nazi and violent jihadi ideologues shaped modern terrorism*. Lexington Books.

Morselli, C., & Décary-Hétu, D. (2013). Crime facilitation purposes of social networking sites: A review and analysis of the "cyberbanging" phenomenon. *Small Wars & Insurgencies, 24*(1), 152–170.

Moses, A. D. (2019). "White genocide" and the ethics of public analysis. *Journal of Genocide Research, 21*(2), 201–213.

Moule, R. K., Decker, S. H., & Pyrooz, D. C. (2017). Technology and conflict: Group processes and collective violence in the Internet era. *Crime, Law and Social Change, 68*(1), 47–73.

Moule, R. K., Pyrooz, D. C., & Decker, S. H. (2014). Internet adoption and online behaviour among American street gangs: Integrating gangs and organizational theory. *The British Journal of Criminology, 54*(6), 1186–1206.

Moynihan, C. (2019, October 22). 2 Proud Boys sentenced to 4 years in brawl with anti-fascists at Republican club. *The New York Times*. https://www.nytimes.com/2019/10/22/nyregion/proud-boys-antifa-sentence.html

Moynihan, C., & Winston, A. (2018, December 23). Far-right Proud boys reeling after arrests and scrutiny. *The New York Times*. https://www.nytimes.com/2018/12/23/nyregion/gavin-mcinnes-proud-boys-nypd.html

Mudde, C. (2005). Racist extremism in Central and Eastern Europe. *East European Politics and Societies, 19*(2), 161–184.

Mudde, C. (2018). *The far right in America*. Routledge.

Mudde, C. (2019). *The far right today*. Polity.

Muñiz, A. (2014). Maintaining Racial Boundaries: Criminalization, Neighborhood Context, and the Origins of Gang Injunctions. *Social Problems, 61*(2), 216–236.

Muñiz, A. (2015). *Police, power, and the production of racial boundaries*. Rutgers University Press.

Myre, G. (2018, March 6). *Deadly connection: Neo-Nazi group linked to 3 accused killers*. Retrieved October 28, 2019, from NPR. https://www.npr.org/2018/03/06/590292705/5-killings-3-states-and-1-common-neo-nazi-link

Nagle, A. (2017). *Kill all normies: The online culture wars from Tumblr and 4chan to the alt-right and Trump*. Zero Books.

Nakamura, K., Tita, G., & Krackhardt, D. (2019). Violence in the "balance": A structural analysis of how rivals, allies, and third-parties shape inter-gang violence. *Global Crime*. doi: 10.1080/17440572.2019.1627879

National Gang Center. (2016). *Brief review of federal and state definitions of the terms "gang," "gang crime," and "gang member."* https://www.nationalgangcenter.gov/content/documents/definitions.pdf

NBC Left Field. (2017). *Far-right Proud Boys cultivate male angst*. YouTube [Video]. https://www.youtube.com/watch?v=nGZ-rw1Zgjw

Neiwert, D. (2016, October 14). The chilling story of how Trump took hate groups mainstream. *Mother Jones*. https://www.motherjones.com/politics/2016/10/donald-trump-hate-groups-neo-nazi-white-supremacist-racism/

Neiwert, D. (2017). *Alt-America*. Verso Books.

Neiwert, D. (2018, September 19). *Is that an OK sign? A white power symbol? Or just a right-wing troll?* Retrieved April 23, 2019, from Southern Poverty Law Center. https://www.splcenter.org/hatewatch/2018/09/18/ok-sign-white-power-symbol-or-just-right-wing-troll

Neiwert, D. (2019, February 11). Portland far-right "Patriot" street brawlers in disarray as Proud Boys part ways amid violent talk. Retrieved April 29, 2019, from *Daily Kos.* https://www.dailykos.com/story/2019/2/11/1833783/-Portland-far-right-Patriot-street-brawlers-in-disarray-as-Proud-Boys-part-ways-amid-violent-talk

Newman, O. (1972). *Defensible space: People and design in the violent city.* Architectural Press.

Newton, C. (2019, April 26). *Why Twitter has been slow to ban white nationalists.* Retrieved May 28, 2019, from The Verge. https://www.theverge.com/interface/2019/4/26/18516997/why-doesnt-twitter-ban-nazis-white-nationalism

Norris, M. (2018, April). As America changes, some anxious whites feel left behind. Retrieved December 11, 2018, from *National Geographic Magazine.* https://www.nationalgeographic.com/magazine/2018/04/race-rising-anxiety-white-america/

Novak, M. (2015, January 21). *Oregon was founded as a racist utopia.* Retrieved April 25, 2019, from Gizmodo. https://gizmodo.com/oregon-was-founded-as-a-racist-utopia-1539567040

NPR. (2017, September 22). *White haze.* Retrieved April 25, 2019, from NPR *This American Life.* https://www.thisamericanlife.org/626/white-haze

NPR. (2018). FBI categorizes Proud Boys as extremist group with ties to white nationalism. Retrieved April 23, 2019, from NPR. https://www.npr.org/2018/11/20/669761157/fbi-categorizes-proud-boys-as-extremist-group-with-ties-to-white-nationalism

Nuño, L. E., & Katz, C. M. (2019). Understanding gang joining from a cross classified multi-level perspective. *Deviant Behavior, 40*(3), 301–325.

O'Brien, L. (2017, December). The making of an American Nazi. *The Atlantic.* Retrieved from https://www.theatlantic.com/magazine/archive/2017/12/the-making-of-an-american-nazi/544119/

O'Connell, H. A. (2019). Historical shadows: The links between sundown towns and contemporary black–white inequality. *Sociology of Race and Ethnicity, 5*(3), 311–325.

O'Connell, H. A. (2020). Monuments outlive history: Confederate monuments, the legacy of slavery, and black-white inequality. *Ethnic and Racial Studies, 43*(3), 460–478.

O'Deane, M. D. (2012). *Gang injunctions and abatement: Using civil remedies to curb gang-related crimes.* CRC Press.

O'Neal, G. S. (1997). Clothes to kill for: An analysis of primary and secondary claims-making in print media. *Sociological Inquiry, 67*(3), 336–349.

Ong, A. (2003). *Buddha is hiding: Refugees, citizenship, the new America.* University of California Press.

Oropeza, L. (2005). *¡Raza sí! ¡Guerra no!* University of California Press.

Ortiz, E. (2019, February 15). *"Disturbing" texts between Oregon police and far-right group prompt investigation.* Retrieved April 29, 2019, from NBC News. https://www.nbcnews.com/news/us-news/disturbing-texts-between-oregon-police-far-right-group-prompts-investigation-n972161

Owen, T. (2018, February 6). *This new mapping tool shows where neo-Nazi trolls live in the U.S.* Retrieved March 15, 2018, from VICE. https://www.vice.com/en_ca/article/d3w8vq /this-new-mapping-tool-shows-where-neo-nazi-trolls-live-in-the-us

Owen, T. (2019, October 7). How Telegram became white nationalists' go-to messaging platform. Retrieved October 20, 2019, from VICE. https://www.vice.com/en_us/article /59nk3a/how-telegram-became-white-nationalists-go-to-messaging-platform

Owen, T., & Hume, T. (2019, November 8). *A U.S. marine used the neo-Nazi site Iron March to recruit for a "racial holy war."* Retrieved November 9, 2019, from VICE. https://www .vice.com/en_us/article/d3aq8a/exclusive-a-us-marine-used-the-neo-nazi-site-iron -march-to-recruit-for-a-race-war

Padilla, F. M. (1996). *The gang as an American enterprise.* Rutgers University Press.

Palmer, E. (2019, May 2). *Far-right groups and Antifa clash again in Portland after police praise peaceful May Day protests.* Retrieved May 18, 2019, from Newsweek. https://www .newsweek.com/portland-proud-boys-patriot-prayer-antifa-may-day-rallies-1412607

Panfil, V. R., & Peterson, D. (2015). Gender, sexuality, and gangs: Re-envisioning diversity. In S. H. Decker & D. C. Pyrooz (Eds.), *The handbook of gangs.* Wiley Blackwell.

Panofsky, A., & Donovan, J. (2019). Genetic ancestry testing among white nationalists: From identity repair to citizen science. *Social Studies of Science, 49*(5), 653–681.

Papachristos, A. V. (2005). Gang world: Street gangs are proliferating around the globe. *Foreign Policy* (147), 48–55.

Papachristos, A. (2009). Murder by structure: Dominance relations and the social structure of gang homicide. *American Journal of Sociology, 115*(1), 74–128.

Papachristos, A. V., Hureau, D. M., & Braga, A. A. (2013). The corner and the crew: The influence of geography and social networks on gang violence. *American Sociological Review, 78*(3), 417–447.

Parsons, E. F. (2015). *Ku-Klux: The birth of the Klan during Reconstruction.* University of North Carolina Press.

Patton, D. U., Eschmann, R. D., & Butler, D. A. (2013). Internet banging: New trends in social media, gang violence, masculinity and hip hop. *Computers in Human Behavior, 29*(5), A54–A59.

Patton, D. U., Frey, W. R., & Gaskell, M. (2019). Guns on social media: Complex interpretations of gun images posted by Chicago youth. *Palgrave Communications, 5*(1), 1–8.

Paxton, R. (2018). The alt-right, post-truth, fake news, and the media. In A. Waring (Ed.), *The new authoritarianism: Vol 1: A risk analysis of the US alt-right phenomenon* (pp. 337–362). Ibidem-Verlag.

PBS (Public Broadcasting System). (2018a). *Documenting hate: Charlottesville. Frontline,* Season 36 Episode 13. https://www.pbs.org/video/documenting-hate-charlottesville -1120-ieomod/

PBS (Public Broadcasting System). (2018b). *Documenting hate: New American Nazis. Frontline,* Season 36 Episode 17. https://www.pbs.org/video/documenting-hate-new -american-nazis-vrbezk/

Pelz, M. E., Marquart, J. W., & Pelz, C. T. (1991). Right-wing extremism in the Texas prisons: The rise and fall of the Aryan Brotherhood of Texas. *The Prison Journal, 71*(2), 23–37.

Perry, B. (2001). *In the name of hate: Understanding hate crimes.* Routledge.

Perry, B., & Blazak, R. (2010). Places for races: The white supremacist movement imagines U.S. geography. *Journal of Hate Studies, 8*(1), 29–51.

Perry, B., Hofmann, D. C., & Scrivens, R. (2018). "Confrontational but not violent": An assessment of the potential for violence by the anti-authority community in Canada. *Terrorism and Political Violence.* doi: 10.1080/09546553.2018.1516210

Perry, B., & Scrivens, R. (2018). A climate for hate? An exploration of the right-wing extremist landscape in Canada. *Critical Criminology, 26*(2), 169–187.

Perry, B., & Scrivens, R. (2019). *Right-wing extremism in Canada.* Palgrave

Petersen, R. D., & Valdez, A. (2005). Using snowball-based methods in hidden populations to generate a randomized community sample of gang-affiliated adolescents. *Youth Violence and Juvenile Justice, 3*(2), 151–167.

Peterson, D. (2012). Girlfriends, gun-holders, and ghetto-rats? Moving beyond narrow views of girls in gangs. In S. Miller, L. D. Leve & P. K. Kerig (Eds.), *Delinquent Girls: Contexts, Relationships, and Adaptation* (pp. 71–84). Springer.

Peterson, D., Carson, D. C., & Fowler, E. (2018). What's sex (composition) got to do with it? The importance of sex composition of gangs for female and male members' offending and victimization. *Justice Quarterly, 35*(6), 941–976.

Peterson, D., & Esbensen, F.-A. (2004). The outlook is G.R.E.A.T.: What educators say about school-based prevention and the Gang Resistance Education and Training (G.R.E.A.T.) Program. *Evaluation Review, 28*(3), 218–245.

Peterson, D., Miller, J., & Esbensen, F.-A. (2001). Impact of sex composition on gangs and gang member delinquency. *Criminology, 39*(2), 411–440.

Peterson, D., & Panfil, V. R. (2017). Toward a multiracial feminist framework for understanding females' gang involvement. *Journal of Crime and Justice, 40*(3), 337–357.

Peterson, D., Taylor, T. J., & Esbensen, F.-A. (2004). Gang membership and violent victimization. *Justice Quarterly, 21*(4), 793–815.

Peterson, J., & Densley, J. (2017). Cyber violence: What do we know and where do we go from here? *Aggression and Violent Behavior, 34*, 193–200.

Phillips, M., Bagavathi, A., Reid, S. E., Valasik, M., & Krishnan, S. (2018, November 29). The daily use of Gab is climbing. Which talker might become as violent as the Pittsburgh synagogue gunman? *Washington Post.* https://www.washingtonpost.com/news/monkey-cage/wp/2018/11/29/the-daily-use-of-gab-is-climbing-which-talker-might-become-as-violent-as-the-pittsburgh-synagogue-gunman/

Phillips, M. D., & Valasik, M. (2017, November 21). The Islamic State is more like a street gang than like other terrorist groups. *Washington Post.* https://www.washingtonpost.com/news/monkey-cage/wp/2017/11/15/the-islamic-state-is-more-like-a-street-gang-more-than-its-like-other-terrorist-groups/

Phillips, S. A. (1999). *Wallbangin': Graffiti and gangs in L.A.* University of Chicago Press.

Phillips, S. A. (2016). Deconstructing gang graffiti. In J. I. Ross (Ed.), *Routledge Handbook of Graffiti and Street Art* (pp. 48–60). Routledge.

Phillips, W. (2015). *This is why we can't have nice things: Mapping the relationship between online trolling and mainstream culture.* MIT Press.

Picciolini, C. (2018). *White American youth: My journey into and out of America's most dangerous hate movement.* Hachette Books.

Pickering, J., Kintrea, K., & Bannister, J. (2012). Invisible walls and visible youth: Territoriality among young people in British cities. *Urban Studies, 49*(5), 945–960.

Pieslak, J. R. (2015). *Radicalism & music: An introduction to the music cultures of Al-Qa'ida, racist skinheads, Christian-affiliated radicalism, and eco-animal rights militants.* Wesleyan University Press.

Pilkington, H. (2010). No longer "on parade": Style and the performance of skinhead in the Russian far north. *The Russian Review, 69*(2), 187–209.

Pilkington, H. (2016). *Loud and proud: Passion and politics in the English Defence League.* Manchester University Press.

Pilkington, H., Omel'chenko, E. L., & Garifzianova, A. (2010). *Russia's skinheads: Exploring and rethinking subcultural lives.* Routledge.

Pollard, J. (2016). Skinhead culture: The ideologies, mythologies, religions and conspiracy theories of racist skinheads. *Patterns of Prejudice, 50*(4–5), 398–419.

Pollard, T. (2018). Alt-right transgressions in the age of Trump. *Perspectives on Global Development and Technology, 17*(1–2), 76–88.

Popkin, S. J., Gwiasda, V. E., Olson, L. M., Rosenbaum, D. P., & Buron, L. (2000). *Hidden war: Crime and the tragedy of public housing in Chicago.* Rutgers University Press.

Posner, S., & Neiwert, D. (2016, October 14). The chilling story of how Trump took hate groups mainstream. Retrieved October 20, 2019, from *Mother Jones.* https://www.motherjones.com/politics/2016/10/donald-trump-hate-groups-neo-nazi-white-supremacist-racism/

Proud Boys. (2019). Proud Boys. Retrieved October 20, 2019, from Proud Boys website. http://proudboysusa.com/

Puffer, J. A. (1912). *The boy and his gang.* Houghton.

Putnam, M. T., & Littlejohn, J. T. (2007). National Socialism with Fler? German hip hop from the right. *Popular Music and Society, 30*(4), 453–468.

Pyrooz, D. C. (2014). From colors and guns to caps and gowns? The effects of gang membership on educational attainment. *Journal of Research in Crime and Delinquency, 51*(1), 56–87.

Pyrooz, D. C., & Decker, S. (2011). Motives and methods for leaving the gang: Understanding the process of gang desistance. *Journal of Criminal Justice, 39*(5), 417–425.

Pyrooz, D. C., & Decker, S. (2019). *Competing for control: Gangs and the social order of prisons.* Cambridge Univeristy Press.

Pyrooz, D. C., Decker, S. H., & Moule, R. K. (2015). Criminal and routine activities in online settings: Gangs, offenders, and the internet. *Justice Quarterly, 32*(3), 471–499.

Pyrooz, D., Decker, S. H., & Webb, V. J. (2014). The ties that bind: Desistance from gangs. *Crime & Delinquency, 60*(4), 491–516.

Pyrooz, D. C., & Densley, J. A. (2018). On public protest, violence, and street gangs. *Society, 55*(3), 229–236.

Pyrooz, D. C., LaFree, G., Decker, S. H., & James, P. A. (2018). Cut from the same cloth? A comparative study of domestic extremists and gang members in the United States. *Justice Quarterly, 35*(1), 1–32.

Pyrooz, D. C., & Mitchell, M. M. (2015). Little gang research, big gang research. In S. H. Decker & D. C. Pyrooz (Eds.), *The handbook of gangs* (pp. 28–58). Wiley Blackwell.

Pyrooz, D. C., & Sweeten, G. (2015). Gang membership between ages 5 and 17 years in the United States. *Journal of Adolescent Health, 56*(4), 414–419.

Pyrooz, D. C., Sweeten, G., & Piquero, A. R. (2013). Continuity and change in gang membership and gang embeddedness. *Journal of Research in Crime and Delinquency, 50*(2), 239–271.

Pyrooz, D. C., Turanovic, J. J., Decker, S. H., & Wu, J. (2016). Taking stock of the relationship between gang membership and offending: A meta-analysis. *Criminal Justice and Behavior, 43*(3), 365–397.

Quicker, J. C. (1983). *Homegirls: Characterizing Chicana gangs.* International Universities Press.

Rafael, T. (2007). *The Mexican mafia.* Encounter Books.

Randle, A. (2018, September 22). Alleged member of white nationalist group Proud Boys gets into fight in Westport. Retrieved October 20, 2019, from *Kansas City Star.* https://www.kansascity.com/news/local/article218805510.html

Reid, S. E., & Maxson, C. L. (2016). Gang youth and friendship networks in California correctional facilities: Examining friendship structure and composition for incarcerated gang and non-gang youth. In Cheryl L. Maxson & F. A. Esbensen (Eds.), *Gang transitions and transformations in an international context* (pp. 95–114). Springer.

Reid, S. E., & Valasik, M. (2018). Ctrl+ALT-RIGHT: Reinterpreting our knowledge of white supremacy groups through the lens of street gangs. *Journal of Youth Studies, 21*(10), 1305–1325.

Reid, S. E. Valasik, M., & Bagavathi, A. (2020). "Examining the physical manifestation of alt-right gangs: From online trolling to street fighting." In C. Melde & F. Weerman (Eds.), *Understanding gangs in the era of internet and social media.* Springer.

Reitman, J. (2018, November 3). U.S. law enforcement failed to see the threat of white nationalism. Now they don't know how to stop it. *The New York Times.* https://www.nytimes.com/2018/11/03/magazine/FBI-charlottesville-white-nationalism-far-right.html

Ridgeway, G., Grogger, J., Moyer, R. A., & MacDonald, J. M. (2019). Effect of Gang Injunctions on Crime: A study of Los Angeles from 1988–2014. *Journal of Quantitative Criminology. 35*(3), 517–541.

Ridgeway, J. (1995). *Blood in the face: The Ku Klux Klan, Aryan Nations, Nazi skinheads, and the rise of a new white culture.* Thunder's Mouth Press.

Roediger, D. R. (1999). *The wages of whiteness: Race and the making of the American working class.* Verso.

Rogan, J. (2017). *Joe Rogan Experience #920—Gavin McInnes* [Video]. YouTube. https://www.youtube.com/watch?v=qm9lfWTGmDY

Roman, C. G., Link, N. W., Hyatt, J. M., Bhati, A., & Forney, M. (2018). Assessing the gang-level and community-level effects of the Philadelphia Focused Deterrence strategy. *Journal of Experimental Criminology.* doi: 10.1007/s11292-018-9333-7

Roose, K., & Winston, A. (2018, November 4). Far-right internet groups listen for Trump's approval, and often hear it. *The New York Times.* https://www.nytimes.com/2018/11/04/us/politics/far-right-internet-trump.html

Rosenfeld, R., Bray, T., & Egley, A. (1999). Facilitating violence: A comparison of gang-motivated, gang-affiliated, and nongang youth homicides. *Journal of Quantitative Criminology, 15,* 495–516.

Ross, J. I. (2014). Misidentified and misunderstood: Extremists and extremist groups incarcerated in U.S. correctional facilities. In G. Michael (Ed.), *Extremism in America* (pp. 274–293). Univeristy Press of Florida.

Roy, J. M. (2008). Brotherhood of blood: Aryan tribalism and skinhead cybercrews. In T. Adams & S. A. Smith (Eds.), *Electronic tribes the virtual worlds of geeks, gamers, shamans, and scammers.* University of Texas Press.

Sack, R. D. (1983). Human territoriality: A theory. *Annals of the Association of American Geographers, 73*(1), 55–74.

Saini, A. (2019). *Superior: The return of race science.* Beacon Press.

Salagaev, A. L., & Safin, R. R. (2014). Capitalizing on change: Gangs, ideology, and the transition to a liberal economy in the Russian Federation. In J. M. Hazen & D. Rodgers (Eds.), *Global Gangs* (pp. 65–84). University of Minnesota Press.

Salagaev, A. L., Shashkin, A., Sherbakova, I., & Touriyanskiy, E. (2005). Contemporary Russian gangs: History, membership, and crime involvement. In *European street gangs and troublesome youth groups: Findings from the Eurogang research program* (pp. 169–191). AltaMira.

Salter, M. (2017). From geek masculinity to Gamergate: The technological rationality of online abuse. *Crime, Media, Culture, 14*(2), 247–264.

Samuels, K. L. (2019). Deliberate heritage. *The Public Historian, 41*(1), 121–132.

Sarabia, D., & Shriver, T. E. (2004). Maintaining collective identity in a hostile environment: Confronting negative public perception and factional divisions within the skinhead subculture. *Sociological Spectrum, 24*(3), 267–294.

Sarnecki, J. (2004). Girls and boys in delinquent networks. *International Annals of Criminology, 42*(1/2), 29–52.

Saslow, E. (2018). *Rising out of hatred: The awakening of a former white nationalist.* Anchor.

Schafer, J. A. (2002). Spinning the web of hate: Web-based hate propagation by extremist organizations. *Journal of Criminal Justice and Popular Culture, 9*(2), 69–88.

Schneider, E. C. (1999). *Vampires, dragons, and Egyptian kings: Youth gangs in postwar New York.* Princeton University Press.

Scott, D. (2018a). A comparison of gang- and non-gang-related violent incidents from the incarcerated youth perspective. *Deviant Behavior, 39*(10), 1336–1356.

Scott, D. (2018b). A mixed methods comparison of gang and race motivated violent incident involvement in a youth correctional setting. *Journal of Ethnicity in Criminal Justice, 16*(3), 177–204.

Scott, D. (2019). Connecting setting and subculture: A qualitative examination of violent incidents related to gangs, race, and other personal issues from the incarcerated youth perspective. *International Journal of Law, Crime and Justice, 56*, 53–69.

Scott, D. W., & Maxson, C. L. (2016). Gang organization and violence in youth correctional facilities. *Journal of Criminological Research, Policy and Practice, 2*(2), 81–94.

Scrivens, R., Bowman-Grieve, L., Conway, M., & Frank, R. (2018). *Sugar and spice, and everything nice? Exploring the Online roles of women in the far-right extremist movement* [Conference presentation]. VOX-Pol's Third Biennial Conference—Violent Extremism, Terrorism, and the Internet: Present and Future Trends, Amsterdam, Netherlands. August 21, 2018. https://www.voxpol.eu/wp-content/uploads/2018/09/2018-VOX-Pol-Conference-Role-of-RWE-Women-PPT.pdf

Scrivens, R., Davies, G., & Frank, R. (2018). Measuring the Evolution of radical right-wing posting behaviors online. *Deviant Behavior, 41*(2), 216–232. doi: 10.1080/01639625.2018.1556994.

Sela-Shayovitz, R. (2012). Gangs and the web: Gang members' online behavior. *Journal of Contemporary Criminal Justice, 28*(4), 389–405.

Semuels, A. (2016, July 22). The racist history of Portland, the whitest city in America. Retrieved April 25, 2019, from *The Atlantic.* https://www.theatlantic.com/business/archive/2016/07/racist-history-portland/492035/

Shallwani, P., & Weill, K. (2018, October 15). *NYPD looks to charge 9 Proud Boys with assault for Manhattan fight.* Daily Beast. https://www.thedailybeast.com/nypd-looks-to-charge-9-proud-boys-with-assault-for-manhattan-fight

Shapiro, A. (2017, May 30). *Portland train murders highlight Oregon's history of white supremacy.* Retrieved April 25, 2019, from NPR. https://www.npr.org/2017/05/30/530769807/portland-train-murders-highlight-oregons-history-of-white-supremacy

Shashkin, A. (2008). Origins and development of racist skinheads in Moscow. In F. van Gemert, D. Peterson & I. L. Lien (Eds.), *Street gangs, migration and ethnicity* (pp. 97–114). Willan.

Shekhovtsov, A. (2011). The creeping resurgence of the Ukrainian radical right? The case of the Freedom Party. *Europe-Asia Studies, 63*(2), 203–228.

Shekhovtsov, A. (2012). *White power music: Scenes of extreme-right cultural resistance.* Searchlight Magazine Ltd.

Shekhovtsov, A. (2013). European far-right music and its enemies. In R. Wodak & J. E. Richardson (Eds.), *Analysing fascist discourse European fascism in talk and text.* Routledge.

Shelden, R. G., Tracy, S. K., & Brown, W. B. (2012). *Youth gangs in American society.* Cengage Learning.

Sheldon, H. D. (1898). The institutional activities of American children. *The American Journal of Psychology, 9*(4), 425–448.

Shifman, L. (2014). *Memes in Digital Culture.* MIT Press.

Short, J. F. Jr. (1974). Youth, gangs and society: Micro- and macrosociological processes. *The Sociological Quarterly, 15*(1), 3–19.

Short, J. F. Jr. (1996). Diversity and change in US gangs. In *Gangs in America.* Sage.

Short, J. F. Jr., & Moland, J. (1976). Politics and youth gangs: A follow-up study. *The Sociological Quarterly, 17*(2), 162–179.

Short, J. F. Jr., & Strodtbeck, F. L. (1965). *Group process and gang delinquency.* University of Chicago Press.

Sibley, C. G., Robertson, A., & Wilson, M. S. (2006). Social dominance orientation and right-wing authoritarianism: additive and interactive effects. *Political Psychology, 27*(5), 755–768.

Siedler, T. (2011). Parental unemployment and young people's extreme right-wing party affinity: Evidence from panel data. *Journal of the Royal Statistical Society: Series A (Statistics in Society), 174*(3), 737–758.

Simi, P. (2006). Hate groups or street gangs? The emergence of racist skinheads. In J. F. Short Jr. & L. A. Hughes (Eds.), *Studying youth gangs* (pp. 145–60). AltaMira Press.

Simi, P. (2009). Skinhead street violence. In B. Perry & R. Blazak (Eds.), *Hate crime: Hate offenders* (vol. 4, pp. 157–169). Praeger.

Simi, P. (2010). Why study white supremacist terror? A research note. *Deviant Behavior, 31*(3), 251–273.

Simi, P., Blee, K., DeMichele, M., & Windisch, S. (2017). Addicted to hate: Identity residual among former white supremacists. *American Sociological Review, 82*(6), 1167–1187.

Simi, P., & Futrell, R. (2006). Cyberculture and the endurance of white power activism. *Journal of Political and Military Sociology; DeKalb, 34*(1), 115–142.

Simi, P., & Futrell, R. (2015). *American swastika: Inside the white power movement's hidden spaces of hate.* Rowman & Littlefield.

Simi, P., Futrell, R., & Bubolz, B. (2016). Parenting as activism: Identity alignment and activist persistence in the white power movement. *The Sociological Quarterly, 57*(3), 491–519.

Simi, P., Smith, L., & Reeser, A. M. S. (2008). From punk kids to public enemy number one. *Deviant Behavior, 29*(8), 753–774.

Simi, P., Sporer, K., & Bubolz, B. F. (2016). Narratives of childhood adversity and adolescent misconduct as precursors to violent extremism: A life-course criminological approach. *Journal of Research in Crime and Delinquency, 53*(4), 536–563.

Simi, P., & Windisch, S. (2018) Why radicalization fails: Barriers to mass casualty terrorism. *Terrorism and political violence.* doi: 10.1080/09546553.2017.1409212

Simi, P., Windisch, S., & Sporer, K. (2016). *Recruitment and radicalization among US far-right terrorists.* National Consortium for the Study of Terrorism and Responses to Terrorism. (START).

Simon, D., & Burns, E. (1997). *The corner: A year in the life of an inner-city neighborhood.* Broadway Books.

Simpson, P. A., & Druxes, H. (2015). *Digital media strategies of the far right in Europe and the United States.* Lexington Books.

Skarbek, D. (2014). *The social order of the underworld: How prison gangs govern the American penal system.* Oxford University Press.

Smith, J. (2018, January 12). This is fashwave, the suicidal retro-futurist art of the alt-right. Retrieved April 29, 2019, from *Mic.* https://mic.com/articles/187379/this-is-fashwave-the-suicidal-retro-futurist-art-of-the-alt-right

Smith, R. C. (2002). Gender, ethnicity and race in the school outcomes of second generation Mexican Americans. In M. M. Suárez-Orozco & M. Páez (Eds.), *Latinos: Remaking America* (pp. 110–125). University of California Press.

Smolík, J. (2015). The skinhead subculture in the Czech Republic. *Kultura-Społeczeństwo-Edukacja, 7*(1).

Sonmez, F. (2018, October 18). Rep. Steve King's endorsement of white nationalist mayoral candidate in Canada draws rebuke from conservative news outlet. Retrieved October 28, 2019, from *Washington Post.* https://www.washingtonpost.com/politics/rep-steve-kings-endorsement-of-white-nationalist-mayoral-candidate-in-canada-draws-rebuke-from-conservative-news-outlet/2018/10/18/3923b7ac-d2fa-11e8-83d6-291fcead2ab1_story.html

Sottile, L. (2019). Bundyville: The remnant [audio podcast]. https://longreads.com/bundyville/

Spergel, I. A. (1995). *The youth gang problem: A community approach.* Oxford University Press.

Speri, A. (2017, January 31). *The FBI has quietly investigated white supremacist infiltration of law enforcement.* Retrieved October 28, 2019, from The Intercept. https://theintercept .com/2017/01/31/the-fbi-has-quietly-investigated-white-supremacist-infiltration-of -law-enforcement/

SPLC. (2001, August 29). *White power music festival Hammerfest 2000 draws international fans to Atlanta.* Retrieved April 29, 2019, from Southern Poverty Law Center. https:// www.splcenter.org/fighting-hate/intelligence-report/2001/white-power-music-festival -hammerfest-2000-draws-international-fans-atlanta

SPLC. (2006, October 19). *A look at racist skinhead symbols and tattoos.* Retrieved April 29, 2019, from Southern Poverty Law Center. https://www.splcenter.org/fighting-hate /intelligence-report/2006/look-racist-skinhead-symbols-and-tattoos

SPLC. (2012, June 25*). Racist skinheads: Understanding the threat.* Southern Poverty Law Center. https://www.splcenter.org/sites/default/files/d6_legacy_files/downloads /publication/IR_Special_Skinhead_Report_2012_web_0.pdf

SPLC. (2014). *White homicide worldwide.* Retrieved May 28, 2019, from Southern Poverty Law Center. https://www.splcenter.org/20140331/white-homicide-worldwide

SPLC. (2017). *A waning storm: Once the world's most popular white nationalist website, Stormfront is running out of steam.* Retrieved October 20, 2019, from Southern Poverty Law Center. https://www.splcenter.org/hatewatch/2017/02/22/waning-storm-once -world%E2%80%99s-most-popular-white-nationalist-website-stormfront-running-out

SPLC. (2018). *Alt-right.* Retrieved April 24, 2019, from Southern Poverty Law Center. https://www.splcenter.org/fighting-hate/extremist-files/ideology/alt-right

SPLC. (2019a). *Proud Boys.* Retrieved April 24, 2019, from Southern Poverty Law Center. https://www.splcenter.org/fighting-hate/extremist-files/group/proud-boys

SPLC. (2019b). *Racist skinhead.* Retrieved April 24, 2019, from Southern Poverty Law Center. https://www.splcenter.org/fighting-hate/extremist-files/ideology/racist-skinhead

St. Cyr, J. L., & Decker, S. H. (2003). Girls, guys, and gangs: Convergence or divergence in the gendered construction of gangs and groups. *Journal of Criminal Justice, 31*(5), 423–433.

Starbuck, D., Howell, J. C., & Lindquist, D. J. (2004). Hybrid and other modern gangs. In F.-A. Esbensen, S. G. Tibbetts & L. K. Gaines (Eds.), *American youth gangs at the millennium.* Waveland Press.

Stephenson, S. (2012). The violent practices of youth territorial groups in Moscow. *Europe-Asia Studies, 64*(1), 69–90.

Stephenson, S. (2015). *Gangs of Russia: From the streets to the corridors of power.* Cornell University Press.

Stern, A. M. (2019). *Proud Boys and the white ethnostate: How the alt-right is warping the American imagination.* Beacon Press.

Steward, S. (2018, September 26). Proud Boys crash local pub. Retrieved October 20, 2019, from *Fort Worth Weekly.* https://www.fwweekly.com/2018/09/26/proud-boys-crash -local-pub/

Storrod, M. L., & Densley, J. A. (2017). "Going viral" and "Going country": The expressive and instrumental activities of street gangs on social media. *Journal of Youth Studies, 20*(6), 677–696.

Strickland, P. (2018, October 30). *Hate before the vote: Pipe bombs, shootings, incitement.* Retrieved April 30, 2019, from Al Jazeera. https://www.aljazeera.com/news/2018/10/midterms-marred-violence-experts-point-finger-trump-181030150744871.html

Struyk, R. (2006). Gangs in our schools: Identifying gang indicators in our school population. *The Clearing House: A Journal of Educational Strategies, Issues and Ideas, 80*(1), 11–13.

Stuart, F. (2019). Code of the tweet: Urban gang violence in the social media age. *Social Problems* spz010.

Suall, I., & Lowe, D. (1988). *The hate movement today: A chronicle of violence and disarray.* Anti-Defamation League of B'nai B'rith.

Sullivan, M. L. (1989). *"Getting paid": Youth crime and work in the inner city.* Cornell University Press.

Suttles, G. D. (1968). *The social order of the slum: Ethnicity and territory in the inner city.* University of Chicago Press.

Suttles, G. D. (1972). *The social construction of communities.* University of Chicago Press.

Sweeten, G., Pyrooz, D. C., & Piquero, A. R. (2013). Disengaging from gangs and desistance from crime. *Justice Quarterly, 30*(3), 469–500.

Swenson, K. (2017, July 10). The alt-right's Proud Boys love Fred Perry polo shirts. The feeling is not mutual. *Washington Post.* https://www.washingtonpost.com/news/morning-mix/wp/2017/07/10/the-alt-rights-proud-boys-love-fred-perry-polo-shirts-the-feeling-is-not-mutual/

Taniguchi, T. A., Ratcliffe, J. H., & Taylor, R. B. (2011). Gang set space, drug markets, and crime around drug corners in Camden. *Journal of Research in Crime and Delinquency, 48*(3), 327–363.

Tapia, M. (2019). Modern Chicano street gangs: Ethnic pride versus "gangsta" subculture. *Hispanic Journal of Behavioral Sciences, 41*(3), 312–330.

Tarasov, A. (2001). Offspring of reforms—shaven heads are skinheads. *Russian Politics & Law, 39*(1), 43–89.

Tarasov, A. (2008). Changing subcultures: Observations on skinheads. *Russian Politics & Law, 46*(1), 31–49.

Taylor, T. J., Freng, A., Esbensen, F.-A., & Peterson, D. (2008). Youth gang membership and serious violent victimization: The importance of lifestyles and routine activities. *Journal of Interpersonal Violence, 23*(10), 1441–1464.

Teitelbaum, B. R. (2017a). *Lions of the north: Sounds of the new Nordic radical nationalism.* Oxford University Press.

Teitelbaum, B. R. (2017b). Rap, reggae, and white minoritization. In F. Holt & A. Kärjä (Eds.), *The Oxford handbook of popular music in the Nordic countries* (pp. 345–362). Oxford University Press.

Templeton, A., & Wilson, C. (2018, December 4). *Portland FBI head clarifies statement on Proud Boys.* Retrieved April 24, 2019, from OPB. https://www.opb.org/news/article/portland-fbi-proud-boys-clarifies-statement/

Tenold, V. (2018). *Everything you love will burn: Inside the rebirth of white nationalism in America.* Nation Books.

Terrell, A. D. (1989). Racial violence and the underclass. *Forum, 4*, 3–6.

Thompson, A. C. (2017, October 19). *Racist, violent, unpunished: A white hate group's campaign of menace.* Retrieved April 24, 2019, from ProPublica. https://www.propublica.org/article/white-hate-group-campaign-of-menace-rise-above-movement

Thompson, A. C., Winston, A., & Hanrahan, J. (2018, May 3). *Ranks of notorious hate group include active-duty military.* Retrieved April 24, 2019, from ProPublica. https://www.propublica.org/article/atomwaffen-division-hate-group-active-duty-military

Thompson, C. Y., Young, R. L., & Burns, R. (2000). Representing gangs in the news: Media constructions of criminal gangs. *Sociological Spectrum, 20*(4), 409–432.

Thornberry, T. P., Kearley, B., Gottfredson, D. C., Slothower, M. P., Devlin, D. N., & Fader, J. J. (2018). Reducing crime among youth at risk for gang involvement: A randomized trial. *Criminology & Public Policy, 17*(4), 953–989.

Thornberry, T. P., Krohn, M. D., Lizotte, A. J., Tobin, K., & Smith, C. A. (2003). *Gangs and delinquency in developmental perspective.* Cambridge University Press.

Thrasher, F. M. (1927). *The gang: A study of 1,313 gangs in Chicago.* University of Chicago Press.

Tita, G. E. (1999). *An ecological study of violent urban street gangs and their crime* [Doctoral dissertation]. Carnegie Mellon University.

Tita, G. E., Cohen, J., & Engberg, J. (2005). An ecological study of the location of gang "set space." *Social Problems, 52*(2), 272–299.

Tita, G. E., & Radil, S. M. (2011). Spatializing the social networks of gangs to explore patterns of violence. *Journal of Quantitative Criminology, 27*(4), 521–545.

Tobar, H. (1991, October 12). Deputies in "neo-Nazi" gang, judge found: Sheriff's Department: Many at Lynwood office have engaged in racially motivated violence against blacks and Latinos, jurist wrote. Retrieved October 28, 2019, from *Los Angeles Times.* https://www.latimes.com/archives/la-xpm-1991-10-12-me-107-story.html

Touchberry, R. (2018, October 13). The violent far-right, pro-Trump group Proud Boys hits New York streets, and Fox News sees them as victims. Retrieved April 25, 2019, from *Newsweek.* https://www.newsweek.com/violent-far-right-group-fox-news-victims-1168454

Trammell, R. (2011). *Enforcing the convict code violence and prison culture.* Lynne Rienner.

Travis, T., & Hardy, P. (2012). *Skinheads: A guide to an American subculture.* ABC-CLIO.

Tuters, M. (2019). LARPing & liberal tears: Irony, belief and idiocy in the deep vernacular web. In M. Fielitz & N. Thurston (Eds.), *Post-digital cultures of the far right: Online actions and offline consequences in Europe and the US* (pp. 37–48). Transcript Velag.

Tynes, B. M., Rose, C. A., & Markoe, S. L. (2013). Extending campus life to the internet: Social media, discrimination, and perceptions of racial climate. *Journal of Diversity in Higher Education, 6*(2), 102–114.

Updegrove, A. H., Cooper, M. N., Orrick, E. A., & Piquero, A. R. (2018). Red states and Black lives: Applying the racial threat hypothesis to the Black Lives Matter movement. *Justice Quarterly, 37*(1), 1–24.

Urbanik, M. M., & Haggerty, K. D. (2018). "#It's dangerous": The online world of drug dealers, rappers and the street code. *The British Journal of Criminology, 58*(6), 1343–1360.

Urbanik, M. M., Thompson, S. K., & Bucerius, S. M. (2017). "Before there was danger but there was rules. And safety in those rules": Effects of neighbourhood redevelopment on criminal structures. *The British Journal of Criminology, 57*(2), 422–440.

Usher, L. E., & Kerstetter, D. (2015). Surfistas locales: Transnationalism and the construction of surfer identity in Nicaragua. *Journal of Sport and Social Issues, 39*(6), 455–479.

Valasik, M. A. (2014). *"Saving the world, one neighborhood at a time": The role of civil gang injunctions at influencing gang behavior* [Doctoral dissertation]. University of California, Irvine. ProQuest ID: Valasik_uci_0030D_12935. Merritt ID: ark:/13030/m5j406sh. Retrieved from https://escholarship.org/uc/item/2065d17s.

Valasik, M. (2018). Gang violence predictability: Using risk terrain modeling to study gang homicides and gang assaults in East Los Angeles. *Journal of Criminal Justice, 58*, 10–21.

Valasik, M., Barton, M. S., Reid, S. E., & Tita, G. E. (2017). Barriocide: Investigating the temporal and spatial influence of neighborhood structural characteristics on gang and non-gang homicides in East Los Angeles. *Homicide Studies, 21*(4), 287–311.

Valasik, M, Brault, E., & Martinez, S. (2019). Forecasting homicide in the red stick: Risk terrain modeling and the spatial influence of urban blight on lethal violence in Baton Rouge, Louisiana. *Social Science Research, 80*, 186–201.

Valasik, M., Gravel, J., Tita. G. E., Brantingham, P. J., & Griffiths, B. (Forthcoming). "Territory, residency and routine activities: A typology of gang member mobility patterns with implications for place-based interventions."

Valasik, M., & Phillips, M. (2017). Understanding modern terror and insurgency through the lens of street gangs: ISIS as a case study. *Journal of Criminological Research, Policy and Practice, 3*(3), 192–207.

Valasik, M., & Phillips, M. (2018). Drive-bys in Chiraq or ethnic genocide in Iraq: Can violent street gangs inform our comprehension of the Islamic State? In J. L. Ireland, P. Birch & C. A. Ireland (Eds.), *The Routledge international handbook of human aggression* (pp. 288–399). Routledge.

Valasik, M., & Reid, S. (2018a, December 4). *White nationalist groups are really street gangs, and law enforcement needs to treat them that way.* Retrieved April 30, 2019, from The Conversation. http://theconversation.com/white-nationalist-groups-are-really-street -gangs-and-law-enforcement-needs-to-treat-them-that-way-107691

Valasik, M., & Reid, S. E. (2018b). Alt-right gangs and white power youth. *Oxford Bibliographies Online: Criminology.* https://www.oxfordbibliographies.com/view/document/obo -9780195396607/obo-9780195396607-0243.xml

Valasik, M., & Reid, S. E. (2019a). The Schrödinger's cat of gang groups: Can street gangs inform our comprehension of skinheads and alt-right groups? *Deviant Behavior, 40*(10), 1245–1259.

Valasik, M., Reid, S. E., & Phillips, M. D. (2016). CRASH and burn: Abatement of a specialised gang unit. *Journal of Criminological Research, Policy and Practice, 2*(2), 95–106.

Valasik, M, Reling, T., & Reid, S. E. (Forthcoming). *The (non)threatening nature of "white power" music.*

Valasik, M., & Tita, G. (2018). Gangs and space. In G. J. N. Bruinsma & S. D. Johnson (Eds.), *The Oxford handbook of environmental criminology* (pp. 839–837). Oxford University Press.

Valasik, M. & Torres, J. (Forthcoming). Civilizing space or criminalizing place: Using routine activities theory to better understand how legal hybridity spatially regulates "deviant populations." *Critical Criminology.*

Valdez, A. (1999, March). Nazi low riders. *Police: The Law Enforcement Magazine, 23*(3), 46–48.

Valeri, R. M., Sweazy, N. E., & Borgeson, K. (2017). An analysis of skinhead websites and social networks, a decade later. *Michigan Sociological Review, 31,* 76–105.

van der Valk, I. (2019). Wilders' Party for Freedom and the Dutch alt-right. In A. Waring (Ed.), *The new authoritarianism: Vol 2: A risk analysis of the European alt-right phenomenon* (pp. 251–272). Ibidem Verlag Stuttgart.

van Gemert, F., Peterson, D., & Lien, I. L. (2012). *Street gangs, migration and ethnicity.* Routledge.

Van Hellemont, E., & Densley, J. A. (2019). Gang glocalization: How the global mediascape creates and shapes local gang realities. *Crime, Media, Culture, 15*(1), 169–189.

Van Valkenburgh, P., & Osborne, J. F. (2012). Home turf: Archaeology, territoriality, and politics. *Archeological Papers of the American Anthropological Association, 22*(1), 1–27.

Vasquez, E. A., Wenborne, L., Peers, M., Alleyne, E., & Ellis, K. (2015). Any of them will do: In-group identification, out-group entitativity, and gang membership as predictors of group-based retribution. *Aggressive Behavior, 41*(3), 242–252.

Ventsel, A. (2008). Punx and skins united: One law for us, one law for them. *The Journal of Legal Pluralism and Unofficial Law, 40*(57), 45–100.

VICE. (2017). *Charlottesville: Race and terror.* [Video]. YouTube https://www.youtube.com/watch?v=RIrcB1sAN8I

VICE. (2018). *We camped out with the antifa activists plotting to disarm the alt-right* [Video]. Retrieved October 20, 2019, from VICE. https://video.vice.com/en_ca/video/we-met-the-working-class-activists-of-antifa-plotting-to-disarm-the-alt-right/5aea5192f1cdb30f804d1723

VICE. (2019) *8chan: Hate and the internet* [Video]. VICE. https://video.vice.com/en_asia/video/8chan-hate-and-the-internet-i-vice-news-tonight-special-report/5d700cb1be40775a11535dcf

Vigil, J. D. (1988a). *Barrio gangs: Street life and identity in Southern California.* University of Texas Press.

Vigil, J. D. (1988b). Group processes and street identity: Adolescent Chicano gang members. *Ethos, 16*(4), 421–445.

Vigil, J. D. (1996). Street baptism: Chicano gang initiation. *Human Organization, 55*(2), 149–153.

Vigil, J. D. (2002). *A rainbow of gangs: Street cultures in the mega-city.* University of Texas Press.

Vigil, J. D. (2007). *The projects: Gang and non-gang families in East Los Angeles.* University of Texas Press.

Vigil, J. D. (2009). *Gangs and life on the streets.* Southern Utah University.

Vigil, J. D. (2016). Multiple marginality: A comparative framework for understanding gangs. In *Methods that matter* (pp. 284–305). University of Chicago Press.

Vigil, J. D., & Yun, S. C. (2002). A cross-cultural framework for understanding gangs: Multiple marginality and Los Angeles. In C. R. Huff (Ed.), *Gangs in America* (3rd ed., pp. 161–174). Sage.

Vitolo-Haddad, C. (2019). The blood of patriots: Symbolic violence and "the West." *Rhetoric Society Quarterly Rhetoric Society Quarterly, 49*(3), 280–296.

Wachowski, L., & Wachowski, A. (1999). *The matrix.* [Film]. Warner Bros.

Wade, W. C. (1998). *The fiery cross: The Ku Klux Klan in America.* Oxford University Press.

Waldner, L. K., Martin, H., & Capeder, L. (2006). Ideology of gay racialist skinheads and stigma management techniques. *Journal of Political and Military Sociology; DeKalb, 34*(1), 165–184.

Walsh, C. (2003). Dispersal of rights: A critical comment on specified provisions of the anti-social behaviour bill. *Youth Justice, 3*(2), 104–111.

Walton, E. (2018). Habits of whiteness: How racial domination persists in multiethnic neighborhoods. *Sociology of Race and Ethnicity.* doi: 10.1177/2332649218815238

Ward, G. (2018). Living histories of white supremacist policing: Towards transformative justice. *Du Bois Review: Social Science Research on Race, 15*(1), 167–184.

Ward, T. W. (2013). *Gangsters without borders: An ethnography of a Salvadoran street gang.* Oxford University Press.

Ware, J. (2008). Siege: The Atomwaffen Division and rising far-right terrorism in the United States. *Terrorism and Political Violence, 20,* 417.

Waring, A. (2018). *The new authoritarianism: Vol. 1: A risk analysis of the U.S. alt-right phenomenon.* Ibidem-Verlag.

Waring, A. (2019). *The new authoritarianism: Vol 2: A risk analysis of the European alt-right phenomenon.* Ibidem-Verlag.

Waring, A., & Paxton, R. (2018). Psychological aspects of the alt-right phenomenon. In A. Waring, *The new authoritarianism: Vol. 1: A risk analysis of the U.S. alt-right phenomenon.* Ibidem-Verlag.

Watkins, A. M., & Melde, C. (2018). Gangs, gender, and involvement in crime, victimization, and exposure to violence. *Journal of Criminal Justice, 57*(C), 11–25.

Watkins, A. M., & Taylor, T. J. (2016). The prevalence, predictors, and criminogenic effect of joining a gang among urban, suburban, and rural youth. *Journal of Criminal Justice, 47,* 133–142.

Watts, M. W. (2001). Aggressive youth cultures and hate crime: Skinheads and xenophobic youth in Germany. *American Behavioral Scientist, 45*(4), 600–615.

Webb, V. J., Katz, C. M., & Decker, S. H. (2006). Assessing the validity of self-reports by gang members: Results from the arrestee drug abuse monitoring program. *Crime & Delinquency, 52*(2), 232–252.

Weerman, F. M., Maxson, C. L., Esbensen, F.-A., Aldridge, J., Medina, J., & Van Gemert, F. (2009). *Eurogang program manual.* University of Missouri–St. Louis. https://www.umsl.edu/ccj/Eurogang/EurogangManual.pdf

Weill, W. S. (2019, March 15). *New Zealand suspect mixed death and disinformation.* The Daily Beast. https://www.thedailybeast.com/new-zealand-shooting-brenton-tarrant-tried-to-trick-the-world-in-manifesto-video

Weimann, G. (2016). Terrorist migration to the Dark Web. *Perspectives on Terrorism, 10*(3).

Weitzer, R., & Kubrin, C. E. (2009). Misogyny in rap music: A content analysis of prevalence and meanings. *Men and Masculinities, 12*(1), 3–29.

Wendling, M. (2018). *Alt-right: From 4chan to the White House.* Pluto Press.

White, K. (2017, April 19). Is Alex Jones an extreme conspiracy theorist or a giant troll? Here's why the answer matters. Retrieved April 30, 2019, from *Los Angeles Times.* https://www.latimes.com/opinion/op-ed/la-oe-white-alex-jones-character-20170419 -story.html

Whitman, J. Q. (2017). *Hitler's American model.* Princeton University Press.

Whittaker, A., Densley, J., Cheston, L., Tyrell, T., Higgins, M., Felix-Baptiste, C., & Havard, T. (2020). Reluctant gangsters revisited: The evolution of gangs from postcodes to profits. *European Journal on Criminal Policy and Research, 26*(1), 1–22.

Whyte, W. F. (1955). *Street corner society: The social structure of an Italian slum.* University of Chicago Press.

Wicentowski, D. (2018, September 26). Inside St. Louis' Proud Boys, the far-right frat accused of fascism. Retrieved October 20, 2019, from *Riverfront Times.* https://www .riverfronttimes.com/stlouis/inside-st-louis-proud-boys-the-far-right-frat-accused-of -fascism/Content?oid=24876365

Wilson, A. F. (2017). The bitter end: Apocalypse and conspiracy in white nationalist responses to the Islamic State attacks in Paris. *Patterns of Prejudice, 51*(5), 412–431.

Wilson, J. (2018a, March 19). The alt-right is in decline. Has antifascist activism worked? *The Guardian.* Retrieved from https://www.theguardian.com/world/2018/mar/19/the -alt-right-is-in-decline-has-antifa-activism-worked

Wilson, J. (2018b, August 5). Portland far-right rally: Police charge counterprotesters with batons drawn. *The Guardian.* Retrieved from https://www.theguardian.com/us-news /2018/aug/04/patriot-prayer-to-carry-guns-at-portland-rally-as-fears-of-violence-rise

Wilson, J. (2019, August 16). Portland prepares for city's largest far-right rally of the Trump era. *The Guardian.* Retrieved from https://www.theguardian.com/us-news/2019/aug/15 /portland-oregon-far-right-rally

Windisch, S., Ligon, G. S., & Simi, P. (2017). Organizational [dis]trust: Comparing disengagement among former left-wing and right-wing violent extremists. *Studies in Conflict & Terrorism, 42*(6), 559–580.

Windisch, S., & Simi, P. (2017). Neo-Nazi music subculture. In S. E. Brown & O. Sefiha (Eds.), *Routledge handbook of deviance* (pp. 111–121). Routledge.

Windisch, S., Simi, P., Ligon, G. S., & McNeel, H. (2016). Disengagement from ideologically-based and violent organizations: A systematic review of the literature. *Journal for Deradicalization, 9*, 1–38.

Winston, A. (2019, October 7). *FBI crackdown on Atomwaffen Division heats up with new arrests.* The Daily Beast. https://www.thedailybeast.com/fbi-crackdown-on-atomwaffen -division-heats-up-with-new-arrests-13

Winter, A. (2019). Online hate: From the far-right to the "alt-right" and from the margins to the mainstream. In K. Lumsden & E. Harmer (Eds.), *Online othering: Exploring digital violence and discrimination on the web* (pp. 39–63). Palgrave Macmillan.

Wisdom in Chains. (2015). Skinhead gang. Retrieved from https://wisdom-in-chains .bandcamp.com/track/skinhead-gang

Wise, T. (2010). *Colorblind: The rise of post-racial politics and the retreat from racial equity.* City Lights Books.

Wohlfeil, S. (2018, November 29). How Spokane's downtown bar scene is reacting to a local chapter of Proud Boys. Retrieved October 20, 2019, from *Inlander.* https://www.inlander.com/spokane/how-spokanes-downtown-bar-scene-is-reacting-to-a-local-chapter-of-proud-boys/Content?oid=15109837

Wolf, S. (2012). Mara Salvatrucha: The most dangerous street gang in the Americas? *Latin American Politics and Society, 54*(1), 65–99.

Wood, J. L. (2014). Understanding gang membership: The significance of group processes. *Group Processes & Intergroup Relations, 17*(6), 710–729.

Wood, R. T. (1999). The indigenous, nonracist origins of the American skinhead subculture. *Youth & Society, 31*(2), 131–151.

Wooden, W. S., & Blazak, R. (2001). *Renegade kids, suburban outlaws: From youth culture to delinquency.* Wadsworth.

Woodhouse, L. A. (2017, September 21). *After Charlottesville, the American far right is tearing itself apart.* Retrieved April 25, 2019, from The Intercept. https://theintercept.com/2017/09/21/gavin-mcinnes-alt-right-proud-boys-richard-spencer-charlottesville/

Woods, B. (2017, October 25). The Proud Boys and the litigious "alt-lite." *Flagpole Magazine.* https://flagpole.com/news/democracy-in-crisis/2017/10/25/the-proud-boys-and-the-litigious-alt-lite

Worley, M. (2013). Oi! Oi! Oi! Class, locality, and British punk. *Twentieth Century British History, 24*(4), 606–636.

Worley, M., & Copsey, N. (2016). White youth: The far right, punk and British youth culture. *JOMEC Journal, 9,* 27–47.

Wright, J. D. (2005). The constitutional failure of gang databases. *Stanford Journal of Civil Rights & Civil Liberties, 2,* 115.

Wright, S. A. (2009). Strategic framing of racial-nationalism in North America and Europe: An analysis of a burgeoning transnational network. *Terrorism and Political Violence, 21*(2), 189–210.

Wu, J., & Pyrooz, D. C. (2016). Uncovering the pathways between gang membership and violent victimization. *Journal of Quantitative Criminology, 32*(4), 531–559.

Yogeeswaran, K., Nash, K., Sahioun, R., & Sainudiin, R. (2018). *Seeded by hate? Characterizing the Twitter networks of prominent politicians and hate groups in the 2016 US election.* Preprint. http://lamastex. org/preprints/2017HateIn2016USAElection.pdf

Young, K., & Craig, L. (1997). Beyond white pride: Identity, meaning and contradiction in the Canadian skinhead subculture. *Canadian Review of Sociology/Revue Canadienne de Sociologie, 34*(2), 175–206.

Zadrozny, B., & Siemaszko, C. (2018, November 20). *The boys and girls of white nationalism: "Proud" groups labeled "extremist."* Retrieved October 28, 2019, from WXXV 25. https://www.wxxv25.com/2018/11/20/the-boy-and-girls-of-white-nationalism-proud-groups-labeled-extremist/

Zannettou, S., Bradlyn, B., De Cristofaro, E., Kwak, H., Sirivianos, M., Stringini, G., & Blackburn, J. (2018a). What is Gab: A bastion of free speech or an alt-right echo chamber. *Companion Proceedings of the Web Conference 2018,* 1007–1014.

Zannettou, S., Caulfield, T., Blackburn, J., De Cristofaro, E., Sirivianos, M., Stringhini, G., & Suarez-Tangil, G. (2018b). *On the origins of memes by means of fringe web communities*. Arxiv. http://arxiv.org/abs/1805.12512.

Zeskind, L. (2009). *Blood and politics: The history of the white nationalist movement from the margins to the mainstream*. Farrar Straus Giroux.

INDEX

Founded in 1893,
UNIVERSITY OF CALIFORNIA PRESS
publishes bold, progressive books and journals
on topics in the arts, humanities, social sciences,
and natural sciences—with a focus on social
justice issues—that inspire thought and action
among readers worldwide.

The UC PRESS FOUNDATION
raises funds to uphold the press's vital role
as an independent, nonprofit publisher, and
receives philanthropic support from a wide
range of individuals and institutions—and from
committed readers like you. To learn more, visit
ucpress.edu/supportus.